# ECONOMIC EPISODES IN CIVICS AND American Government

M. Scott Niederjohn
Mark C. Schug
Signè Thomas
William C. Wood

WOHL PUBLISHING

## A Note from the Publisher

The authors of this textbook are extraordinarily talented and accomplished educators, and I am very proud to be the publisher of *Economic Episodes in Civics and American Government*, as well as their related textbook, *Economic Episodes in American History* (winner of the Gold Award of Excellence from the National Association of Economic Educators).

It has been a great honor to work with this outstanding author team, as well as the publishing professionals and educators that have contributed so importantly to the entire effort. We hope that you will find the results of their work to be valuable to you and your students, and that you will decide to integrate this textbook into your curriculum by having your school adopt it for classroom use.

This textbook has several goals. The first is to teach students about the economic way of thinking, which helps us understand the choices people make across all disciplines and all walks of life. The second goal is to help students become more engaged and knowledgeable citizens by applying that economic way of thinking to our government and to our elected officials. And lastly, the textbook explains in non-technical language the economic and financial institutions, activities, and decisions that are integral to our government decisions and policies.

*Economic Episodes in Civics and American Government* is a unique teaching tool. There is no other supplemental textbook in today's market that successfully integrates the principles of economics with civics and American government at the high school level. We greatly appreciate, and are inspired by, your dedication to your students and to the teaching profession. We recognize that the need is greater than ever for innovative teaching materials that engage students in new and creative ways about issues that really matter. We hope that you find this book to be such a text, and that the teaching and learning that occurs in your classes every day are enriched by its use.

—Rich Wohl

**Copy Editor:** Theresa Kay
**Book Design and Photo Editor:** Jeremy C. Munns
**Indexer:** Heather Dubnick
**Printer:** Kennington Media Solutions

**Credits and acknowledgments** for materials borrowed from other sources and reproduced, with permission, in this textbook appear on the appropriate page within the text and/or in the credits section at the end of this book.



Wohl Publishing, Inc.
45 S. Park Place #223
Morristown, NJ 07960
www.wohlpublishing.com

ISBN 978-1-935938-01-9

# MEET THE AUTHORS

M. Scott Niederjohn, Ph.D.

**M. Scott Niederjohn** is Professor of Economics and Director of the Free Enterprise Center at Concordia University Wisconsin in Mequon. Scott is a widely known scholar in the areas of economic education and public policy analysis. He has published more than 80 journal articles, book chapters, monographs, reports, and curricular materials. Scott is also the co-author of two books: *Economic Episodes in American History*, Second Edition (Wohl Publishing) and *Teachers Can Be Financially Fit: Economists' Advice for Educators* (Springer). Scott serves on the Wisconsin Governor's Council for Financial Literacy and has received the Governor's Financial Literacy Award in 2011, 2012, 2015, and 2018. During the fall of 2013, he was awarded a Fulbright Scholarship to teach at the University of Luxembourg.

Mark C. Schug, Ph.D.

**Mark C. Schug** is Professor Emeritus at the University of Wisconsin Milwaukee and President of Mark Schug Consulting Services. Mark taught for 36 years at the middle school, high school, and university levels. A widely recognized scholar, he has written and edited over 230 articles, books, and national curriculum materials. He has been the guest co-editor of 12 issues of *Social Education*, the flagship journal of the National Council for the Social Studies. His latest books are *Economic Episodes in American History* published by Wohl Publishing and co-authored by William C. Wood, Tawni Hunt Ferrarini, and M. Scott Niederjohn, now in its second edition. The same author team of Ferrarini, Niederjohn, Schug, and Wood wrote *Teachers Can Be Financially Fit: Economists' Advice for Educators,* which was published in 2020 by Springer Nature.

Signè Thomas

**Signè Thomas** is the K. W. Davis Visiting Lecturer at Trinity College, where she teaches courses within the Formal Organizations minor. Prior to joining Trinity, she was the Project Director for the Stavros Center for the Advancement of Free Enterprise and Economic Education at Florida State University (FSU). Her role included advancing economic literacy through teaching, textbook and curriculum development, and programs. While at FSU she also served as Research Associate for the DeVoe Moore Center and taught courses for the Jim Moran College of Entrepreneurship. She is heavily involved in promoting economic literacy across North America—particularly through partnering with organizations such as the Foundation for Economic Education and the Fraser Institute to train educators via teacher workshops and webinars, and to teach college and high school students via student seminars.

William C. Wood, Ph.D.

**William C. Wood *(editor and special topics author)*** is Professor of Economics and Director of the Center for Economic Education at James Madison University. Bill was the recipient of teaching awards at the University of Virginia and at James Madison University, where he was the 2001–2002 Distinguished Teacher in the College of Business. He was named in 2002 as an inaugural winner of the Southern Economic Association's Kenneth G. Elzinga Distinguished Teaching Award. Bill is also a past recipient of the Alpha Kappa Psi-Clifford D. Spangler award for research in risk and insurance and Best Paper award for the *Journal of Private Enterprise*. He is the author of four books, more than 60 scholarly articles, and national economic education materials for school and adult audiences. In 2016, Bill received the Henry H. Villard Award from the National Association of Economic Educators for career achievement in economic education research.

# Preface

To be intelligently engaged in American government at all levels, you have to understand the economic way of thinking. That's what this book is about. We believe that economic thinking is a critical-thinking tool that allows you to clearly grasp the behavior of people in government as well as the role played by government and nongovernment institutions. Economic thinking might change how you view your nation's government and its history. It might even change your life!

Your author team enjoys teaching. One of the most satisfying times we have in the classroom is introducing students to compound interest. That probably sounds pretty dull (and maybe we *are* just economics geeks), but bear with us. Compound interest is so powerful that smart people have referred to it as "magic."

Imagine you get a birthday gift of $600 each year. Whoop, whoop! Free money! What do you want to do with it? Buy a new electronic gadget? New clothes? Car repair? How about blowing it all by taking friends to a concert?

But wait. Is that money really free? Consider this. Beginning at age 18, if you saved $600 every year and earned an annual interest rate of 8%, you would have earned more than $310,000 in lifetime wealth by age 65, even though you contributed a little over $28,000. Skeptical? Go to **https://www.econedlink.org/resources/compound-interest-calculator** and do the math.

How can this be? It's called the magic of compounding interest. Albert Einstein called it the eighth wonder of the world. It's the secret sauce of becoming financially independent. (Turn to Chapter 18 to learn more about compounding and how citizens can become financially independent.)

Economists explain compound interest in the context of *opportunity cost*. Every choice has a cost, even ones that involve "free" money. Whatever you give up when you make a decision is called your opportunity cost. It turns out that

spending $600 each year comes with a high opportunity cost. The dollar cost of, say, taking your friends to a concert each year is $600. But the opportunity cost is what that money, set aside, could have earned in an investment account. That's $310,000.

A common principle of economic thinking is that people try to make the best decisions they can—ones that are in their self-interest—given the information they currently possess. What if no one ever told you about compound interest? You might never have considered getting started saving at a young age. Knowing about compound interest and opportunity cost has the potential to change your life and the lives of those around you.

Elected officials constantly make choices. Just like your choices, their choices involve an opportunity cost.

- What do candidates give up when they decide to run for office?
- What does a winning candidate give up by serving in office?
- What are the opportunity costs involved in decisions made by elected officeholders?
- What does an elected official give up when deciding to return to life as a private citizen?

When it comes to decisions about spending tax dollars, government is a world of nearly endless opportunity costs. In 2021, the U.S. government spent nearly $7 trillion. (One trillion is a thousand billion; one billion is a thousand million.) Florida spent more than $100 billion in 2021. New York spent $186 billion. California spent nearly $300 billion. The opportunity cost of federal and state spending is mind numbing even to economists.

The economic way of thinking is the focal point of *Economic Episodes in Civics and American Government*. The point is *not* to teach economics. Rather, the point is to help you learn to apply a few principles of economics to help you understand the behavior of people in government and governmental institutions. We do our best to help you analyze politics by referring to the following questions:

- What choices are being made by individual politicians and citizens?
- What are the costs of those choices? All choices involve an opportunity cost. Nothing is free.
- What are the incentives driving those choices? Incentives can be anything elected officials and citizens find rewarding. It may be money but it might be something else that they find valuable.
- How does the political system with its rules and regulations influence the choices that are made by individuals in the private sector, including private businesses and nonprofit organizations?
- Is voluntary trade taking place? Are there mutual gains from trade? Or are choices being influenced by coercion or force?
- What are the primary effects—the obvious and visible effects—of public and private choices?
- What are the secondary effects—the less obvious or invisible effects—of the choices? What could go wrong?

## The Organization of *Economic Episodes in Civics and American Government*

The overall design of this book tracks the structure of a traditional civics or American government course. You will find topics on the following:

- The fundamentals of democratic systems
- The role of government including the legislative, executive, and judicial branches
- Monetary policy and the Federal Reserve

- The role played by state governments
- Current issues including the economics of voting, the media, and international trade
- The roles of citizens in the public and private sectors

Three chapters are distinctive. Chapter 1 provides an introduction to the economic way of thinking as applied to government. Chapter 17 focuses on civil society, the nonprofit and volunteer sector. Chapter 18 features a citizen's guide to financial independence.

Chapter 1's introduction to the economic way of thinking is organized through six principles of economic thinking that are applied throughout the rest of the book. For this reason, Chapter 1 is a good place for readers to begin before moving to other chapters.

Each chapter is self-contained and can be used independently. All have a similar organization.

- At the top of the first page in each chapter, you will find the **key economic concepts** in the chapter set off in a box. The idea is to provide a preview of what you are about to be reading.
- The text of each chapter opens with a personal story. It might be a famous person or a not-so-famous person. You will have the chance to meet some interesting characters such as Adam Smith (the founding economist), but also Sergey Brin, Yeonmi Park, Rosa Parks, Ida Fuller, Judge Kenesaw Mountain Landis, Robert Latham Owen, David Ricardo, Suze Orman, and many others.
- The next section is called **The Civics Context**. This section is meant to be a bridge between traditional civics or American government content and the economics content in this chapter. In civics you learn about the U.S. Constitution as a political document. In Chapter 2 you will learn how the U.S. Constitution established the conditions for the development of a market economy.
- Now we come to the economics section. This section applies the economic way of thinking to the civics content. The economic concepts are introduced and explained. Chapter 4, for example, explains the difference between capitalism, socialism, and communism. Chapter 6 explains the economic statistics that every citizen should know.
- This is followed by a section called **Civics Questions & Economic Answers**. This section extends the economic analysis. Chapter 5, for example, explains how African American parents were the unsung heroes of the Civil Rights Movement. Chapter 11 discusses the role of federal regulations.
- Next is the **Primary Source** section. These focus on a photograph, original quote, map, chart, or graph. All of these primary sources provide firsthand evidence for you to consider. Chapter 3, for example, features a quote from Muhammad Yunus (a social entrepreneur and Nobel Prize winner) on poverty. Chapter 12 features an excerpt from *Hamilton: An American Musical.*
- What follows is a **Contemporary Connection**. The idea here is to show a connection between the content of the chapter and a current issue. Chapter 3 discusses the erosion of economic freedom in Hong Kong. Chapter 12 features a section on cryptocurrencies. The minimum wage is the focus in Chapter 15.
- Each chapter concludes with a **Web Quest** section. Here you will find several websites that allow you to dig deeper into the chapter topics. Included are a few suggested questions to guide the process. The Web Quest in Chapter 3 invites you to explore the Fraser Institute's *Economic Freedom of the World Index*. Chapter 6 connects you to the Bureau of Economic Analysis where you can get the most current information on economic growth.

We wish you the best in your economics-guided journey through civics and American government.

# BOARD OF ADVISORS

The author team wishes to express its thanks and appreciation to the members of the Board of Advisors who provided us with numerous insightful comments that helped guide this project.

**Derek D'Angelo**
President
Michigan Council on Economic Education

**Marianna Davidovich**
Director, External Relations
Foundation for Economic Education

**Joe DiFiglia**
School of Business
New Jersey City University

**Dr. Lucien Ellington**
UC Foundation Professor of Education
University of Tennessee at Chattanooga

**Kim Holder**
Director, Center for Economic Education and Financial Literacy
University of West Georgia

**Carroll Lavallee**
Social Studies Instructor
Sarasota County Schools, FL

**Charlie Lemberger**
Social Studies Teacher
Valders High School, WI

**Kristen McDaniel**
Social Studies Consultant
Wisconsin Department of Public Instruction

**Dr. James Nelson**
Social Studies Department Chair
Golda Meir School
Milwaukee, WI

**Dr. Mary Suiter**
Assistant Vice President, Research Division
Federal Reserve Bank of St. Louis

# Table of Contents

## PART 1 An Introduction to the Economic Way of Thinking

## PART 2 Economic Freedom and Democracy

## PART 3 The Economic Role of Government:

### Legislative, Executive, and Judicial Branches, Federal Reserve, and State Government

We the People

CHAPTER 11

CHAPTER 12

CHAPTER 13

## PART 5 Your Role in the Public and Private Sectors

CHAPTER 17

CHAPTER 18

CHAPTER
# 1

# How Can Economics Illuminate Civics? Meet Adam Smith, the Founding Economist

*A statue of Adam Smith in Edinburgh, Scotland.*

# Adam Smith: Founder of Economics

Adam Smith was the founder of economics. Because this book is designed to help you learn how to use economics to better understand government, it makes sense to begin with the original economist. After all, Smith's ideas have influenced the British government and policies, the U.S. Constitution, and the constitutions of nations around the world.

Adam Smith was born in 1723 in Kirkcaldy, Scotland, a small coastal trading town. Out of his back windows, Smith watched its bustling seaport: salt and coal going out, scrap metal coming in for the local nail factories.

Adam's father, a customs official, died at age 43, five months before his son was born. Smith was raised by his mother Margaret. He was an unhealthy child. While not impoverished, Adam's young mother often struggled financially.

After attending the University of Glasgow and Oxford in England, Smith became a professor at the University of Glasgow from 1751 to 1763. Smith developed a reputation as a great teacher and a scholar. He traveled widely, even resigning his position at Glasgow to travel with Henry Scott, the Third Duke of Buccleuch, as the duke's tutor. Together they traveled through much of Europe and interacted with the continent's top minds.

Smith returned to Scotland in 1767 to care for his mother. But through all these years he continued writing. Smith's best-known book is *An Inquiry into the Nature and Causes of the Wealth of Nations*, commonly shortened to *The Wealth of Nations*.[1]

Through much of his life, Smith enjoyed visiting, entertaining, and discussing ideas. He had a reputation for being absent-minded. Adam Smith's friends included his closest friend David Hume, a philosopher; Edmund Burke, the British statesman and philosopher; and British prime ministers. He even knew that world-famous American, Benjamin Franklin. He never married.

### KEY ECONOMIC CONCEPTS

**capital resources**
**economic system**
**economic way of thinking**
**human resources**
**incentives**
**invisible hand**
**laissez-faire**
**mercantilism**
**opportunity cost**
**primary and secondary effects**
**scarcity**
**self-interested behavior**
**voluntary trade**

## The Civics Context

The principles of economics inspired by Adam Smith and further developed by today's economists apply to all types of activities, choices, and institutions. It makes sense, then, that the economic way of thinking might be used to improve our understanding of how people in governments behave. In this sense, economics is like disciplines such as history and geography, which also help us understand civics and government.

What does a historical perspective contribute to understanding government? American governmental institutions were shaped by English law stretching back to the Magna Carta in 1215. The Magna Carta established due process of law as a fundamental right. Ideas about government continued to develop in England through the centuries. When Thomas Jefferson wrote the Declaration of Independence and James Madison shaped the U.S. Constitution, both were reflecting the influence of the 17th-century English philosopher John Locke. Locke was a strong advocate of individual natural rights, freedom, and equality before the law.

Geography is also fundamental to understanding government. Much of government is organized according to location, including a local school district, village, city, county, state, and nation. Government often functions somewhat differently at each geographic level. School board members, for example, have different powers than do state legislators, which are, in turn, different from the powers of state governors, and so forth.

Economics, like history and geography, provides important insights into the workings of government. What might those be? The economic way of thinking is all about choices, costs, incentives, economic systems, trade, and primary and secondary effects.

*Adam Smith, author of* The Wealth of Nations.

## The Economic Way of Thinking

Adam Smith's *The Wealth of Nations*, published in 1776, challenged then-prevailing ideas about what made a nation wealthy. The dominant thinking of the time, called **mercantilism**, called for nations to hoard precious metals such as gold and silver. The British Empire's government favored exports and discouraged imports.

In contrast, Smith explained that the wealth of a nation depended on the prosperity of the people who lived there, not the amount of precious metals held by the crown. Smith showed how people would prosper with the economic freedom to trade and seek profitable uses of their resources. He argued against government dominance of markets including state-sponsored monopolies. The idea that people could direct their economic affairs without being told what to do by a monarchy seemed radical in 1776.

Starting with Smith but including insights developed across the centuries, economists have developed what is known at the "economic way of thinking." We define the **economic way of thinking** as a way to analyze behavior in the private and public sectors with the application of six principles.

***1. People make choices because they face scarcity.***

The first principle of the economic way of thinking is that as we face **scarcity**, we all have to make choices.

People's desires for goods and services are vast, but we have a limited amount of productive resources, which means we can't have everything that we desire. For example, we have a finite amount of natural resources such as farmland, clean water, and minerals such as copper and oil. We also have a limited amount of **capital resources**, defined in economics as tools used to produce goods and services such as factories and computers. Finally, we have a limited number of **human resources**: people are who willing to produce goods and services. Since our desires outstrip our limited resources, we need to make choices.

The fact that people make choices seems pretty obvious. But in everyday life, don't we often deny that we are making choices? Julia, a student we know, recently said, "I couldn't do my homework last night because I had to work." Was Julia making a choice? Of course she was. She decided that the benefits of working were greater than the benefits of doing the homework assignment. She almost certainly could have found a way to complete the assignment, but she chose not to because it wasn't worth it to her.

Behavior in government involves a nearly endless supply of individual choices. Citizens choose whether they will vote. If they do, then they have to decide on candidates to support. But that's complicated. Voters often face many choices on the same ballot, including candidates running for local offices, state offices, the U.S. Congress, and, every four years, the president. There may be other things on the ballot as well, including votes on changing the state constitution. (Chapter 14 is about the economics of voting.)

Elected officials are busy making individual choices too. Should individuals choose to run for office? What political party should they choose? On what specific policies should they run? What are the best ways to raise campaign funds? If elected, how should they vote on specific legislation? Should they seek reelection? How should they communicate with voters? And so forth.

***2. People's choices involve costs.***

The second principle of the economic way of thinking is that all choices involve a cost. Many choices involve monetary costs. Buying a pair of running shoes involves paying the price that is asked for the shoes. To run for office, candidates often pay a filing fee. To get a driver's license, you pay a fee.

Economics stresses that while many choices involve dollar costs, all choices involve an **opportunity cost**, defined as what you sacrifice when you make a decision. If you decide to play soccer instead of studying for an Advanced Placement exam, your opportunity cost might be a low test score. An old saying among economists is, "There is no such thing as a free lunch." That means that all choices involve a cost, even if there is not a direct monetary cost.

Elected officials sometimes suggest that some things are "free." Perhaps you have heard someone say that public schools are "free." Public schools are "free" in the limited sense that parents do not have to pay tuition. Even so, public schools incur all kinds of costs: paying teachers, administrators, cooks, and custodians. In addition, there are the costs of computers, books, desks, and buildings. Taxpayers at all levels pay the costs. And spending for schools could be used differently. The alternative use is the opportunity cost.

***3. People respond to incentives in predictable ways.***

The third principle of the economic way of thinking is that people respond to incentives in predictable ways. **Incentives** are anything that people find rewarding. Money is a powerful incentive because you can turn it into anything that it can buy. That $50 graduation gift from your Aunt Agnes can be saved or spent. If you spend it, you face many choices.

Let's consider the case of Molly Jackson. Molly is thinking about throwing her hat in the ring to run for a seat on the local school board. What incentives does she face? She and her spouse have two sons; both are in elementary school. One incentive for her might be help to make sure the school district is well run so that the students, including her children, get a great education. But there might be other incentives at work. Molly might have a particular issue in mind such as improving the math curriculum. She might have noticed that school board members receive a modest salary for serving. She might even be thinking about one day running for Congress. To do that, usually you have to have experience at other levels of government. There's no one incentive that will definitely make Molly decide to run, but there are many that might have an influence.

***4. People create economic systems that influence individual decisions.***

The economy is shaped by many factors, including formal and informal rules. The formal rules of the **economic system** are decided by local, state, and national governments. And those rules influence individual choices. Want to buy a car? The government has rules about how titles of automobile ownership are transferred from one party to another. Want to rent an apartment? Governments have rules that govern relationships between tenants and landlords.

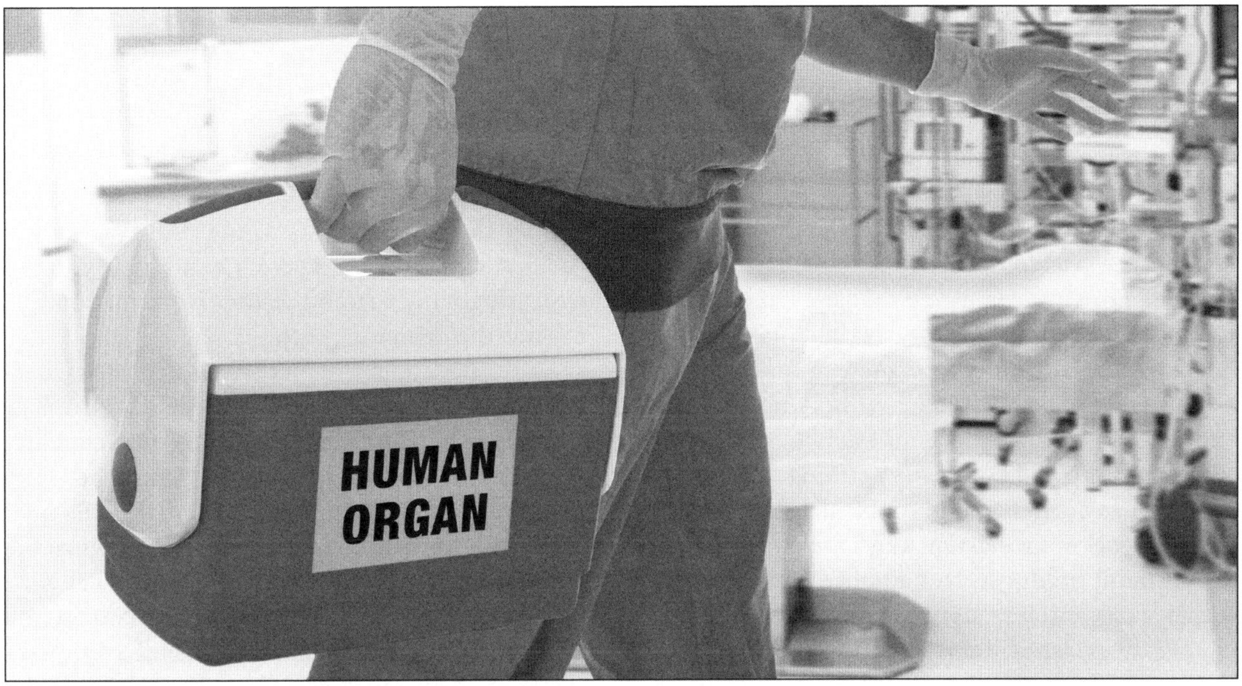


*Organ donation laws are one example of how changes to the rules of a market economy can change behvaior.*

The economy involves many rules of the game. Here are some of the rules for a market economy:

- Most of the economy is managed by the private sector, not the government.
- Governments at nearly all levels are involved in regulating the private sector.
- Private property ownership is widespread and enforced by government laws.
- Businesses compete with each other to persuade consumers to buy the goods and services they offer.
- Governments have rules that try to keep widespread competition in the economy.
- Unlike government, an important motive for businessowners is to earn a profit.
- Federal and state governments impose taxes on corporate profits.
- To earn a profit, businesses have to please their customers.
- Exchanges between producers and consumers are voluntary, not forced by government.

If the rules of the economic system change, so will the behavior of consumers and producers. For example, states have laws regarding organ donation. They often involve you making a decision. When you get your first driver's license from the state, you are asked a question: Would you donate your organs if your life were lost in an accident? Some choose "yes," knowing the difference that donated organs can make to kidney or heart patients. Some choose "no." And most of us would rather not think about it. But organ donation involves a rule of the game. Traditionally, if you do nothing, then you're not an organ donor.

Advocates of organ donation, however, are now proposing that state laws allow you to become an organ donor *unless you specifically choose not to*. This change, it is thought, would result in many more organ donations every year. That's just one example of how a change in the rules of the game changes behavior.

***5. People gain when they trade voluntarily.***

For people to gain from an exchange, it must be voluntary. From buying a new phone to purchasing a movie ticket, millions of voluntary exchanges happen 24 hours a day. These are win–win trades where both sides—businesses and consumers—are better off.

Voluntary trade encourages cooperation among strangers and encourages specialization. Do you suppose people in Vermont could grow peaches? It is a northern state, so the climate doesn't seem welcoming to peaches. But peaches could be grown in large greenhouses. Do you suppose that people in Georgia could make maple syrup? Georgia has a good climate for growing trees, so it seems reasonable to think that maple trees could be grown there.

But it is an expensive proposition to grow peaches in Vermont and produce maple syrup in Georgia. The more efficient alternative would be for Vermont producers to specialize in making maple syrup and for Georgia farmers to specialize in growing peaches. Then, producers in both states can trade, which makes all parties better off. Another "win–win" outcome.

### 6. *People's choices sometimes create unintended consequences.*

The economic way of thinking involves thinking critically about the **primary and secondary effects** of government policies. A primary effect is a result intended by, for example, a piece of legislation. It is usually pretty obvious. The secondary effect is more difficult to see. It requires thinking about the future consequences of a piece of legislation that might even produce harmful results.

The Endangered Species Act of 1973 called for the government to maintain a list of wildlife at risk of becoming extinct. Under this law, many species such as whooping cranes and gray wolves were brought back from the edge of extinction. This was the primary effect.

But think about the incentives of a landowner who discovers a nesting pair of golden-cheeked warblers on personally owned Texas ranch land. Following the law would mean reporting the warblers to the authorities and *taking the land out of use*—no logging, no grazing, no clearing for crops. Ranchers typically don't brag openly about doing such things, but some have been known to give the advice that, when an endangered species is discovered on ranchland, "shoot, shovel, and shut up." The authors of the Endangered Species Act did not want to give an incentive to shoot endangered animals, but the incentive was a secondary effect. An alternative idea that might still protect endangered species is to figure out a way to compensate ranchers for their losses, maybe by using funds raised from private or public sources or both.

*Protection of the golden-cheeked warbler under the Endangered Species Act has put the bird in conflict with Texas ranchers.*

## Civics Questions & Economic Answers

### Did Adam Smith want to keep the government totally out of economic matters?

No, not totally. In some textbooks, you may have read that Smith opposed state intervention in the economy. Scholars often say that Smith was **laissez-faire**, the French term for "leave alone" or "to allow to be." Laissez-faire is the belief that economies work best when there is no interference by the government. Smith seems to agree. In the following quote from *The Wealth of Nations*, there is no explicit mention of the role of government.

"Every man, as long as he does not violate the laws of nature, is left perfectly free to pursue his own interest his own way, and to bring both his industry and his capital into competition with those of any other man, or order of men." (page 687)

But Smith never used the term laissez-faire. Instead, Smith argued that government plays a fundamental role in establishing the conditions for an economy to grow and to promote human happiness. Among the government roles he favored were the following:

- Protection of citizens' property and persons against violence
- Strong impartial courts
- Promotion of education
- Infrastructure spending on roads, canals, bridges, and harbors
- Military protection

Thus, Smith favored an important but limited role for government in the economy.

### What is the "invisible hand"?

The **invisible hand** is a metaphor originated by Smith that suggests voluntary exchange of goods and services often results in unintended and widespread benefits. Business owners might only desire to earn a profit. But, to earn a profit, they have to offer to consumers goods and services that they are voluntarily willing to purchase.

Profits are an incentive to producers in free-market economies to voluntarily provide goods and services for consumers. Governments in unfree economies, such as today's Cuba or North Korea, use coercion to make enterprises produce and workers work. Violating government orders to produce and work in these unfree nations results in many bad things happening to individuals and their family members, up to and including death.

Many of us love our phones. Do you think Apple and Samsung produce phones because they care about you? Probably not. They don't even know you. The owners of the companies care about earning more income, which they hope will result in a profit. The people who work for those companies care about earning income to take care of their families and do the things they enjoy.

Companies and their employees are guided by their own self-interest to provide you with a phone. The fact that you are happy is a result of Smith's invisible hand. Visit a grocery store or a big box hardware store. How did all the goods arrive there in more or less the right quantities? We attribute it to Smith's invisible hand. Things like this happen so often in our daily life that they mainly go unnoticed.

### Questions for Discussion

1. Who was Adam Smith?
2. What is the economic way of thinking?
3. Why should Georgia grow peaches and Vermont produce maple syrup?
4. What is the role of government in the economy according to Smith?
5. What is Smith's invisible hand?
6. How are profits incentives?

# Reading Adam Smith's *The Wealth of Nations*

PRIMARY SOURCE

## Role of Government

Some people say they have heard of Adam Smith, but few have read excerpts from *The Wealth of Nations*. Let's give it a try. It might be a challenge. Remember, he was writing 250 years ago.

What does Smith view as the proper role of government in the economy? Here is an excerpt from *The Wealth of Nations*:

> According to the system of natural liberty, the sovereign has only three duties to attend to: first, the duty of protecting the society from violence and invasion of other independent societies; secondly, the duty of protecting, as far as possible, every member of the society from the injustice or oppression of every other member of it, or the duty of establishing an exact administration of justice; and, thirdly, the duty of erecting and maintaining certain public works and certain public institutions which it can never be in the interest of any individual, or small number of individuals, though it may frequently do much more than repay it to a great society. (pages 687–688)

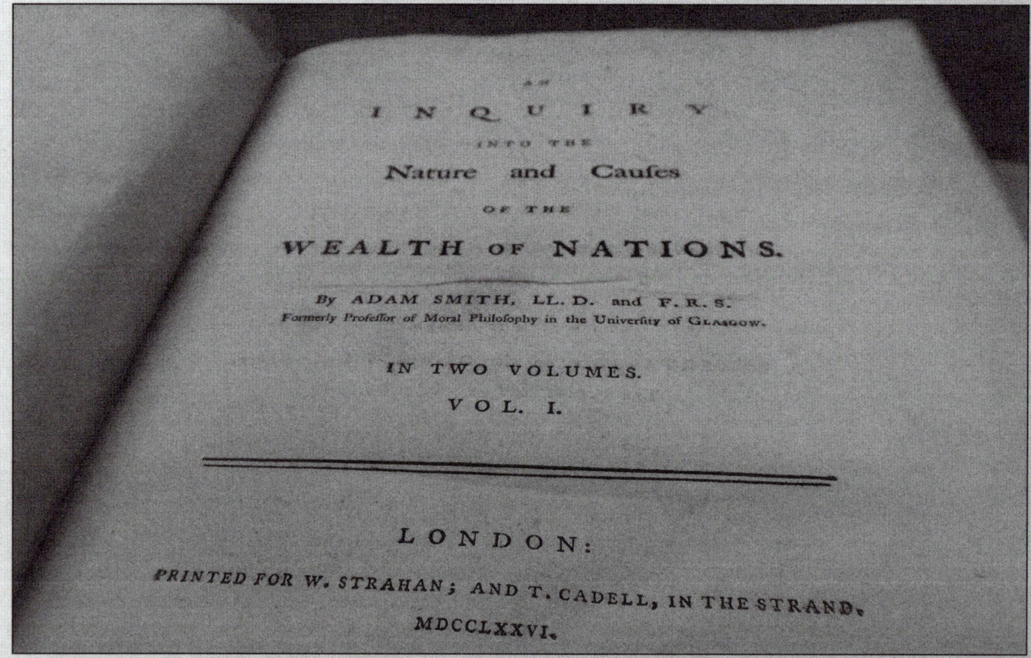
AN
INQUIRY
INTO THE
Nature and Caufes
OF THE
WEALTH OF NATIONS.
By ADAM SMITH, LL.D. and F.R.S.
Formerly Profeffor of Moral Philofophy in the Univerfity of GLASGOW.
IN TWO VOLUMES.
VOL. I.
LONDON:
PRINTED FOR W. STRAHAN; AND T. CADELL, IN THE STRAND.
MDCCLXXVI.

*Title-page of the first edition of Adam Smith's* The Wealth of Nations.

### Self-Interested Behavior

Smith is well-known for making a distinction between selfish behavior and **self-interested behavior**. Selfish behavior occurs when people put themselves unfairly ahead of others, seeking their own advantage over others. Most of us don't find selfishness to be a desirable trait.

Self-interested behavior means that we are pursuing outcomes that we value. This might include studying hard at school, finding a satisfying career, starting an innovative business, providing for your family, doing volunteer work, and protecting your community.

Smith maintains that while some of us are selfish, we all are self-interested. Here is a quote from Adam Smith in *The Wealth of Nations* that provides his explanation of self-interested behavior:

> Man has almost constant occasion for help from his brethren, and it is in vain for him to expect it from their benevolence only. ... It is not from the benevolence of the butcher, the brewer, or the baker, that we expect our dinner, but from their regard to their own interest. We address ourselves, not to their humanity but to their self-love, and never talk to them of our necessities but of their advantages. (pages 26–27)

## QUESTIONS for DISCUSSION

1. What are the three key functions of government according to Smith?
2. Provide an example of government today performing each of these three duties.
3. What might be reasons for government to limit its role to Smith's three duties?
4. What might be reasons for a more expansive role of government?
5. What is the difference between selfishness and self-interest? Provide an example of each.

Contemporary Connection

## Want to Go for a Run?

The Swiss are famous for voting on nearly everything. The Swiss have a representative democracy like most democracies, but they also operate something close to a direct democracy, which means involving voters directly in making many decisions.

In the United States, we don't vote as much as the Swiss, but we do vote a lot. There are about 520,000 politicians in the United States. The vast majority of these (about 500,000) are at the local level. This includes city council members, mayors, county officials, and school board members. There are another 19,000 at the state level and 537 at the national level.

There are many opportunities for citizens to run for political office. But do they? Obviously, many do. When Kathy Tran ran for the Virginia state legislature for the first time, her only political experience was serving as president of the Parent Teacher Association at her children's school. Tran came to the United States as a refugee from Vietnam. She became interested in immigration issues. She campaigned hard and won. Today, she is the representative of Virginia House of Delegates District 42.

Most people are not like Tran. Research done by the Pew Research Center suggests that only about 2 percent of Americans say they have ever run for federal, local, or state

*Kathy Tran represents District 42 in the Virginia House of Delegates.*

elected office. Why do so few Americans run for political office? Let's use the economic way of thinking to see why.

People choose. Many Americans who are eligible to seek public office choose not to do so. Apparently, many people think running for office involves a high opportunity cost. That is understandable. Time spent attending endless campaign meetings, speaking at rallies, going door to door, attending meet and greets, and raising campaign funds can turn your life upside down.

Incentives, however, do motivate some to run. Tran was worried about immigration policy. Others might be concerned about taxes, the homeless, climate change, and so forth. But there are other incentives as well. Some people are highly motivated by a sense of serving their community. Others might enjoy being well-known in the local community, or they might be interested in obtaining experience to run for higher office. Most elected officials are compensated for their work.

The rules of the political game are important and influence the decisions of potential lawmakers. A potential candidate has to be qualified to get on the ballot (for example, live in the district) and must file an application. But that is just the beginning. Office seekers face a thicket of campaign finance laws and regulations. Candidates need to know how much in campaign funds they can legally raise and spend. The tougher these rules are, the less likely it is that people will seek office.

Campaigns involve voluntary trade. Candidates strive to develop ideas and themes that appeal to potential voters, campaign volunteers, and donors. Conversely, potential voters, volunteers, and donors are looking for candidates they can support. Successful candidates work hard to shape strategies that appeal to all of these groups.

Finally, office seekers face primary and secondary effects. A primary effect is winning office and then getting to work on the issues that persuaded the voters. But secondary effects can hold potential candidates back. Campaigns can get nasty. Candidates might face personal attacks from the opposition and the media. Politics sometimes requires a thick skin.

## QUESTIONS for DISCUSSION

1. Which points in the economic way of thinking (choices, costs, incentives, rules of the game, voluntary trade, primary and secondary effect) do you think would encourage you to seek elected office?
2. Which points in the economic way of thinking (choices, costs, incentives, rules of the game, voluntary trade, primary and secondary effect) do you think would discourage you from seeking elected office?

## Web Quests

**Enter any of the links below and use the questions to get you started on your own web quest.**

### An Animal That Trades

*Here you can watch a high-quality video on the life and contemporary relevance of Adam Smith.*

**https://www.adamsmithworks.org/life_times**

1. What is Smith's invisible hand?
2. What does the title *An Animal That Trades* suggest about human nature?
3. What does Smith mean by division of labor?
4. What, according to Smith, should be the role of government in society?

### More on the Economy Way of Thinking

*Paul Heyne, a modern pioneer of the economy way of thinking, expands on the topic in this essay. Heyne taught economics at the University of Washington.*

**https://oll.libertyfund.org/page/heyne-economics-as-a-way-of-thinking**

1. Heyne summarizes the economic way of thinking into one sentence. Explain his definition in your own words by considering what he means by choices, costs, and benefits.
2. What does it mean to make decisions at the margin?
3. How does Heyne view opportunity cost?
4. What does Heyne mean by economizing behavior?
5. Why are prices so important to Heyne?

### The Essential Adam Smith

*Here you can downland an easy-to-read book on the life and ideas of Adam Smith written by James Otteson, a professor at the University of Notre Dame.*

**https://www.essentialscholars.org/smith**

1. What does Smith mean by a "mutual sympathy of sentiments" (Chapter 1)?
2. What does Smith mean when he suggests that people desire "not only to be loved but to be lovely" (Chapter 3)?
3. What are Smith's three rules of justice (Chapter 4)?
4. In your own words, explain Smith's invisible hand idea (Chapter 8).
5. According to Smith, what is the essential role of government (Chapter 10)?

### Would You Run?

*Do you think that you might wish to seek elected office? Check out this website to learn more about what is involved:*

**https://www.onlinecandidate.com/articles/running-for-office-faqs-and-tips**

1. What are some of the key steps in running for public office?
2. Which of these steps do you think you would be good at handling?
3. Which of these steps do you think you would be bad at handling?

CHAPTER 2

# Did Adam Smith Attend the Constitutional Convention? The Economic Principles in the U.S. Constitution

*"Scene at the Signing of the Constitution of the United States" by artist Howard Chandler Christy.*

# Adam Smith, James Madison, and the U.S. Constitution

Adam Smith, the founder of economics, published his famous book *The Wealth of Nations* in 1776, the same year as the Declaration of Independence. But did he attend the Constitutional Convention 11 years later in 1787?

No. Smith was strongly interested in Britain's North American colonies, but he never made the trip. Perhaps it is more correct to say that Smith did not physically travel to North America, but his ideas did. You can find them embedded in the Constitution if you know where to look.

The delegates to the Constitutional Convention were well aware of Smith's *The Wealth of Nations*. George Washington, who was elected unanimously to preside over the Constitutional Convention and later elected the first president of the United States, had a copy of *The Wealth of Nations* in his library. He had written notes in it. James Madison, who served as the fourth president of the United States, nominated *The Wealth of Nations* to be one of the books in a proposed congressional library. Madison is widely regarded as the primary architect of the U.S. Constitution.

### KEY ECONOMIC CONCEPTS

**checks and balances**
**Commerce Clause**
**Contract Clause**
**free trade**
**free trade zone**
**interest group**
**Takings Clause**
**tariff**
**Taxation Clause**
**slavery**

## The Civics Context

The Articles of Confederation represented the first attempt by the newly independent Americans to establish a new government. Worried about the problems they endured under British rule, many of our Founders were reluctant to grant much power to a central government. The Articles granted most political power to the states. The Articles were more like a treaty among 13 separate countries than a single government's charter.

Over time, the weaknesses in the Articles became apparent. George Washington, like Madison, began to argue that the new nation was in danger. On January 18, 1784, Washington wrote to Virginia governor Benjamin Harrison that the government was "a half starved, limping Government, that appears to be always moving upon crutches, & tottering at every step."[1]

Three fundamental economic problems faced the new nation under the Articles.

***1. Debt***

By the end of the war, the new nation had accumulated an enormous debt. The Continental Congress (made up of delegates from the 13 colonies during the war) borrowed money from other nations. Benjamin Franklin succeeded in securing loans of more than $2 million from France. John Adams, later to be the second president of the United States, obtained a loan from Dutch bankers. In addition, many individual Americans purchased government debt in the form of government bonds.

As the war ended in 1783, the nation was on the verge of bankruptcy. Under the Articles, the new Congress of the Confederation had no power to tax. The power to tax was retained by the states. The Congress could only request money from states. Not surprisingly, states would provide only a portion of the request or nothing at all. Between 1781 and 1787, Congress only received $1.5 million of the $10 million that it had requested from the states.

*Drafting the Articles of Confederation.*

***2. Tariff Wars***

A **tariff** is a tax imposed on imported goods. Under the Articles, the states retained the power to set tariffs on other states and foreign nations. Tariff wars frequently erupted between states. Pennsylvania placed tariffs on goods passing through Philadelphia. New Jersey residents paid more for goods imported from Philadelphia and New York because of state tariffs. The Articles failed to provide Congress the power to regulate interstate commerce. While tariffs were a source of revenue for some states, tariffs harmed the living standards of consumers by making goods more expensive.

***3. Military Weakness***

At the end of the American Revolution, the nation's military forces were exhausted. Yet, the new nation faced threats on all sides. Britain refused to abandon its forts and trading posts in the Northwest Territory. Spain limited American access to the Mississippi. The Barbary States of North Africa raided American ships in the Mediterranean. Without the power to tax, Congress had no way to raise and maintain an army or a navy.

But it wasn't all bad news. Under the Articles, Congress passed a series of land ordinances including the Northwest Ordinance of 1787. These ordinances provided a process for adding new states to the Union. They required that new states be treated as equals of the original states. Civil liberties were protected under a bill of rights. The Northwest Ordinance banned slavery in the new territories after 1800.

Washington, Madison, and others recognized the weaknesses of the Articles. The Annapolis Convention was called in the fall of 1785. It included 12 delegates from five states. The delegates quickly realized that not enough states were represented to make real progress. Madison and Alexander Hamilton encouraged the Annapolis Convention to issue a call for a constitutional convention to be held in Philadelphia in 1787. The hope was that more states would be represented, and the delegates could address the broad range of problems faced under the Articles.

The Philadelphia Convention convened in 1787 to revise the Articles. Madison played a pivotal role in framing the Constitution that replaced the Articles of Confederation. His "Virginia Plan" formed the basis of the Constitution. A key feature of his plan was the establishment of a federal government with checks and balances that divided power between the legislative, executive, and judicial branches and between the federal government and the states.

After the Constitutional Convention drafted the Constitution, Madison worked vigorously for its ratification. He along with Alexander

Hamilton and John Jay coauthored 85 articles and essays called *The Federalist Papers*. Madison also wrote the early drafts of what was to become the Bill of Rights, the first 10 amendments to the Constitution that provided written guarantees for the freedoms of speech and religion, the right to bear arms, and the right not to be forced to testify against oneself.

## The Economic Features of the Constitution

A principle of the economic way of thinking (see Chapter 1) is that people create economic systems or rules of the game that influence individual decisions. The Constitution established the broad rules of our political system. It also significantly shaped future development of the economic system.

The Constitution's framers worried about the role that **interest groups** would play in the new republic. In a free nation, citizens enjoy the freedom to organize groups to further their own interests. Today, we have thousands of interest groups from the National Education Association to the U.S. Chamber of Commerce.

James Madison called interest groups "factions." He feared that factions might capture the political process to further their narrow interests rather than the broad interests of the new nation as a whole.

In *Federalist 10*, Madison argued that forming interest groups is human nature. He wrote,

> It is in vain to say enlightened statesman adjust these clashing interests and render them all subservient to the public good. Enlightened statesmen will not always be at the helm.[2] (page 44)

So, what could be done? Madison suggested that the way to handle the situation was to prevent interest groups from controlling the political system. How do you do that? By creating a system of **checks and balances** to limit the power of the central government. This was done by providing for three separate branches, including the legislative branch (U.S. Congress), executive branch (the presidency), and judicial branch (the Supreme Court and other federal courts). Each branch has its own system of checks on the

*Detail from "The Constitution" by Barry Faulkner—a mural at the rotunda of the National Archives building.*

others, and each possesses distinct and separate powers. Congress may pass a bill—a new piece of legislation. But a bill requires the signature of the president before it can take effect. If the president decides to veto or reject a bill, Congress can vote to override it with a two-thirds majority in the House of Representatives and the Senate. And even if Congress approves and the president signs a bill, it remains possible that the Supreme Court may toss it by finding it to be unconstitutional.

Madison's prime consideration was to constrain the power of interest groups desiring to use the political process to further their well-being. But the system of checks and balances seems slow and cumbersome. It is. Today, thousands of bills are introduced into Congress each year, but only a handful eventually become law. This, however, is the process that the Founders intended. The process makes it hard to pass legislation that promotes narrow group interests but does not have broad popular support.

What are the more specific economic features of the Constitution? Let's take a closer look.

**The Taxation Clause**: As we mentioned earlier, the Articles of Confederation did not provide the central government with the ability to collect taxes. Article I, Section 8 of the Constitution states that Congress shall have the power "to lay and collect taxes." This power enables the federal government to use tax revenue to pay for goods and services. It gives the federal government the ability to establish military forces to protect the rights of the nation, its citizens, and its commerce. It also allows the federal government to borrow money.

**The Commerce Clause**: We described earlier how trade wars were flaring up between the states. Article I, Section 8 states that Congress shall have the power to "regulate commerce with foreign nations, and among the several states, and with Indian tribes." This clause prevents states from doing their own regulating of interstate commerce. It stops them from imposing tariffs on imports from other states.

Today, we take it for granted that the United States is a **free trade zone**, where states impose no tariffs on goods from other states. But in 1787 this was a debatable proposition. Adam Smith was a consistent advocate of **free trade** within and between nations. The Commerce Clause is strong evidence of the impact of Smith's ideas on Madison and others.

**The Contract Clause**: Article I, Section 10 states that "no state shall … pass any ... law impairing the obligation of contracts." This provision protects the enforcement of contracts by the court system. The administration of justice through a court system is vital to economic growth. It would be nearly impossible for business owners and consumers to prosper unless people are protected from violence and feel secure in their ownership of personal property and businesses.

Again, we can find Adam Smith's fingerprints all over the Contract Clause. Smith wrote in *The Wealth of Nations*:

> Commerce and manufactures can seldom flourish long in any state which does not enjoy a regular administration of justice, in which the people do not feel themselves secure in the possession of their property, in which the faith of contracts is not supported by law.[3] (page 910)

**The Takings Clause**: The "takings clause" of the Fifth Amendment states that government may not take property for public purposes without "just compensation." The Fifth Amendment limits the ability of the government to restrict property ownership and ensured rule of law. In other words, even the federal government has to obey the law.

This is not always the case around the world. In nations such as Cuba, China, North Korea, and Venezuela, the property rights of families and business owners are not safe. Would you invest in a new business or keep your savings in financial institutions if you feared that the government could take it away from you without compensation? Unlikely. By establishing the Takings Clause, the Founders provided an incentive for people to save, invest, and start new enterprises.

## Civics Questions & Economic Answers

### Did the Constitution protect slavery, or did it envision the end of slavery?

This is a controversial question. The Constitution did not abolish slavery. One view is that it protected slavery. For example, it delayed ending the external slave trade until 1808. And it is true that many of the signers of the Constitution were slaveholders, including James Madison himself, sometimes called the "Father of the Constitution."

Another view is that the Founders believed slavery would fade away. Many thought that its inefficiencies and immoral nature would cause it to eventually collapse. History appeared to be on the side of slavery's decline. In 1772, Lord Chief Justice Mansfield, head of the British court system, ruled in *Somerset v Stewart* that slavery had no basis in common law and had never been formerly approved by Parliament. (Great Britain did not end the slave trade until 1807. In 1884, it ended slavery in most of its colonies.)

Soon after independence, 10 of 13 of the American states abolished the slave trade. In addition, many delegates regarded slavery as morally repugnant. Several delegates including Benjamin Franklin, James Wilson, and Gouverneur Morris were abolitionists. Others, such as John Adams, spoke out forcefully against slavery.

### How did the Founders resolve the slavery dispute?

As debate continued, South Carolina and Georgia threatened to walk out of the Convention if slavery was threatened. What might happen next? The Founders had two worries. First, the new nation would crumble into a combination of confederacies or independent states. The new nation would resemble Europe, with unending conflicts and wars destroying lives and prosperity. Second, they feared the establishment of a separate, sovereign slaveholding nation in North America operating with few internal restraints.

Many of the Founders believed that keeping slave states within the union provided a better chance to abolish slavery over the long term. A measure called the *three-fifths compromise* illustrates this point. Delegates who *supported* slavery wished to count all people, free and enslaved, for the purposes of representation. The supporters of counting all people hoped that this approach to allocating representatives would strengthen the power of the slave states in Congress and thus make emancipation less likely.

Delegates who *opposed* slavery wished to count only free citizens. They hoped that this approach would weaken the power of the slave states in Congress and thus make emancipation more likely. Unable to agree on counting zero slaves or all slaves by state, the Founders decided that enslaved individuals would be counted as three-fifths of a person by counting three-fifths of the slaves for representation.

The best opportunity to abolish slavery almost certainly occurred at the Constitutional Convention of 1787 when the delegates debated it. But they failed. Slavery became profitable with changes in the production of cotton. It would take the bloody Civil War to finally abolish it.

### What did the Founders learn from Adam Smith regarding slavery?

Smith argued forcefully against slavery. His first book was titled *The Theory of Moral Sentiments*, and Smith wrote that it is cruel

> to reduce them [enslaved people] into the vilest of all states, that of domestic slavery, and to sell them, man, woman, and child, like so many herds of cattle to the highest bidder in the market.[4] (page 282)

In *The Wealth of Nations*, Smith wrote,

> The experience of all ages and nations, I believe, demonstrates that the work done by free men comes cheaper in the end than the work performed by slaves. ... Whatever work he does, beyond what is sufficient to purchase

> his own maintenance, can be squeezed out of him by violence only and not by any interest of his own.[5] (pages 387–388)

Smith understood that slavery is the opposite of a free market. Coercion was required at all times to make slavery work.

The first principle of economic freedom is that individuals own themselves and their labor. Exchanges under slavery were coerced, not voluntary. Enslaved individuals were regarded as the property of their owners. They were not permitted to act in their own self-interest to obtain an education, work for wages, own land, or own a business. They were denied the opportunity to use the profit motive to benefit themselves. It was the opposite of the voluntary exchange fundamental for a free market.

### Was the Constitution in part an economic document? Did good timing have anything to do with its success?

In addition to being a political document, the Constitution established a set of institutional rules such as limiting the role of interest groups through checks and balances and encouraging free trade through the Commerce Clause. These rules significantly shaped the future development of the U.S. market economy. And yes, the extraordinary economic success of the original Constitution was, in part, a result of good timing. It was written at a critical period in U.S. history. It was forged by a group with immense ability led by the great minds of people such as James Madison. It is hard to imagine that this set of unique circumstances would ever happen again.

## QUESTIONS for DISCUSSION

1. In what sense did Adam Smith attend the Constitutional Convention of 1787?
2. What were three weaknesses of the Articles of Confederation that you regard as most important?
3. What did James Madison consider to be the greatest threat to the new republic? How did he address it in the Constitution?
4. What are four other economic features of the Constitution?
5. Of the four, which two do you consider to be the most important? Why?
6. Why did the Founders fail in abolishing slavery?
7. What were Adam Smith's views on slavery?

## James Madison on the Economic Role of Government

PRIMARY SOURCE

James Madison agreed with Smith that the role of government in the economy should be limited. Madison argued that the laws of the nation should be few and easily understood. He believed that great injury comes to commerce from the operation of an unstable government. Stability assures producers that investing in new enterprises will have minimal interference from the government. Why would farmers work to clear trees and dig out stones to start a farm if they feared the government would take their land, steal their crops, or impose impossibly high taxes? Limiting the role of government and ensuring stability provides the context for commerce to flourish.

Here are Madison's own words from the *Federalist Papers: The Federalist No. 62* (February 27, 1788):

> What prudent merchant will hazard his fortunes in any new branch of commerce, when he knows not but that his plans may be rendered unlawful before they can be executed? What farmer or manufacturer will lay himself out for the encouragement given to any particular cultivation or establishment, when he can have no assurance that his preparatory labors and advances will not render him a victim to an inconstant government? In a word no great improvement or laudable enterprise, can go forward, which requires the auspices of a steady system of national policy.[6] (page 306)

*James Madison*

### QUESTIONS for DISCUSSION

1. Do Madison and Smith appear to agree on the role of government in the economy? How?
2. In your own words, what is the main point that Madison makes in *Federalist 62*?

Contemporary Connection

## Africa's Free Trade Zone

As mentioned earlier, Adam Smith was a proponent of free trade. Smith argued that nations should specialize at producing goods and services and then trade with others. The idea is that open trade within states, among and between states, and among and between nations improves the standard of living of all trading partners. Some gain more and some gain less, but everyone who trades is better off with trade than without trade.

The benefits of free trade are not a secret. Smith inspired the Commerce Clause, which unleased trade between and among the states of the new American nation. This helped the new nation prosper. Both the European Union and the United States, Mexico, and Canada Agreement (USMCA) follow the same principle.

Many nations of continental Africa today are placing bets on more open trade as a way to develop wealth and reduce poverty. In January 2021, the African Continental Free Trade Area (AfCFTA) created a new market estimated to be as large as 1.3 billion people across 55 countries. It has an estimated combined Gross Domestic Product (GDP) of $3.4 trillion. GDP is the total value of all goods produced within the borders of a nation. The agreement is believed to have the potential to lift up to 30 million Africans out of extreme poverty. The World Bank defines extreme poverty as living on $1.90 per day or less per person. In addition, it is hoped that the AfCFTA will help African countries diversify their exports, accelerate economic growth, and attract direct investment from other nations.

How does it work? The most important element of the AfCFTA is the reduction of tariffs among the member nations. Tariffs on 90 percent of affected items will be eliminated over a five-year period for the least developed nations and a 10-year period for the more developed nations.

*African heads of states and governments pose during African Union Summit for the agreement to establish the African Continental Free Trade Area.*

The agreement aims to develop continentwide regulations that, much like regulations in the European Union, will allow businesses in one country to produce goods and services that can be readily sold to consumers or businesses in other member countries.

Current projections show that the implementation of the AfCFTA could increase real income on average by 7 percent by 2035. The expectation is that the volume of total exports will increase by almost 30 percent by 2035. Manufacturing is expected to benefit the most.

Much could go wrong. It remains to be seen if the projections are correct and nations keep their commitments. In the meantime, perhaps you wish to do a little research to see how this latest application of Smith's ideas regarding trade is progressing.

## QUESTIONS for DISCUSSION

1. What is the African Continental Free Trade Agreement (AfCFTA)?
2. How does the AfCFTA work?
3. What are the projected results of the AfCFTA?

## Web Quests

**Enter any of the links below and use the questions to get you started on your own web quest.**

### James Madison

*The link below includes a video where historian Joseph Ellis discusses the lives and contributions of Alexander Hamilton and James Madison.*

**https://www.mountvernon.org/library/digitalhistory/digital-encyclopedia/article/james-madison/**

1. What was Madison's relationship with George Washington and Thomas Jefferson? How did it change over time?
2. After watching the video of Joseph Ellis, compare the lives and contributions of Alexander Hamilton and James Madison.

### Slavery and the Constitution

*Follow this link to learn more about the Founders and slavery.*

**https://billofrightsinstitute.org/essays/slavery-and-the-constitution**

1. In what ways have some scholars suggested that the Constitution was designed to protect slavery?
2. What were the beliefs of most of the Founders regarding slavery?
3. Compare the views of Abraham Lincoln and Stephen Douglas regarding constitutional rights and slavery.
4. Explain the argument that the Constitution was written in such a way as to eventually eliminate slavery.

### The African Continental Free Trade Area

*Here you can take a deeper dive regarding free trade in Africa.*

**https://www.worldbank.org/en/topic/trade/publication/the-african-continental-free-trade-area**

1. What is the African Continental Free Trade Area (AfCFTA)?
2. How does the AfCFTA propose to make continental Africa more prosperous?
3. Would Adam Smith have agreed with the goals and policies of the AfCFTA? Explain.

# CHAPTER 3

# Is Economic Freedom the First Civil Liberty?

*Sergey Brin, co-founder of Google.*

# Sergey Brin Succeeds in a Land of Opportunity

You may have never heard of Sergey Brin, but almost everyone reading this textbook has heard of Google. This is the story of a man who immigrated to the United States to pursue a better life and became a highly successful entrepreneur as a founder of Google.

Sergey Brin was born in 1973 in Moscow. Young Sergey was 6 years old when he and his family escaped Russia to avoid persecution from the then-ruling Communist Party. In the United States, Brin had earned a B.S. in computer science by the age of 19. In graduate school while studying computer science at Stanford University, he met Larry Page. Finding they had common interests, they worked together to build the algorithms that resulted in the most popular search engine used today: Google.[1] As of September 2021, the Bloomberg Billionaires Index estimates that Brin is the seventh richest person in the world, with an estimated net worth of $124 billion.

What does it mean to call Brin an **entrepreneur**? It means he possesses the type of creative personality, desire to innovate, and courage to take significant financial risks to bring a new product or service to the market. What else contributed to Brin's success? Brin is an immigrant who left the former Soviet Union, where economic freedom was sharply limited. Would this successful, talented mind have been able to create the Google empire had he stayed in his home country? Likely not. For entrepreneurship to be able to thrive, it needs the right environment to grow. In this chapter, we explore the type of environment needed for entrepreneurship to thrive.

### KEY ECONOMIC CONCEPTS

**civil liberties**
**economic freedom**
**economic growth**
**economic institutions**
**entrepreneur**
**gross domestic product (GDP)**
**political freedom**
**political institutions**
**pork-barrel legislation**
**rent-seeking**
**special interest group**

## The Civics Context

### Political Freedom and Economic Freedom

Civics textbooks pay specific attention to political freedom, characterizing societies by how democratic or autocratic they are. Political freedom is the presence of institutions that foster free and fair elections and that constrain the behavior of governmental leaders. A democratic country has high levels of political freedom, while an autocratic country has low levels of political freedom. Economic freedom is not the same as political freedom, but it is critical to the flourishing of a society.

For individuals to release their entrepreneurial spirits and talents, they need to be in an environment of economic freedom. Individuals have economic freedom when property they acquire without the use of force, fraud, or theft is protected from physical invasion by others, and they are free to use, exchange, or give their property as long as their actions do not violate the identical rights of others. The cornerstones of economic freedom are the following:[2]

- Personal choice
- Voluntary exchange coordinated by markets
- Freedom to enter and compete in markets
- Protection of persons and their property from aggression by others

The Fraser Institute publishes the Economic Freedom of the World (EFW) Index, which measures economic freedom on a scale of 0 to 10 (where 10 is the highest level of economic freedom). The EFW Index is split into five main areas:[3]

*1. Size of Government (government spending and taxes)*

The components of this area indicate the extent to which countries rely on the political process to allocate resources, goods, and services. In general, lower levels of government spending and lower tax rates result in higher levels of economic freedom.

*2. Legal System and Property Rights*

The key elements of a legal system consistent with economic freedom are rule of law, security of property rights, an independent and unbiased judiciary, and impartial and effective enforcement of the law. The more property rights are protected by the rule of law (and contracts are enforced in an evenhanded manner), the higher the level of economic freedom.

*3. Access to Sound Money*

An absence of sound money undermines gains from trade. For example, high and volatile rates of inflation alter the terms of long-term contracts and make it hard for people to plan for the future. Thus, having long-term price stability (a low and stable rate of inflation) results in greater economic freedom.

*4. Freedom to Trade Internationally*

Protectionist policies that limit or prohibit international trade make it more costly for people to engage in voluntary exchange. Lowering barriers to trade (such as fewer tariffs and fewer quotas) results in more economic freedom.

*5. Regulation of Credit, Labor, and Business*

Government regulation restricts entry into markets and therefore limits freedom of exchange in the credit, labor, and product markets. Therefore, less government regulation results in more economic freedom.

Below is a map depicting data from the Economic Freedom of the World 2021 Annual Report, where the countries have been organized into quartiles based on their level of economic freedom: most free, 2nd quartile, 3rd quartile, and least free.

**MAP 1 Economic Freedom of the World**

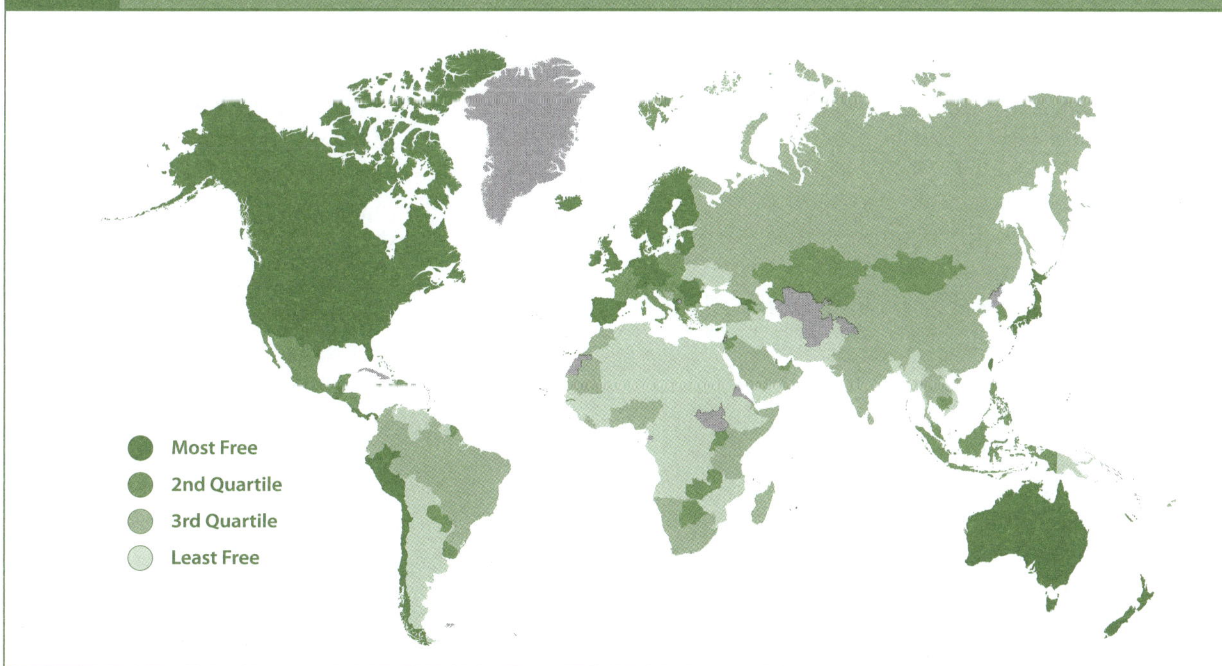


*Source:* The Fraser Institute's *Economic Freedom of the World: 2021 Annual Report*

## The Economics of "Rules of the Game"

The rules of the game—the economic institutions in place—directly affect the incentives within the economy and thus also the outcomes present within that society. Imagine that you are taxed 30 percent at your job, and then the next year you are taxed 75 percent. Would you work as many hours as you did before? Would you put in as much effort? Perhaps it's no longer worth it to you to pick up an additional shift. The same thought process will be true of other workers, innovators, and employers within the economy. This example connects with Area 1 of the Economic Freedom of the World (EFW) Index, Size of Government. How much you're taxed limits the personal choices you're able to make, which directly affects your incentives and economic freedom.

Most individuals in the United States don't think much about property rights. We are accustomed to having strong private property rights and rule of law here. Imagine you are a farmer cultivating your field of crops, and after a year of hard work of planting, sowing, and harvesting your field, someone takes half of what you harvested. What recourse do you have?

In the United States you could work with the police and the court system to get your property returned or be compensated for your loss. But what about countries such as Somalia, North Korea, Venezuela, Sudan, or Syria, where the rule of law is not secure and stable? What if there's not a fair court or police system? That is going to have a devastating impact on the incentives of individuals in all sectors of the economy. This illustrates the importance of Area 2 of the EFW Index, Legal System and Property Rights. This area is essential for a society to have an incentive structure in place that rewards productivity and innovation.

What if you couldn't trust the value of your currency to be stable from one day to the next, or from one week to the next? In the United States, it's common for workers to get paid once every two weeks or even once a month. But if your currency lost value nearly every day, you would

*German children play with stacks of money in 1923.*

want to be paid every day so you could purchase food for the week before the money depreciated any further in value. Venezuela, Zimbabwe, and Germany are a few examples where inflation has been high and volatile before. After World War I, Germany experienced hyperinflation. At one point the exchange rate between the U.S. dollar and the German mark was one trillion marks to one dollar, and a wheelbarrow full of marks would not even buy a newspaper. These examples showcasing inflation correspond to Area 3 of the EFW Index, Access to Sound Money.

Imagine for a moment that you could only consume what you had personally produced: housing, clothing, food, cars, computers, phones, and other electronics. What would the quality and variety of these various items look like? Now imagine you are able to trade with others within your country. No longer limited by your abilities, you would get better quality, greater variety, all at lower prices! Now imagine you are able to trade with anyone in the world. Just think of the additional variety that you'll be able to enjoy—products and foods that you have never heard of before! When you are free to trade with individuals in other countries (without trade barriers), this increases the economic freedom of the trading partners in each country. This is measured within Area 4 of the EFW Index, Freedom to Trade Internationally.

Let's say you decide to open your own business. But what if you lived in a country with a lot of regulations that made it hard to legally get started? In the United States, it only takes on average four days to start a business. This 2019 figure comes from the World Bank's "Doing Business" survey project. But in Venezuela, it takes on average 230 days—more than 7 months! In Haiti, it is estimated to take about 97 days (more than 3 months). Such governmental regulations certainly affect our economic freedom, which is why the "Doing Business" survey data by the World Bank is included as one of the variables in Area 5 of the EFW Index, Regulation of Credit, Labor, and Business.

As these examples show, economic freedom will certainly affect the incentives you face and, thus, your choices and actions. The same will be true for others in your society, which is why we see such differences in wealth and prosperity across countries. Those with high levels of economic freedom prosper, while those with poor economic institutions (inconsistent with economic freedom) suffer from dire poverty.

## Civics Questions & Economic Answers

### Why might economic freedom be thought of as the first "civil liberty"?

Freedom of speech, the right to assemble, and protections against unjust imprisonment are classic civil liberties. But having the right to a fair trial is not only a civil liberty; it is part of what makes a strong legal system and rule of law, a key element of economic freedom.

Are civil liberties and economic freedom connected in other ways, too? One aspect of economic freedom is having protection of private property, which includes having the right to control my own labor. I can choose whether to work, for whom to work, and at what wage. That is precisely the civil right that was not allowed when slavery existed. Slave labor is a violation of an individual's civil rights, and it is also a clear violation of their economic rights, too, which is why some may consider economic freedom as the first civil liberty. But when exercising economic freedom, people express themselves in many ways—not just in the work they perform and the businesses they start, but also in the places they travel and the clothes they wear. In this regard, civil rights and economic freedom are inextricably linked.

### Are natural resources the key to economic growth and prosperity?

People often wonder whether geography, culture, political institutions, natural resources, and other variables are the keys to economic growth. In years past, it was commonly believed that having a large endowment of natural resources was the key to a nation's prosperity. However, in reality many countries that have abundant natural resources are poor countries with little economic growth. This counterintuitive trend is so consistent that economists have labeled it the "natural resources curse."

Scholars are still debating why some countries succumb to the natural resources curse while others seemingly do just fine. One explanation is that countries with abundant natural resources are likely to experience a great deal of corruption. In such countries, individuals or special interest groups spend their time, money, and other resources lobbying government officials to get special kickbacks and favors, an activity known as **rent-seeking**.

Researchers have found that rent-seeking hinders growth and development within the economy. Natural resource extraction concessions (special privileges) are usually given to large enterprises—whether governmental or privately owned. In such a situation, future competition is reduced and the early winners then have a strong incentive to protect their status and positions.

This might include bribing governmental officials, one of many forms of rent-seeking. This differs from the healthy competition we see in many other sectors of the economy and could be one reason why resource-abundant countries are prone to rent-seeking and corruption.[4]

### Does international trade result in one country "winning" while the other "loses"?

If opening up trade to allow someone in Florida to trade with someone in North Carolina is a good thing because it makes both trading partners better off, then the same is true when we open up trade between people in different countries. Perhaps an aspiring fashion entrepreneur in the United States would like to purchase textiles from a business in China. Or a young mom in China wants to purchase infant milk formula from a factory based in New Zealand. A coffee shop owner in New Zealand buys sugar from El Salvador. In all of these cases, both parties are better off when two individuals voluntarily trade with one another—regardless of how close in proximity they are to each other. When we use the term *trade* here, keep in mind a "trade" doesn't have to be one item traded for another item. Almost always, there is a transfer of money for goods.

### Should trade always be balanced between individuals?

Suppose a person buys a lot from a trading partner but sells that trading partner little or nothing at all. If you become a history teacher and buy groceries locally, you do so because you'd rather have the food while the grocery store owner would rather have your dollars. In a single week, you might buy $75 worth of groceries and not sell the grocery store owner anything. By one way of thinking, you have a **trade deficit** of $75 with the grocer.

But there is no reason the grocer should consume your services such as a lecture on what led to World War II. You don't need to sell anything to the grocer for you to both be better off and enjoy what you received out of the trade. The school board buys your history teaching services, and you use the dollars to buy groceries. Or perhaps you are a surgeon who likes to frequent your local bookstore. You spend your dollars at the bookstore. But you do not think the bookstore owner needs to spend those earned dollars at your hospital requesting a surgery, right?

### Should trade always be balanced internationally?

Just as we don't expect a history teacher and a neighborhood grocery store to run a trade balance, there's no reason we should expect trade to be balanced between countries. After all, trade between countries is just the aggregate of the trades between individuals in each country. This means that when discussing international trade, the country-level figures are just adding up a bunch of individual trades (transactions) made by ordinary individuals and businesses.

Think about what happens if the United States runs a "trade deficit" with China (this means that American individuals bought more from Chinese businesses than what Chinese individuals bought from American businesses). The Americans purchasing the Chinese goods consider the products to be more valuable than the money; in return, the Chinese received U.S. currency from the transaction. Is it a bad thing to receive more products from someone (or a country) than what they buy from you?

As long as the trade is voluntary (not forced or coerced), then both trading partners gain from the trade. There is no reason to expect the seller of a given item to buy what the purchaser happens to produce. Nor is there any reason why individuals and businesses in the United States should try to buy exactly as much from the businesses in China as what those in China buy from people in the United States.

That's the beauty of using currency: it eliminates the need for "coincidence of wants," so you can make your trade and then use the money you earned to purchase what you desire.

This concept often seems like common sense when put in terms of two local individuals, such as the grocer in the United States not wanting to consume any history lessons from a customer who is a teacher (or the bookstore owner not needing services from the surgeon). Still, many people get confused by the same concept once they start thinking in terms of international trade. Hopefully now you'll recognize these concepts when you hear international trade being discussed on the news, in your local newspaper, or in your social media newsfeeds.

## QUESTIONS for DISCUSSION

1. What is economic freedom?
2. How does economic freedom differ from political freedom?
3. In what five areas does the Fraser Institute measure economic freedom? Why are these five areas important?
4. Can you personalize economic freedom? That is, what are a few aspects of economic freedom that you're able to enjoy in your own life?
5. How does economic freedom affect incentives and entrepreneurs in your hometown? What could make your city or hometown more prosperous?
6. Do nations rich with natural resources automatically prosper? Why or why not?
7. When trading, is it typically true that one side of the trade wins while the other side loses? What if one trading partner is already wealthier than the other? What if the trading partners are in different countries?
8. What would it mean for trade to be "balanced" between you and your favorite grocery store? Would that be a good thing?
9. Let's say that two people want to engage in a trade and they are doing so of their own volition, but you—a third party who is not a participant in the transaction—don't think the trade should occur (perhaps you believe one of the individuals is getting ripped off). Do you think you would/should lobby the government to prohibit such a trade from occurring? Why or why not? What if you were wanting to participate in a trade (and your trading partner also wanted the trade to happen!), but someone else lobbied the government and got a law passed to prohibit or hinder such types of trades/transactions from occurring? Does your opinion change if you're the one being prevented from engaging in the voluntary transaction?

## Muhammad Yunus Quote from the Film *Poverty, Inc.*

PRIMARY SOURCE

Muhammad Yunus is a social entrepreneur, banker, and economist in Bangladesh who won the Nobel Peace Prize in 2006 for founding Grameen Bank and for his work helping impoverished people in Bangladesh through microcredit (small-scale) loans. In the film *Poverty, Inc.*, Muhammad Yunus says:

> When I talk about poverty, one example I like to give is the bonsai tree. Go and look at the tallest tree in the forest, and pick the best seed of that tallest tree, and plant it in a flowerpot. You get about a meter high or less than a meter high plant. So what's wrong with this little one? The wrong thing is the flowerpot. If you had planted in the real soil, it would be as tall as the tree you saw in the forest. Poor people are bonsai people. Society does not provide them the base. The laws, and the institutions, and the policies do not allow them the base. So they remain stunted, and we call them poor people.

*Muhammad Yunus*

Here Yunus is pointing out that a country needs to have economic institutions consistent with economic freedom for its people to prosper and flourish. Economic institutions are the legal, regulatory, and social constraints that affect the security of property rights, enforcement of contracts, and one's choice of when and how to participate in an exchange. These "rules of the game" exert a major impact on the incentive to engage in productive activities, innovate,

and realize gains from trade, particularly when the trading partners do not know each other.

All of this explains why the countries on the Economic Freedom of the World map with high levels of economic freedom also tend to be the countries with the greatest prosperity. Prosperity can be measured many different ways: income (GDP per capita) and economic growth, health measures like infant and child mortality rates, life expectancy at birth, or education measures such as literacy rates or educational attainment. It's not surprising, then, that we find a negative relationship between economic freedom and poverty (such as the extreme and moderate poverty rates measured by the World Bank).

## Questions for Discussion

1. Why does the story of the bonsai tree make a good metaphor when discussing entrepreneurship, economic institutions, and prosperity versus poverty?
2. How might the availability of small loans (microcredit) help a nation achieve greater economic freedom?
3. What do you consider to be a good measure of prosperity?

Contemporary Connection

## Freedom Threatened in Hong Kong

As of the *Economic Freedom of the World: 2021 Annual Report*, the EFW Index measures the economic freedom of 165 countries—well, technically 164 countries and 1 territory. That one territory is Hong Kong, which has managed to remain ranked #1 on the EFW Index since its inception in 1975, with the exception of two years (2002 and 2003) when Hong Kong temporarily slipped to the spot of #2 in the world.

Hong Kong was part of China from ancient times. But after a colonial period when the British occupied Hong Kong during the First Opium War, China signed an agreement in 1898 leasing the territory of Hong Kong to the British for 99 years. The United Kingdom (UK) and China signed the Sino-British Joint Declaration in 1984, which set the conditions in which Hong Kong was peacefully transferred to China in 1997. In this treaty, China agreed to allow the region of Hong Kong to be self-governing with a high degree of political and economic autonomy for 50 years under a framework known as "one country, two systems."

The "one country, two systems" principle is laid out in Hong Kong's constitutional document, the Basic Law. This law allows for Hong Kong to run its own political and economic affairs—including holding its own political elections and having a free-market economic system. This system differs from how the mainland People's Republic of China operates under communism. The Basic Law also protects the civil rights of people in Hong Kong, such as freedom of assembly and freedom of speech. Such civil rights are not present in mainland China.

In 2019, Hong Kong's Chief Executive, Carrie Lam, proposed a bill to change the relationship between Hong Kong and China on criminal matters. Many in Hong Kong took to the streets to protest this bill, fearing that it would put their citizens and foreign nationals at risk by allowing suspects to be sent to mainland China for trial. The fear was that the proposal would ultimately undermine the independence of Hong Kong's legal and judicial system. Lam eventually suspended and withdrew the proposed bill.

*Gao Zhisheng*

Critics maintain that China has a history of disregarding fundamental human rights. Reports of human rights abuses include forced labor, organ harvesting, abusive psychiatric practices, and illegal imprisonment. The reports of illegal imprisonment included everything from arbitrary detention to systematic torture (including sexual abuse and beatings).

Examples of such illegal imprisonment are abundant. Those subjected to illegal imprisonment and other human rights abuses include human rights lawyers Gao Zhisheng and Jian Tianyong and human rights advocates Chen Guancheng and Liu Xiabobo (also a Nobel laureate).

Gao Zhisheng is a well-known lawyer who disappeared at the hands of Chinese officials, was eventually charged with "subverting state power," and tortured during his years in Chinese prisons. In response to his work as a human rights lawyer, Zhisheng was unable to renew his law license. This prevented him from working in his chosen occupation, severely decreasing his economic freedom. Over the years he endured multiple imprisonments and beatings at unknown locations. As of the writing of this book in 2021, no one knows where he is being detained. He is what they call "forcibly disappeared" by Chinese officials.[5] Zhisheng's economic freedom, political freedom, and civil rights have all been severely restricted.

On June 30, 2020, China passed a measure known as the Hong Kong National Security Law. The law was passed weeks after being announced. The text was kept secret from the public and even the Hong Kong government until after it was enacted, and it completely bypassed Hong Kong's legislature.[6] The new law provides an expansive definition of crimes against the government: nearly anything could constitute as "secession," "subversion," "organization and perpetration of terrorist activities," or "collusion with foreign forces or with external elements to endanger national security." Penalties now range up to life imprisonment. China can now exercise jurisdiction over any alleged violations of the National Security Law, and can prosecute and adjudicate the cases in mainland China.

Human rights advocates worry that these vague and broadly defined terms will be used to continue to imprison (and torture) those who politically disagree with mainland China.[7] The citizens of Hong Kong and international observers consider it to be a breach of the agreement between China and the UK that outlined "one country, two systems" until 2047.

In July 2020, pro-democracy activists held a primary to select candidates for Hong Kong's Legislative Council election in September. Lam and Chinese authorities condemned the opposition group and warned that they could be violating the National Security Law by participating in activities that fall within the category of subverting state power. Despite these threats, over 600,000 voters turned out for the primary election. Hong Kong authorities retaliated against their political opponents with raids, arrests, and freezing of funds.[8] Arresting political candidates for participating in a primary election is a prime example of obstructing their political freedom. Freezing the bank accounts of such individuals and making fundraising an illegal activity is an example of restricting their economic freedom.

Throughout 2020 and 2021 there have been mass arrests with police claiming the crime of "subversion." Political freedom and civil rights in Hong Kong have most certainly decreased in recent years, and the economic freedom of the citizens of Hong Kong is in jeopardy, too.

## QUESTIONS for DISCUSSION

1. In your view, has the "one country, two systems" agreement been upheld in Hong Kong? Why?
2. What is subversion, and why does it pose a problem for the citizens of China and Hong Kong?
3. What is the Hong Kong National Security Law, and what does it mean for Hong Kong citizens?
4. What is more important to the happiness of citizens in a nation, their political freedom or their economic freedom? Explain your answer. (Something to keep in mind and consider, is that when Hong Kong was a territory of the UK during the 99 year lease, the people of Hong Kong did not have political freedom—but they had extremely high levels of economic freedom during that time.)

## Web Quests

**Enter any of the links below and use the questions to get you started on your own web quest.**

### *Economic Freedom of the World Index*

*The* Economic Freedom of the World *(EFW)* Index *is published by the Fraser Institute*[8]*, and measures the economic freedom across countries. The index is comprised of 44 variables categorized into 5 main areas.*

**https://www.fraserinstitute.org/economic-freedom**

1. Download the latest copy of the *Economic Freedom of the World Annual Report*. Which exhibit (bar chart graph) showcasing economic freedom's relation to other well-being measures do you consider to be most impressive? Hint: You can find a PDF of the EFW annual reports by clicking the Research tab and then clicking Publications & Commentaries. Look for these exhibits in Chapter 1, prior to the country data tables, which you're likely to find in Chapter 2.
2. Check out the interactive EFW map on the home page. What does each color on the map represent?

### The CIA World Factbook

*This valuable resource provides excellent country descriptions and basic economic and social data on the countries of the world.*

**https://www.cia.gov/the-world-factbook/**

1. Find the entry for Hong Kong in the *CIA World Factbook* and locate the one-page summary. Now compare Hong Kong's one-page summary with that of another country of interest. What is the most striking difference between the two countries you chose?

### The film *Poverty, Inc.*

*In* Poverty, Inc. *(2014), filmmaker Michael Matheson Miller investigates the complex global industry of foreign aid. Time: 1 hour, 34 min. Available via multiple platforms such as Amazon Prime and YouTube.*

**https://www.povertyinc.org**

1. Watch the film *Poverty, Inc.*, and pay special attention to when the interviewees express concern about the human dignity of those living in poverty. What points did the film make about the "global poverty industry" and false perceptions of the poor?
2. What is an example in the film *Poverty, Inc.* in which the well-intentioned efforts of a charity organization harmed the people they were trying to serve? What is an example in the film where the well-intentioned efforts of a social enterprise harmed the people they were trying to serve?
3. In the film *Poverty, Inc.*, what does Magatte Wade think of the charity given to her home country of Senegal? Does she believe the charity to be helpful or harmful? What does she say her people of Senegal actually need to achieve prosperity?

CHAPTER

# 4

# Is Economic Freedom Indispensable to Democracy?

*Students participate in English class at an elite school in Pyongyang, North Korea.*

# Yeonmi Park's Personal Account of Life in a Communist Dictatorship

In her biography *In Order to Live: A North Korean Girl's Journey to Freedom*, Yeonmi Park describes how, as a little girl, she was indoctrinated to believe she was fortunate and lived better than the rest of the world. Yet for much of her childhood she went without food on a regular basis, and she saw bodies in the streets and river from those who starved to death.

Because her village of Hyesan was separated from China by only the Yalu River, she can recall being able to see the lights and smell the aromas of food cooking on the other side of the river. During the worst of the famine, she and her sister would catch and eat bugs to fight hunger. Yeonmi was taught that their "Dear Leaders"—dictators Kim Jong-Il and Kim Jong-un—could read their minds. No religion was allowed, and only the Kims could be revered.

Yeonmi explains how North Korea had an endless list of crimes. It was illegal to wear jeans or to dye or cut your hair in a way not approved by the government. All forms of foreign media were forbidden. The government controlled every aspect of life. Yeonmi and her fellow North Koreans were unable to climb the economic ladder based on their work ethic, intelligence, or interests. Instead, everyone in North Korea is classified by their "songbun" status. This status system is based on the political, social, and economic background of one's ancestors, as well as their own behavior and the behavior of their relatives. One's songbun status determines everything from job and college opportunities to the amount of food received.

*Yeonmi Parks speaks at a press conference at the 2018 Oslo Freedom Forum.*

### KEY ECONOMIC CONCEPTS

**civil rights (civil liberties)**
**constitutional monarchy**
**economic freedom**
**political freedom**
**republic**

Yeonmi was part of the upper-middle class during her early years of childhood. Even so, she was living in what would be considered poverty by Western standards—no modern plumbing, and the majority of the time she did not have electricity. Then her father was arrested and sent to a prison camp for the crime of buying and selling goods. Once arrested, he was kicked out of the Worker's Party, securing a dismal fate for his entire family as their songbun status was ruined.

Public executions were used to teach citizens the consequences of disobedience. Yeonmi remembers a young man being executed by firing squad for killing and eating a cow. It didn't matter that he was starving. In North Korea, it is a crime to eat beef without special permission from government officials. Cattle are considered too valuable to eat because they are used for plowing fields and dragging carts. Anyone who butchers one is stealing government property.

*Women work on a roadside in North Pyongan province, North Korea.*

Yeonmi Park was able to escape from North Korea in 2007 at age 13 by sneaking into China, where she was caught in human trafficking for a few years. Her journey led her through Mongolia and South Korea on the way to the United States, where she completed a degree in economics from Columbia University in 2018.

What made the North Korean system perform so poorly, economically and politically? As we will see by the end of this chapter, it was not the culture, natural resources, or geography.

## The Civics Context

### Systems of Political Organization

A system is called an autocracy, dictatorship, or totalitarian regime when it has no political freedom and power is concentrated in one individual, entity, or party. Widespread surveillance and control over news and media are common, and the regime displays its police power to intimidate and suppress the population. North Korea is a prime example.

The Center for Systemic Peace publishes a scale of political freedom in countries across the globe by measuring how democratic and autocratic they are. Their Polity5 dataset codes democratic and autocratic patterns of authority and regime changes in all independent countries with a population greater than 500,000 in the most current year. It gives each country a democracy score on a scale of 0 to 10 (where 10 indicates the highest level of democracy), and it also gives each country an autocracy score on a similar scale of 0 to 10. The autocracy score is subtracted from the democracy score to produce a single score on a variable called Polity2. The Polity2 variable can be as low as -10 such as in North Korea, a full autocracy with no political freedom. A Polity2 score of +10 indicates a full democracy.

In a direct democracy, citizens personally vote on all issues. An example of this was in Athens, Greece, in the fifth century BC. Today the word *democracy* usually refers to a representative democracy, or *republic*. The Romans developed the first representative democracy, with different social groups electing their own representatives, who then assembled to vote on the issues.

The United States is an example of a **republic**. U.S. citizens elect two senators from each state, and elect a representative from each congressional district. The elected representatives then assemble as a Congress to vote on the issues. The United States' Polity2 score for 2018 was 5, indicating relatively high levels of political freedom.

The United Kingdom is an example of another form of government called a **constitutional monarchy**. In such a system there is a symbolic monarch (king or queen) who does not make any political decisions but does perform ceremonial functions. In the UK, all political decisions are made by the legislature (Parliament) and the executive (the prime minister and Cabinet). The United Kingdom's Polity2 score for 2018 was 8, indicating a relatively high degree of political freedom.

Republics such as the United States and constitutional monarchies such as the UK tend to have strong levels of political rights and political freedom. Still, other outcomes are possible for these forms of governmental and political systems. Thailand is a constitutional monarchy that has low levels of political freedom. Thailand is often referred to as having a "military dictatorship," as its parliament-based constitutional monarchy is dominated by the military. In 2018, its Polity2 score was -3.

Singapore is described as a parliamentary democratic republic, and yet it is known as being politically unfree. In 2018, its Polity2 score was -2. Thailand's and Singapore's negative Polity2 scores mean that they are classified as being politically unfree. Even so, they have more political freedom than, say, North Korea with its Polity2 score of -10.

*Soldiers march in front of Buckingham Palace, the London residence and administrative headquarters of the monarch of the United Kingdom.*

## The Economics of Government Organization

Who owns productive and natural resources in the economy? The answer to this question allows an economy to be classified as capitalist, socialist, or communist.

In a pure capitalist or market economy, all resources would be privately owned. In such an economy, market prices would allocate goods and services, and property rights would be fully protected. Some countries that are considered market economies have extremely high levels of **economic freedom**, whereas others have medium levels of economic freedom. This is why you'll sometimes hear a country referred to as a "mixed economy," rather than being described as a "market economy." No country has 100 percent economic freedom, so in a sense, almost every economy is some sort of "mixed economy." Varying degrees of economic freedom push every mixed economy either closer to a pure market economy or farther away.

In a pure socialist economy, the government owns the "means of production," which are all inputs used for making output, from natural resources to factories. Individuals continue to own personal property under socialism. A major goal of such an economy is to redistribute the wealth of a nation to reduce the gap between the rich and the poor. Socialist economies face a tradeoff. If they eliminate the profit and loss incentive structure of a market economy, they reduce production and hamper innovation. Nations with highly socialist economies have all faced such problems, including the former Soviet Union, former East Germany, and current-day Cuba and Venezuela. Socialist economies have struggled to produce food and other essentials, let alone luxuries.

Individuals in a communist country have an extremely low amount of economic freedom. In a pure communist economy, the government (state) collectively owns and controls all production and resources. Individuals do not have property rights because the state owns all property, resources, and the means of production. Communism is the opposite of a market economy.

## Civics Questions & Economic Answers

### Can a nation have political freedom without having economic freedom?

Proponents of a view called "democratic socialism" believe so. In their view, a government with extensive control over the means of production could still allow **political freedom**. But history suggests a free market economic system may be needed for political freedom to continue across the years.

Two Nobel Prize–winning economists, Friedrich A. Hayek and Milton Friedman, believed that societies with high levels of political freedom would also have to maintain high levels of economic freedom. This view became known as "the Hayek-Friedman hypothesis." Economists Robert A. Lawson and J. R. Clark found broad support for this hypothesis in a study of 123 nations from 1970 to 2005.[1] They reported finding few instances of societies being able to maintain relatively high political freedom without also having relatively high levels of economic freedom. Even those few cases were becoming rarer over time.

Friedman says while economic freedom is a necessary but not sufficient condition for political freedom, political freedom is neither a necessary nor sufficient condition for economic freedom.[2] Countries with political freedom may end up voting away their economic freedom. Although "economic freedom" is not specifically on the ballot, some policies affect it directly. Examples include government spending and redistribution programs, policies that limit international trade, and occupational licensing that restricts people from some lines of work. Extreme inflation from an expanded money supply will also decrease economic freedom, as would eminent domain policies that weaken individuals' property rights. All of this means that economic freedom can over time become eroded even in countries with high levels of political freedom.

## Can a nation have a free market without democracy?

From history there are several examples of countries that had free market economic arrangements while being politically unfree: Fascist Italy and Fascist Spain, Germany at various times in the last 70 years, Japan before World Wars I and II, and tsarist Russia in the decades before World War I. These examples were highlighted by Friedman.[3]

Singapore today has world-class levels of economic freedom while being politically unfree. For many years Singapore has ranked second on the Economic Freedom of the World Index. However, it has had a Polity2 score of -2 for many years, indicating that the country is relatively unfree politically.

## Are countries like Denmark, Sweden, and Norway socialist?

Many people in the United States who support democratic socialism cite Denmark, Norway, and Sweden as countries where the system can work well. Along with Finland, Iceland, and associated islands, these nations are referred to by the label "Nordic." The Nordic countries have a high quality of life, strong labor unions, and a robust social safety net. Are they examples of socialist countries with good economic results?

The Nordic countries actually show high levels of economic freedom. In the most recent Economic Freedom of the World (EFW) Index,[4] Denmark has the highest level of economic freedom among the Nordic countries, with an overall EFW score of 8.17. This places Denmark as 10th in the world in economic freedom out of

*The Bugis Street Shopping District in Singapore.*

all 165 countries currently measured by the index. The rest of the Nordic countries do well too: Finland is ranked 21st, Iceland 23rd, and Norway and Sweden tie for the rank of 37th in the world.

For comparison, the United States' 2019 EFW score was 8.24 (sixth in the world in economic freedom). Thus the Nordic nations are only slightly less free than the United States in terms of overall economic freedom. Within some sub-areas of the EFW Index, the Nordic nations are even freer than the United States.

So, are these countries properly labeled "socialist"? No. They have a strong legal system—among the best in the world, and stronger than that of the United States. It is true that the Nordic countries have a large welfare state, which does bring their scores down within Area 1 (Size of Government) of the EFW Index. Still, they maintain strong levels of economic freedom in the other four areas of the index. All of the Nordic countries are in the most economically free quartile—the top 25 percent of the world in terms of economic freedom. This is quite different from the system in place within socialist countries such as Venezuela and Cuba.

## How is economic freedom correlated with other measures of well-being and human progress?

Let's take a look at how various well-being measures relate to economic freedom. Since it is important to consider the economic freedom of countries over a lengthy period of time, the data used to construct the following graphs are the average of each country's Economic Freedom of the World (EFW) score from 2000 to 2019; then, the country-level data for each well-being measure are split into four quartiles ordered from least economically free to most economically free.

The data are adjusted for purchasing power parity (PPP) and in constant 2017 U.S. dollars, to be able to make comparisons between the prices and currencies in different countries. When these adjustments are made, we find that the average income (GDP per capita) for countries in the most economically free quartile is $50,619. Those in the least economically free quartile have an average income of about $5,911.

**FIGURE 1** Economic Freedom and Income per Capita

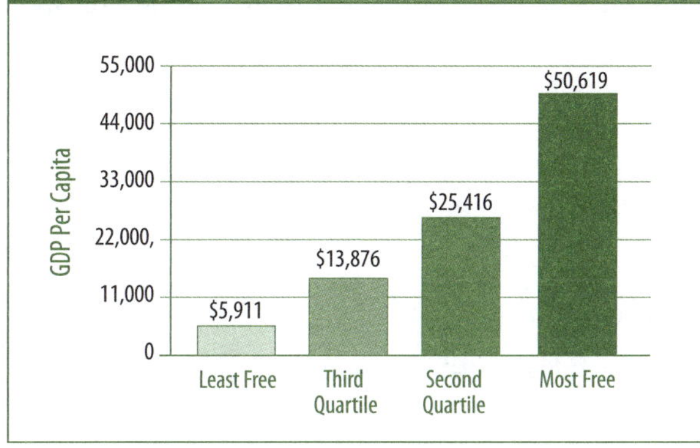


*Sources: Economic Freedom of the World: 2021 Report;* Word Bank, 2021, *World Development Indicators*

How well off are the poorest of the poor in various types of societies? What does it mean to be "poor" in an economically free country versus an economically unfree country? Let's take a look at the average annual income per capita earned by the poorest 10 percent of the population in different societies. In 2021 in the most economically free quartile, the poorest 10 percent of income earners make about $14,400, on average. Meanwhile, the poorest 10 percent of people in countries that are within the least economically free quartile only earn about $1,549.

**FIGURE 2** Economic Freedom and Income Earned by Poorest 10 Percent

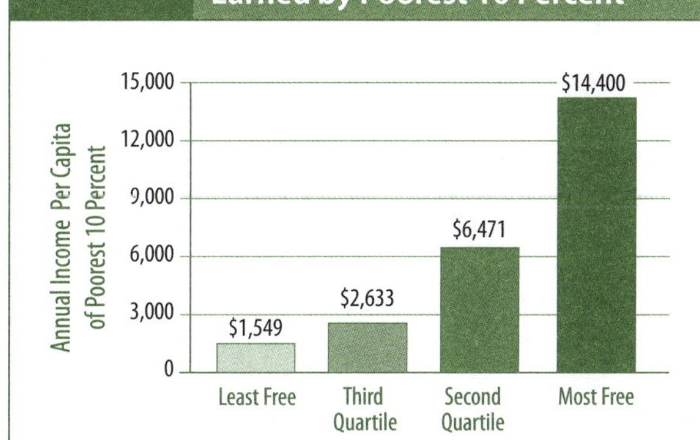


*Sources: Economic Freedom of the World: 2021 Report;* Word Bank, 2021, *World Development Indicators*

How likely are you to be severely poor? The following statistics show the 2021 poverty rate figures from the World Bank's World Development Indicators (again, adjusted for comparability to U.S. dollars). In the most economically free quartile, only 0.94 percent of the population lives on as little as \$1.90 per day. In the least economically free quartile, 34.10 percent of the population lives on \$1.90 per day. Similar conclusions apply when looking at other poverty thresholds of \$3.20 or \$5.50 per day.

**FIGURE 3 Economic Freedom and Poverty Rates**

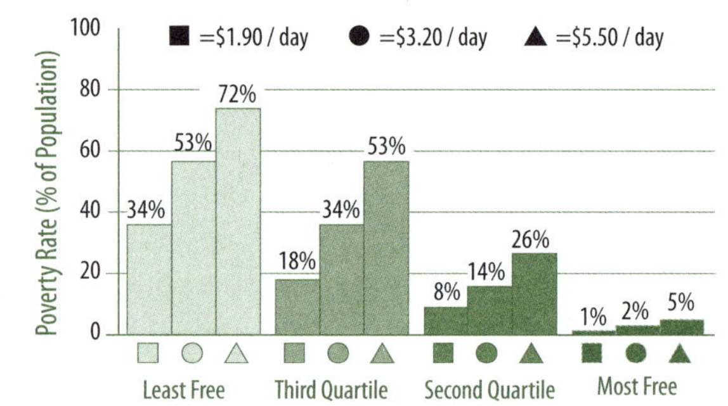


*Sources: Economic Freedom of the World: 2021 Report*; Word Bank, 2021, *World Development Indicators*

How does economic freedom relate to other measures of well-being and human progress, such as educational attainment and health measures? In the following graphs, you can see that:

- Primary and secondary school enrollments are higher in countries with greater economic freedom.
- Infant mortality is nearly 10 times higher in countries that are within the least economically free quartile than in those within the most free quartile.
- Life expectancy at birth is about 15 years longer in countries in the most economically free quartile compared to the least free quartile.

**FIGURE 4 Economic Freedom and School Enrollment**

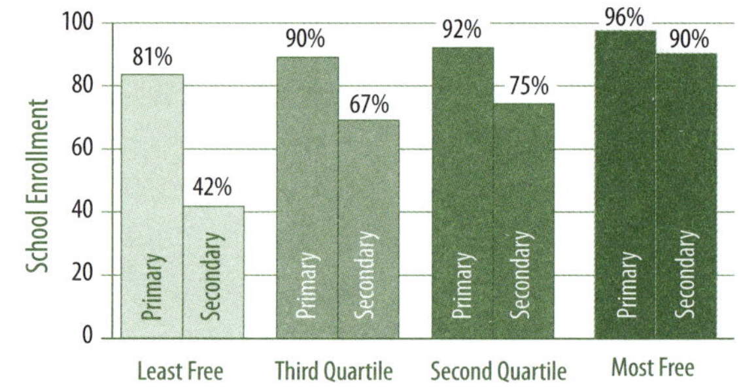


*Sources: Economic Freedom of the World: 2021 Report*; Word Bank, 2021, *World Development Indicators*

**FIGURE 5 Economic Freedom and Infant Mortality**

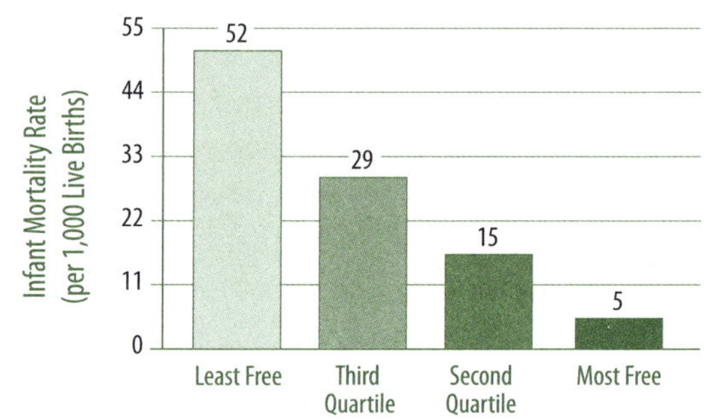


*Sources: Economic Freedom of the World: 2021 Report*; Word Bank, 2021, *World Development Indicators*

**FIGURE 6 Economic Freedom and Life Expectancy**

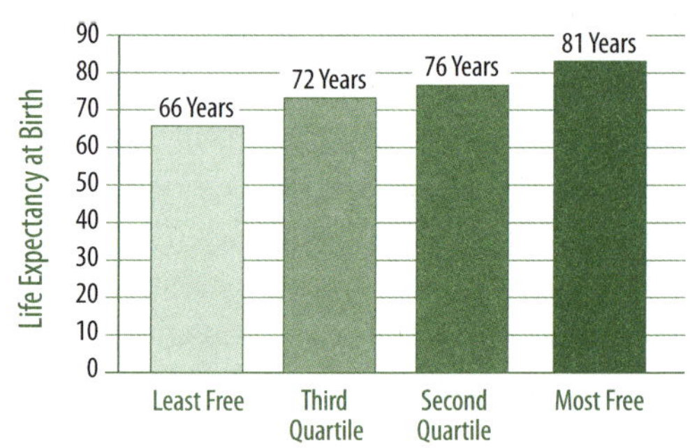


*Sources: Economic Freedom of the World: 2021 Report*; Word Bank, 2021, *World Development Indicators*

*Shoppers buy produce in the San Rafael Market, Havana, Cuba.*

Many sophisticated empirical studies analyzing economic freedom and measures of well-being have been done. They go far beyond just looking at correlations. Such studies consistently find economic freedom positively associated with beneficial outcomes, both those measured in money and those measured in quality of life.[5]

## QUESTIONS for DISCUSSION

1. What does Nobel Prize–winning economist Milton Friedman believe about the relationship between economic freedom and political freedom?
2. How do the Nordic countries do when it comes to economic freedom? What does this mean in terms of their economic system? Are they socialist countries?
3. How do various standard of living and well-being measures differ in countries with a lot of economic freedom versus those with little economic freedom?

## Excerpt from *Capitalism and Freedom*

PRIMARY SOURCE

In his book *Capitalism and Freedom*, Milton Friedman says:

> One feature of a free society is surely the freedom of individuals to advocate and propagandize openly for a radical change in the structure of the society—so long as the advocacy is restricted to persuasion and does not include force or other forms of coercion. It is a mark of the political freedom of a capitalist society that men can openly advocate and work for socialism. Equally, political freedom in a socialist society would require that men be free to advocate the introduction of capitalism. How could the freedom to advocate capitalism be preserved and protected in a socialist society?[6]

*Milton Friedman*

Friedman explains that it would be extremely difficult, if not impossible, to speak for freedom in a strictly socialist society, because a socialist government does not allow its citizens to promote policies that are in direct contradiction of its doctrine. Those who spoke out would likely be out of a job and no longer have a livelihood since the government would be the source of production and all jobs.

Friedman also explains that to spread ideas to the masses, it takes money to circulate ideas. In a free market, you can buy paper and print your viewpoints even if your view is in disagreement with the government or that of the paper company. But in a socialist society, it is not enough to merely have the funds; a supporter of free markets in a socialist society would need to also persuade the factories, printing presses, post offices, etc. owned by the government to have their ideas disseminated. (Keep in mind that Friedman was writing in a time when paper publication was vital to spreading ideas.)

*China's censorship of the internet is known as the "Great Firewall of China."*

In today's age, the internet has become more and more important in spreading ideas. But even in the current technological age, we still see the accuracy of Friedman's assertion that it is nearly impossible for proponents of free markets to be able to advocate their beliefs while living in a socialist economy. For instance, governments of countries such as China and North Korea block all internet websites that oppose the philosophies and ideas of the government officials, so the individuals in such countries do not have access to the information that the rest of the world can discover via the internet.

## QUESTIONS for DISCUSSION

1. According to Friedman, is it feasible for someone in a free market economy who disagrees with the system to promote a move toward socialism? Does Friedman think it is easier or more difficult for someone living in a socialist country to promote a move toward free markets? Do you agree? Explain your answer.
2. How does socialism's ownership of the means of production limit citizens' ability to voice dissent regarding anything happening in their country?
3. How does socialism's ownership of the printing press prevent any freedom of the press from arising, and how does it stifle regular citizens' speech? Are civil liberties such as freedom of the press or freedom of speech able to exist in a socialist country?

Contemporary Connection

## Economic Freedom in North Korea versus South Korea

Take a look at this satellite image showing the darkness of North Korea next to South Korea. South Korea is full of lights, signifying electricity and prosperity. North Korea is in complete darkness, with the exception of the light coming from Pyongyang—the capital of North Korea.

Economic analysts look for "natural experiments." Since they cannot control variables as in a scientific experiment, they seek cases where similar societies have a single but important difference to analyze. South Korea and North Korea were one country, Korea, for centuries prior to 1945. They had the same:

- geography
- natural resources
- culture
- language

Then the end of the Korean conflict in 1953 caused a "natural experiment" to occur, splitting South Korea from North Korea. What is the result after all of these years, as the nations have grown apart? South Koreans are prosperous, while nearly everyone in North Korea lives in dire poverty. The true extent of poverty is masked by North Korea's refusal to report reliable statistics. Most economists believe the difference in economic institutions to be the key reason for the vast difference in well-being measures in the two countries.

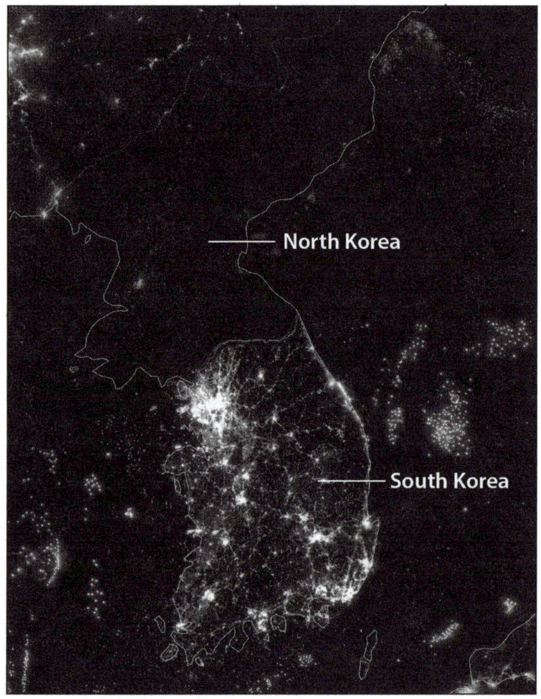


*Satellite imagery of the Korean peninsula at night.*

### QUESTIONS for DISCUSSION

1. What does the satellite image of North and South Korea indicate about the level of prosperity in each country?
2. Why are analysts confident that the differences between North and South Korea are due to economic institutions and not factors such as culture or geography?
3. Why are scientific experiments considered to have an advantage in reliability over observations from social sciences such as psychology, sociology, or economics?

## Web Quests

**Enter any of the links below and use the questions to get you started on your own web quest.**

*Freedom in the World Index*

*The* Freedom in the World Index *published by Freedom House measures the political rights and civil liberties in countries around the world.*[7]

**https://freedomhouse.org/report/freedom-world**

1. Describe the political rights component and the civil rights component of the Freedom in the World Index. What exactly does each component measure, and what is the scale for each?
2. How is the aggregate Freedom in the World score calculated, and what is its scale?

**Polity5 Project**

*The Polity5 dataset is published by the Center for Systemic Peace, and measures how democratic and autocratic each country is.*[8]

**https://www.systemicpeace.org/polityproject.html**

1. How are the autocratic and democratic components of the Polity5 Project measured, and what is the scale for each?
2. How is the "Polity2" variable in the Polity5 Project calculated, and what is its scale?

**Was Milton Friedman Wrong on China?**

*The video "WSJ Opinion: Was Milton Friedman Wrong on China" (time: approx. 4 min.) and its accompanying article by William McGurn, published by the* Wall Street Journal *on June 28, 2021.*

**https://www.wsj.com/articles/was-milton-friedman-wrong-about-china-11624918231**

1. Do you think Friedman was wrong when it comes to China? Why or why not?
2. What does Friedman mean when he says, "Economic freedom is a necessary condition for political freedom, but it is not a sufficient condition. Political freedom, on the other hand, is neither a necessary nor a sufficient condition for economic freedom"?

**The film *Sweden: Lessons for America?***

Sweden: Lessons for America?: A Personal Exploration *by Johan Norberg, produced by the Free to Choose Network in 2018. Time: approx. 57 min.*

**https://www.youtube.com/watch?v=jq3vVbdgMuQ**

1. Who is Anders Chydenius, and what were his beliefs?
2. What is Sweden's "employer fee," and why was it introduced?
3. How is it possible that Astrid Lindgren and Ingmar Bergman had tax rates greater than 100%?
4. What were Sweden's wage earner funds (or employee funds), and how did they impact entrepreneurs and others in Sweden during the 1970s and 1980s?

5. What types of economic reforms did Sweden undertake in the 1990s? Did these reforms decrease or increase Swedes' economic freedom?
6. If there is a program that citizens want to be state funded, does that mean the state also must be the one to provide it? Describe a few examples where private enterprises are the service providers for programs that are paid by Sweden's welfare programs.

**The film *Doctor Zhivago***

*The film* Doctor Zhivago *was released in 1965, and was an adaptation of the acclaimed novel of the same name by Boris Pasternak.[9] Time: 3 hours, 17 minutes. This film is available via multiple platforms such as Amazon Prime, HBO Max, and YouTube.*

**https://www.justwatch.com/us/movie/doctor-zhivago-1965**

1. Who were the Bolsheviks, and what were they seeking?
2. How were the living arrangements of the Gromeko family in Moscow different after Yuri Zhivago returned from World War I? What economic system had been instituted that caused the change in living arrangements? Did the country become more or less prosperous as a result?

**"Leaving North Korea: My Story"**

*"Leaving North Korea: My Story" was originally published in 2018 in* Education About Asia *(Volume 23:2). The author requested to remain anonymous (likely to protect her family members remaining in North Korea from retaliation by government officials).*

**https://www.asianstudies.org/publications/eaa/archives/leaving-north-korea-my-story**

1. What is a songbun?

**Yeonmi Park: My Escape from North Korea**

*Lyse Doucet, Chief International Correspondent for BBC, interviews North Korean defector Yeonmi Park at the Women in the World Summit in 2015. Time: Approx. 20 min.*

**https://www.youtube.com/watch?v=h-hS8A85_RE**

1. What kind of propaganda does North Korea use to indoctrinate their citizens?
2. What happened to Yeonmi Park and her mother once they escaped to China?
3. China implemented a one-child policy from 1980–2016. Since some families chose to abort/kill female babies in the hopes of having a male baby, it left China with 37 million more males than females.[7] Furthermore, while many countries give refugee status (grant asylum) to individuals who are at risk of persecution in their home country, China does not grant such status to North Korean defectors (those who manage to escape North Korea). Instead, to stay on good terms with the North Korean regime, China forcibly repatriates defectors. Defectors sent back to North Korea face torture, imprisonment, sexual violence, forced labor, and possibly death. How do these two Chinese policies create the conditions for the human trafficking of North Korean women in China?

# CHAPTER 5

# Why Did Rosa Parks Succeed Years After Homer Plessy Failed?

Rosa Parks in 1955.

# Homer Plessy and Rosa Parks Take a Stand

Homer Plessy was born in New Orleans in 1862 while the Civil War was still raging. As he was growing up, New Orleans had a large population of formerly enslaved individuals. New Orleans had a long multiracial history, and racial segregation was not as widespread as elsewhere. African American children could attend the same schools as white children and sit anywhere in streetcars.

But in 1890, Louisiana passed the Separate Car Law requiring racial segregation on passenger trains.

In 1892, Homer Plessy and the Citizens' Committee, a group formed to fight segregation, executed a carefully designed plan. Plessy purchased a first-class railroad ticket. He was denied a seat. Then he and the other members of the Citizens' Committee fought that denial and the Louisiana law all the way to the U.S. Supreme Court.

In *Plessy v Ferguson* (1896) the Supreme Court rejected the claim that the Separate Car Law violated the Thirteenth Amendment by perpetuating racial distinctions derived from slavery. The Supreme Court also ruled that "separate but equal" accommodations for African Americans and whites did not violate the equal protection clause of the Fourteenth Amendment.

*Homer Plessy's case goes to the Supreme Court.*

### KEY ECONOMIC CONCEPTS

**boycott**
**comparative advantage**
**human capital**
**opportunity cost**
**rules of the game**

Rosa Parks was born in Tuskegee, Alabama, in 1913. As a young African American, she directly experienced racism. On one occasion, Parks's grandfather stood in front of their house with a shotgun while Ku Klux Klan members marched down the street. Unlike Homer Plessy, she attended racially segregated schools. After graduating from high school, she became active in the National Association for the Advancement of Colored People (NAACP) Montgomery Chapter, where she served as the secretary of the organization.

On December 1, 1955, Rosa Parks, an African American riding on a bus in Montgomery, Alabama, refused to give up her seat to a white passenger. She was arrested and charged with violating city codes. Her action set off the Montgomery Bus Boycott. She challenged the segregation laws underlying this incident, and she won.

What explains the change between 1896 and 1955? Why did Rosa Parks succeed so many years after Homer Plessy had failed?

## The Civics Context

The civic and economic "**rules of the game**" (as explained in Chapter 1) changed after the Civil War with the passage of the Thirteenth, Fourteenth, and Fifteenth Amendments. The Thirteenth Amendment abolished slavery. The Fourteenth and Fifteenth Amendments granted citizenship rights to all persons born or

*Rosa Parks is fingerprinted at her arrest during the Montgomery Bus Boycott of 1956.*

naturalized in the United States. They required states to guarantee equal protection under the law for all citizens and granted voting rights to African American males. Despite these changes, racism was widespread. Many white northern and southern Americans continued to think that some separation between the races was desirable.

By the 1890s, this belief in racial separation was embodied in a system of southern state laws and local ordinances called Jim Crow laws, intended to keep the races apart. In many states these laws established separate schools for white and African American children. In the 1890s, most African Americans were still living in the south. Schools for African American children were separate but hardly equal. Southern schools were poorly financed compared to schools elsewhere, and southern officials spent much less state money on schools for African American children. This practice imposed great hardships on African American parents and children.

But elected officials didn't have to worry much about losing votes from the African American community. Beginning around 1890, Jim Crow laws it made it very difficult for African Americans to register and vote. With so few African Americans voting, white elected officials could ignore African American concerns without fear of losing public office.

## The Economics of Jim Crow

Jim Crow laws resulted in poor business practices. If separate but equal treatment under the law was to be taken seriously, it was an expensive proposition. Two of everything would need to be provided.

Throughout the southern states, by the early 1900s the Jim Crow practices meant that towns often had no libraries, parks, or other public services available for African American residents. Privately owned facilities were also segregated. Jim Crow laws and customs applied to restaurants, stores, hotels, and other facilities, sometimes by extraordinary means. African American customers might be served at separate counters or areas within a store, for example, barricaded off from areas reserved for whites.

Jim Crow laws prevented many African Americans from moving into better paying jobs. In a normally functioning labor market, the concept of **comparative advantage** motivates people to develop their talents. They do what they can do better than other things, producing at their lowest **opportunity cost**. In other words, they work at an occupation where they give up the least to gain the most. Jim Crow thwarted African Americans' ability to deploy their talents fully. African Americans who could have prospered in management, sales, or highly skilled trades were denied these opportunities based on race. Jim Crow laws lasted for decades, severely limiting economic opportunity for African Americans. Others were hurt, too, as they were denied the opportunity of living in an economy where everyone's talents were fully developed.

It gets worse. Why, you might wonder, would white business owners drive away African American customers in the 1890s? These practices surely damaged the profits of these business owners by leaving hotel rooms unoccupied and restaurant seats empty. The answer relates to African American poverty and fear of white boycotts.

Most white business owners felt that by serving African American customers, they would lose their white customers. They were afraid that white customers would not spend money in their stores if African Americans were served on an equal basis. A loss of white customers would cause a major reduction in the store owner's income. The fear was that African Americans did not have enough purchasing power to compensate for

*A family of sharecroppers in Little Rock, Arkansas, 1935.*

a decline in spending by white customers who might boycott.

In the 1890s, African Americans in the South commonly were sharecroppers or tenant farmers. They farmed on lands they did not own. Instead of earning cash, they earned shares of the crops they raised for those who did own the land. With little cash being used, the sharecropping economy depended heavily on credit and a barter system. The debt carried by African American sharecroppers added further to their economic difficulties.

Suppose Homer Plessy had encouraged African Americans to boycott Louisiana railroads. How much influence would such a boycott have had on railroad revenue in the 1890s? Very little, because few African Americans then could travel by first-class passage, given their low incomes.

Even as challenges to Jim Crow laws continued over the years, African Americans took direct action to improve their economic condition. During World War I and World War II, millions of African Americans moved to cities in the North, Midwest, and West to take jobs in the nation's factories. Historians call this the "Great Migration." In their new locations, they earned more than they had as sharecroppers.

Slowly, African American family incomes rose. In 1939, the average annual income of an African American family was $489, a little more than one-third of the average white family income of $1,325. By 1949, the average annual African American family income reached $1,533, nearly half of the $3,138 earned by an average white family. And in 1955, when Rosa Parks refused to give up her seat on a bus, average African American family income had risen to more than half of the average white family income ($2,418 to $4,331).

Racial attitudes were also changing. In 1948, President Harry S. Truman signed Executive Order 9981 calling for the desegregation of the U.S. Armed Forces. While African Americans had served in the armed forces since the American Revolution, it was almost always in segregated units.

Many white Americans joined the struggle to gain equal rights for all citizens. And technological changes made it increasingly difficult to maintain Jim Crow laws. For many white Americans, travel by automobile replaced travel by railroad and bus. As a result, by 1955, most people who rode buses in Montgomery, Alabama, were African Americans. In 1892, when Homer Plessy was denied his seat on a passenger train, the financial consequences of ignoring African American consumers were small. But the situation had changed by 1955. African Americans had gained in economic power.

Soon after Rosa Parks refused to give up her bus seat on December 1, 1955, a group of African American women called the Women's Political Council began circulating flyers calling for a boycott of the Montgomery bus system beginning on December 5. Word spread. African American ministers announced the boycott from their pulpits. On December 5, approximately 40,000 African American bus riders boycotted the bus system. How did people get to work? Leaders organized car pools and taxi rides. Others simply walked to work.

The fight moved to the courts. On June 5, 1956, a Montgomery federal court ruled that African American bus riders were being denied their right to equal protection under the law as specified by the Fourteenth Amendment of the Constitution. On December 20, 1956, the Supreme Court upheld the lower court ruling. The boycott succeeded after lasting 281 days.

The boycott was a game changer for three reasons. First, it demonstrated the economic power of the newly emerging African American middle class. Second, it set the stage for other civil rights protests to end racial discrimination. Finally, it helped establish a young minister named Martin Luther King Jr.—an outspoken supporter of the boycott—as a prominent national civil rights leader.

## Civics Questions & Economic Answers

### Jim Crow laws were on the books for decades. Nonetheless, how did the economic environment for African Americans change between the time of Homer Plessy (1892) and Rosa Parks (1955)?

In the Great Migration, millions of African Americans increased their family incomes by leaving the rural south. In 1892, African American real incomes trailed far behind white incomes. By 1955, while still large, the gap had narrowed.

By 1955, bus ridership in Montgomery, Alabama, was largely made up of African Americans. This situation gave African Americans a new measure of economic power. The bus companies depended on African American ridership to stay in business. Other businesses also depended on African American customers. Business owners could no longer offer poor services, or refuse to provide services, without risking a loss of revenue.

### Did education help African American income to improve?

Yes. Economists often stress the importance of investing in **human capital**. Human capital refers to investments in formal education, on-the-job training, informal education, life experiences, and just plain learning by doing. One factor human-capital economists track is investment in formal education. It turns out that on average, higher levels of educational attainment are strongly and consistently associated with earning higher incomes. For example, according to the U.S. Bureau of Labor Statistics, workers with a bachelor's degree had median weekly earnings of $1,305 in 2020, compared with $781 for workers with a high school diploma. And the unemployment rate for bachelor's-level workers was 5.5 percent, compared with 9.0 percent for those whose highest level of education was a high school diploma.

*A man waits in the segregated area of a bus station in Durham, North Carolina, 1940.*

One of slavery's most pernicious legacies is that it was illegal to teach enslaved individuals how to read. Robert A. Margo (1993) estimated that 90 to 95 percent of newly freed African American adults were unable to read or write.[1]

But generations of African American parents set out to change this even though their schools were not as good as the ones white children attended. They invested in their children's human capital by sending them to school. According to the 1900 census, 37 percent of southern African Americans between the ages of 15 and 24 were completely illiterate. By 1920, the illiteracy rate had declined to 18 percent. Margo (1993) reports that by 1950, 69 percent of African American children were in school, the same as the white attendance rate. He observes that each successive generation of African American children attended school for more years than the previous generation.[2]

### Weren't the segregated schools in the south often of poor quality during the Jim Crow era?

Yes. The "separate but equal" schools called for by *Plessy v Ferguson* (1896) did not exist.

African American children attended largely poorly built and maintained schools with low-paid teachers. Margo (1993) points out that "for every dollar spent per child on instruction in Alabama's white schools in 1920, only 27 cents were spent per black pupil."[3] Had separate but equal been enforced, there is little doubt that African American children would have more quickly reduced the gaps in learning and income. The fact that racial differences in education and income would be reduced over time is largely due to the ordinary African American parents who made the best of an unjust situation. Margo writes, "Thus, black parents are the unsung heroes of the Civil Rights Movement."[4]

### Did improvements in literacy among African Americans have anything to do with the Great Migration?

Yes. African Americans with higher levels of literacy were more likely to learn about the economic conditions in the North, Midwest, and West. Families wrote letters providing valuable information regarding how to make the journey and where the jobs were. Newspapers contained valuable information as well. Thus, African Americans with higher levels of education were more likely to migrate. They were also more likely to succeed in manufacturing jobs that increasingly called for literate workers.[5]

## QUESTIONS for DISCUSSION

1. How were Homer Plessy's and Rosa Parks's actions to end racial segregation similar?
2. How were Homer Plessy's and Rosa Parks's actions to end racial segregation different?
3. Jim Crow laws meant business owners had to turn away customers. Why did business owners often go along with such a poor business scheme?
4. How did Jim Crow thwart the ability of African Americans to use their comparative advantage to earn more income?
5. What is human capital?
6. What is the relationship between human capital and income?
7. How did African American parents invest in their children's human capital?
8. What was the relationship between education and the Great Migration?

# Justices Speak Out in 1896 and 1954

PRIMARY SOURCE

In the law, there is a long tradition of upholding past decisions. The Latin term is *stare decisis*, or "let the decision stand." Rarely, however, courts will admit they got a previous decision wrong and overturn it. That happened in 1954 when the Supreme Court repudiated *Plessy v Ferguson*.

Justice Henry Billings Brown in 1896 had written for the Court:

> We consider the underlying fallacy of the plaintiff's [Plessy's] argument to consist in the assumption that the enforced separation of the two races stamps the colored race with a badge of inferiority. If this be so, it is not by reason of anything found in the act, but solely because the colored race chooses to put that construction upon it ...
>
> The argument also assumes that social prejudice may be overcome by legislation, and that equal rights cannot be secured except by an enforced commingling of the two races. … If the civil and political rights of both races be equal, one cannot be inferior to the other civilly or politically. If one race be inferior to the other socially, the Constitution of the United States cannot put them upon the same plane.

*Henry Billings Brown*

The decision was not a close call, either, with a Supreme Court vote of six to one. Justice John Harlan Marshall was the only dissenter—but history vindicated him.

*Plessy v Ferguson*'s "separate but equal" standard stood until the landmark 1954 ruling in *Brown v Board of Education of Topeka* overturned it. In a complete reversal, the Court ruled that separate but equal educational facilities for African Americans were inherently unequal and a violation of the Fourteenth Amendment's guarantee of equal protection under the law. The decision was unanimous. The opinion was written by Justice Earl Warren. Here is an excerpt:

Earl Warren

In approaching this problem, we cannot turn the clock back to 1868 when the [Fourteenth] Amendment was adopted, or even to 1896 when *Plessy v. Ferguson* was written. We must consider public education in the light of its full development and its present place in American life throughout the Nation. Only in this way can it be determined if segregation in public schools deprives these plaintiffs of the equal protection of the laws.

Today, education is perhaps the most important function of state and local governments. … In these days, it is doubtful that any child may reasonably be expected to succeed in life if he is denied the opportunity of an education. Such an opportunity, where the state has undertaken to provide it, is a right which must be made available to all on equal terms. …

To separate [students] from others of similar age and qualifications solely because of their race generates a feeling of inferiority as to their status in the community that may affect their hearts and minds in a way unlikely to ever be undone. … Whatever may have been the extent of psychological knowledge at the time of *Plessy v. Ferguson*, this finding is amply supported by modern authority. …

We conclude that in the field of public education the doctrine of "separate but equal" has no place. Separate educational facilities are inherently unequal. Therefore, we hold that the plaintiffs and others similarly situated … are, by reason of the segregation complained of, deprived of the equal protection of the laws guaranteed by the Fourteenth Amendment.

## QUESTIONS for DISCUSSION

1. How are the Supreme Court decisions of *Plessy v Ferguson* and *Brown v Board of Education of Topeka* similar?
2. How are the decisions in *Plessy v Ferguson* and *Brown v Board of Education of Topeka* different?
3. In what way was the Supreme Court making a constitutional argument in *Brown v Board of Education of Topeka*?
4. In what way was the Supreme Court making an economic argument in *Brown v Board of Education of Topeka*?

## Contemporary Connection

## The Supreme Court on Affirmative Action

The Civil Rights Movement's initial economic focus was on public accommodations, employment, and housing. The Civil Rights Act of 1964 prohibited race-based discrimination in all of these areas. Its application was obvious in places where Jim Crow laws were still on the books. Following its passage, African Americans and other racial minority groups no longer faced overt discrimination of the kind embodied in "White Only" signs.

But was ending overt discrimination enough? No, according to the proponents of affirmative action, originally defined as "action to ensure that applicants are treated equally without regard to race, color, religion, sex, or national origin." Passively claiming racially neutral treatment would not be enough.

College admissions, as a gateway to economic and social mobility, became a focus of special interest. Colleges and universities wanted to make sure they treated applicants fairly. Is it possible to increase minority admissions without engaging in "reverse discrimination" against nonminority applicants? The courts have struggled with this question since the early days of civil rights enforcement.

Currently it is easier to say what is not permitted than what is permitted in affirmative action admissions. Following

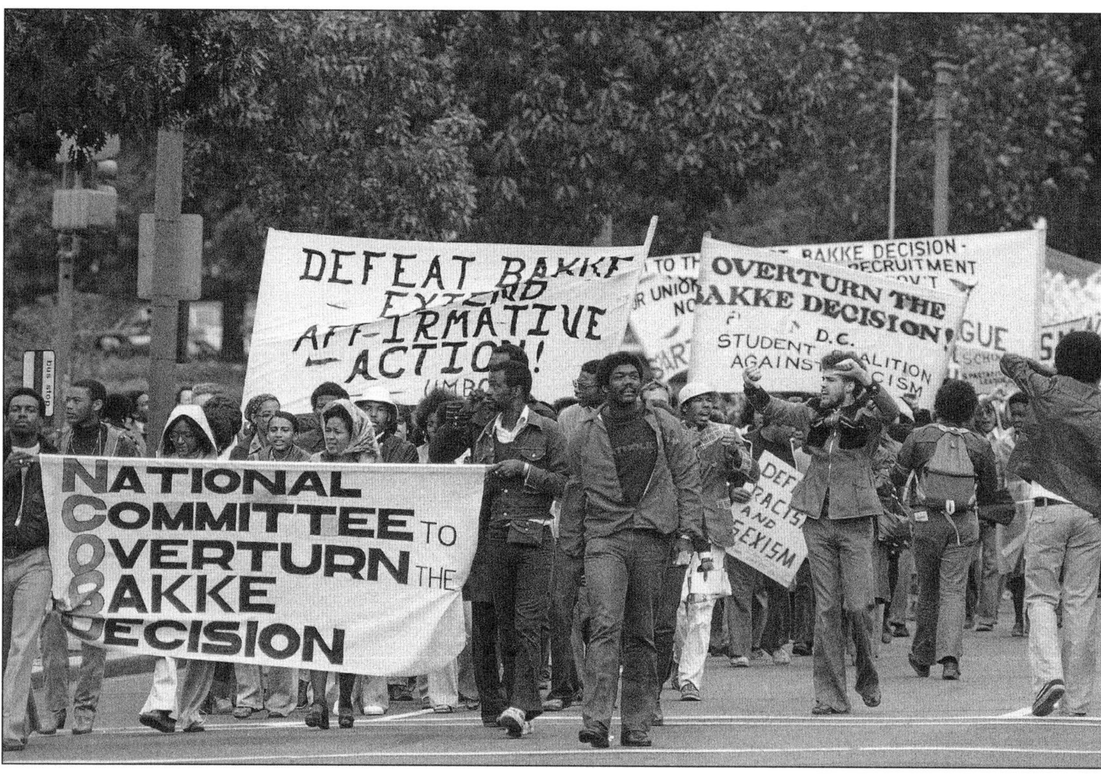


*A protest march in 1977 against the* Bakke *decision in the lower courts, prior to the Supreme Court ruling.*

the decision in *California v Bakke* (1978), it is clear that colleges may not reserve a set number of spaces for minority applicants. *Gratz v Bollinger* (2003) ruled out the awarding of points based on race or ethnicity. But many other cases have allowed minority status as one of several factors favoring admission, provided there are no quotas or specific set-asides.

Opinions on affirmative action remain sharply split. Chief Justice John Roberts, in the 2007 *Parents Involved* decision, argued for race-neutral rules: "The way to stop discrimination on the basis of race is to stop discriminating on the basis of race." Proponents of affirmative action worry that qualified candidates may be excluded by race-biased measures or differential opportunities for education. Associate Justice Sonia Sotomayor, in the 2014 *Schuette* decision, rejected Roberts's simple formulation, writing, "The way to stop discrimination on the basis of race is to speak openly and candidly on the subject of race, and to apply the Constitution with eyes open to the unfortunate effects of centuries of racial discrimination."

## QUESTIONS for DISCUSSION

1. What did the Civil Rights Act of 1964 prohibit in public accommodations, employment, and housing? Why was it necessary in 1964?
2. Why might race-neutral rules leave minority groups at a disadvantage in areas such as college admissions?
3. Would it be legal for a university to set aside a certain number of spaces in an entering first-year class for minority students?
4. How might a college or university increase the number of minority students without using set-asides or awarding points on racial grounds?

## Web Quests

**Enter any of the links below and use the questions to get you started on your own web quest.**

### Homer Plessy

*This link features a video that provides more details regarding Homer Plessy and the earliest days of the Civil Rights Movement.*

**https://www.nps.gov/people/homer-plessy.htm**

1. What was life like for Homer Plessy growing up in New Orleans following the Civil War?
2. How did Louisiana white supremacists react to the new freedoms for African Americans following the Civil War?
3. What was the Separate Car Act?
4. What actions did Homer Plessy and the Citizens' Committee take regarding the Separate Car Act?
5. Why was Judge Harlan's dissent in *Plessy v Ferguson* important?

### Rosa Parks' Journey as a Civil Rights Icon

*This website features an article on the life of Rosa Parks.*

**https://constitutioncenter.org/blog/rosa-parks-journey-as-a-civil-rights-icon**

1. What was the relationship between Rosa Parks and the National Association for the Advancement of Colored People (NAACP)?
2. What role did the Montgomery Improvement Association (MIA) play in the bus boycott?
3. How did Rosa Parks's life change following the Supreme Court ruling of November 13, 1956?

### 120 Years of Literacy: Literacy from 1870 to 1979

*This site features data from the National Center for Educational Statistics on adult literacy.*

**https://nces.ed.gov/naal/lit_history.asp**

1. How did school enrollment rates change for African Americans following the Civil War?
2. How did literacy rates change from 1870 to 1979 among the total population, whites, and African Americans?
3. What are the economic implications of these changes in literacy rates for African Americans?

### A History of Affirmative Action in College Admissions

*This site defines affirmative action and traces the Civil Rights Movement and Supreme Court rulings.*

**https://www.bestcolleges.com/blog/history-affirmative-action-college/**

1. What is affirmative action?
2. How is affirmative action linked to the Civil Rights Movement?
3. Why did white students sue over affirmative action?
4. What has the Supreme Court ruled regarding affirmative action?

# CHAPTER 6

# What Are the Economic Statistics Every Informed Citizen Should Know?

# Can Money Be a Weapon?

Samuel Curtis Upham (1819–1885) was a Philadelphia-based journalist, entrepreneur, and counterfeiter. Some believe Upham's counterfeit work wreaked considerable economic devastation on the Confederacy during the Civil War. Upham claims that Confederate Senator Harry S. Foote said he "had done more to injure the Confederate cause than General McClellan and his army."[1]

Upham, a northerner and a strong supporter of the Union, ran a store that sold stationery, newspapers, and cosmetics. In 1862, after witnessing his customers' interest in Confederate money for its novelty, Upham began printing fake Confederate notes to sell as "funny money." Upham was so proud of his excellent forgeries that he printed his name and address on them. He even advertised his products in *Harper's Weekly* and *The New York Tribune*.

Some of Upham's best customers, it turned out, were southerners who purchased whole sheets of the novelty currency and used them in transactions all around the rebellious southern states. Upham's currency quickly circulated throughout the Confederacy, and rebel soldiers regularly used it in transactions and, in some cases, were even paid their salaries with it. By his own estimate, Upham produced at least $15 million worth of Confederate bills that caused inflation among this currency.

Interestingly, it was the government in Washington, D.C., that forced Upham to cease and desist his dubious work. Leaders of the Union cause were concerned the South would view his actions as a grand Union strategy and retaliate, causing harm to the national economy. Federal investigators were unable to charge Upham with a crime, as Washington didn't recognize the Confederate government in Richmond, meaning he wasn't breaking any actual laws.

## KEY ECONOMIC CONCEPTS

**Consumer Price Index (CPI)**
**economic indicators**
**inflation rate**
**misery index**
**personal consumption expenditure (PCE) price index**
**real GDP per capita**
**real gross domestic product (real GDP)**
**stagflation**
**unemployment rate**

Samuel Upham

History provides many other examples of weaponizing currency during military conflicts. During the American Revolutionary War, two British Tory agents travelled the 13 colonies dispersing wads of fake Continental dollars into circulation, hoping they would undermine colonists' faith in the colonial currency and cause widespread inflation. During World War II, Nazi Germany conscripted concentration camp inmates to produce British pound sterling notes. The plan was to scatter the fake money over British cities using Luftwaffe bombers and create chaos in the U.K.'s economy. The camps were liberated before the plan could be put into action.

And finally, the United States and its allies used counterfeit Iraqi money during the 1991 Gulf War. In this case it wasn't used to undermine the enemy's economy and cause widespread inflation; instead, it was meant to break the fighting spirit of the Iraqi military with propaganda printed in Arabic on the bank notes. One included message was "Saddam lives in luxury while you and your family starve." Others provided details on how to surrender safely to the U.S.-led forces.

*The Herbert C. Hoover Building, home to the U.S. Department of Commerce.*

## The Civics Context

On any given day, citizens reading a news story or watching a cable news show are likely to read or hear reports about the state of the U.S. economy. Often these reports discuss economic indicators. An economic indicator is a statistic that measures something about the current performance of the U.S. economy. The three most commonly reported indicators are **real gross domestic product (GDP)**, the **inflation rate**, and the **unemployment rate**.

As the economic way of thinking in Chapter 1 explains, citizens, business, and governments must make choices. Economic indicators serve those making decisions:

- Investors, on how to allocate their capital
- Consumers, on buying a home or car
- Business owners, on how many workers to employ
- Citizens, in deciding which representatives to vote for and which public policies to support

Citizens must understand these and other uses of economic indicators to fully participate in the economy.

A number of departments, bureaus, and councils are officially charged with measuring economic data, writing official reports, and even testifying in front of the U.S. Congress. A few important examples include the following:

### *Council of Economic Advisors*

Established by Congress in 1946, this organization advises the president on economic policy based on data, research, and evidence. The CEA is composed of three members, with one appointed by the president and confirmed by the Senate to serve as the chair. The CEA produces the annual *Economic Report of the President*, analyzes data and information on economic developments and trends, reviews federal government policies and programs for soundness, and recommends economic policies designed to benefit American workers.

### *Department of Labor*

A number of agencies within the department work on economic data and issues. Best known is the Bureau of Labor Statistics (BLS). The BLS measures labor market activity, working conditions, price changes, and productivity in the U.S. economy to assist government and private sector decision making. Monthly the BLS' releases of the U.S. unemployment rate and Consumer Price Index (CPI) make international news.

***Department of Commerce***

Within the department, the Bureau of Economic Analysis (BEA) provides a wealth of data about the nation's economy. This bureau produces some of the world's most closely watched economic statistics, including U.S. gross domestic product (GDP), foreign trade and investment, and data about specific American industries and sectors. Governments, investors, businesses, and citizens rely on these data to make decisions.

***Federal Reserve***

This system is a quasi-government agency so important that it will be covered more fully in Chapter 12. "The Fed" is involved with much important work including setting the nation's monetary policy, regulating the banking system, and researching the state of the U.S. economy. The agency also produces significant amounts of important economic data. Data on the U.S. money supply, lending, interest rates, and exchange rates fall under their purview. The Fed's work is considered so important that the Chair of their Board of Governors provides a semiannual monetary policy report to the Congress.

## Tracking the National Economy

There are a couple of questions about the macroeconomy that nearly every citizen, business, and policy maker is interested in. First, what is the current level or prices or rate of inflation? Second, what is going on with production of U.S. goods and services? Taken together, these two indicators address an important third question: Do most Americans that want jobs have jobs?

Three key economic statistics are used to monitor these important questions:

- **Real gross domestic product (real GDP)** is a measure of economic output. It is defined as the market value of final goods and services produced in the United States in a year, adjusted for inflation. Real GDP is total output adjusted for inflation by holding prices constant.
  GDP is an important measure of overall economic performance because when our real GDP increases, we are producing more "product" as a nation, and we are usually better off. Changes in real GDP are discussed in the press after every quarterly announcement. Any change in the growth of real GDP will be discussed in news reports as an indicator of the health of the national economy. Real GDP trends are prominently included in discussions of potential slowdowns and economic booms. Economic commentators use decreases in real GDP as indicators of recessions.

- **Inflation** is a rise in the average prices of all goods and services. The consumer price index (CPI) is the most widely reported measure of inflation. The CPI compares the prices of a fixed set of goods and services (called a "market basket") to the prices of those same goods and services in a previous month or year. Any increase in the cost of purchasing this market basket of goods and services means an overall increase in the average level of prices paid by consumers. Thus when the CPI goes up, inflation is said to be present.

- **The unemployment rate** is the percentage of the United States labor force officially counted as "unemployed." It is calculated by dividing the number of unemployed individuals by the sum of those unemployed and those employed. This result is then multiplied by 100 to make unemployment rate a percentage.

  The U.S. labor force equals the number of people who are unemployed added to the number of people who are employed. Anyone who is 16 or older and is actively looking for a job, but cannot find one, is counted as unemployed. Students, individuals who choose not to work, and retirees are not in the labor force, and therefore not counted in the unemployment rate.

In the 1970s and early 1980s, the United States found itself in a novel and precarious economic situation. Inflation was high while production was declining and causing widespread unemployment. In the past, these two problems had not occurred in combination. A hot and expanding economy usually leads to inflation with low unemployment. A period of recession historically tamps down inflation pressure, but it leads to Americans being out of work. This situation was so unique, it was even given a name, "stagflation," a combination of a stagnant economy and inflation.

Further, during this period, the misery index gained attention as a new statistic that combined the inflation rate and unemployment rate, first proposed by economist Arthur Okun in the 1970s. This measure is the simple sum of the unemployment rate and the inflation rate. Clearly, as each of these indicators increases, life gets worse for Americans (hence the misery) as more people are out of work and prices rise.

During the high unemployment and high inflation of the 1970s, this index was frequently used to criticize the economic policies of President Jimmy Carter. The status of the misery index is frequently a good predictor of whether a member of the incumbent president's party will be reelected or replaced[2], as Table 1 indicates.[3]

The fourth column from the left in Table 1 shows the misery index for election years and the previous year from 1975 to 2000. If the misery index declines as an election year approaches, the index predicts that the candidate of the incumbent party will keep control of the White House. As an example, the 1980 misery index rose to 20.6 from 17.1 in 1979. Accurately, this change predicted that incumbent Democrat Jimmy Carter would lose to Republican challenger Ronald Reagan. When the misery index declines in the year before an election, the incumbent party is likely to hold on to the White House.

Overall, the misery index does well in predicting the results of presidential elections. It has correctly predicted the outcomes in 10 of 12 presidential elections. The misery index failed to predict the correct outcome in 1976, the year Democrat Jimmy Carter defeated Republican incumbent Gerald Ford. President Ford issued an

**TABLE 1 The Misery Index: 1975 to 2020**

| YEAR | Unemployment Rate (A) | Inflation Rate (B) | Misery Index (A+B) | Presidential Candidates | Winner Consistent with the Misery Index Prediction? |
|---|---|---|---|---|---|
| 1975 | 8.5 | 9.0 | 17.5 | | |
| 1976 | 8.7 | 6.1 | 13.8 | **Carter(D)**<br>Ford(R) | No |
| 1979 | 5.8 | 11.3 | 17.1 | | |
| 1980 | 7.1 | 13.5 | 20.6 | Carter(D)<br>**Reagan(R)** | Yes |
| 1983 | 9.6 | 3.2 | 12.8 | | |
| 1984 | 7.5 | 4.3 | 11.8 | Mondale(D)<br>**Reagan(R)** | Yes |
| 1987 | 6.2 | 3.6 | 9.8 | | |
| 1988 | 5.5 | 4.1 | 9.6 | Dukakis(D)<br>**Bush(R)** | Yes |
| 1991 | 6.8 | 3.3 | 10.1 | | |
| 1992 | 7.5 | 3.0 | 10.5 | **Clinton(D)**<br>Bush(R) | Yes |
| 1995 | 5.6 | 2.8 | 8.4 | | |
| 1996 | 5.4 | 3.0 | 8.4 | **Clinton(D)**<br>Dole(R) | No Prediction |
| 1999 | 4.2 | 2.2 | 6.4 | | |
| 2000 | 4.0 | 3.4 | 7.4 | Gore(D)<br>**Bush(R)** | Yes |
| 2003 | 6.0 | 2.3 | 8.3 | | |
| 2004 | 5.5 | 2.7 | 8.2 | Kerry(D)<br>**Bush(R)** | Yes |
| 2007 | 4.6 | 2.8 | 7.4 | | |
| 2008 | 5.9 | 3.8 | 9.7 | **Obama(D)**<br>McCain(R) | Yes |
| 2011 | 8.95 | 3.16 | 12.11 | | |
| 2012 | 8.08 | 2.07 | 10.15 | **Obama(D)**<br>Romney(R) | Yes |
| 2015 | 5.28 | 0.12 | 5.40 | | |
| 2016 | 4.87 | 1.26 | 6.13 | Clinton(D)<br>**Trump(R)** | Yes |
| 2019 | 3.7 | 1.74 | 5.44 | | |
| 2020 | 8.1 | 1.25 | 9.35 | **Biden (D)**<br>Trump(R) | Yes |

Presidential winners are in green.
*Source:* U.S. Bureau of Labor Statistics

unpopular pardon of President Richard Nixon, who had resigned from office as a result of the Watergate scandal. This non-economic factor may have influenced the outcome of the election. In 2020, with the COVID-19 pandemic causing the unemployment rate to soar, the misery index again correctly predicted voters would change political parties from incumbent Republican Donald Trump to Democratic challenger Joe Biden.

## Civics Questions & Economic Answers

### Does the state of the economy affect elections?

As indicated by the misery index analysis, no matter what policies a presidential candidate may propose, an incumbent candidate is often blamed for or credited with how well the economy is doing. This is true whether or not the incumbent's policies were responsible. Many voters base their decisions narrowly on how the nation's economy is affecting them or their families at the time. Therefore, in a presidential campaign in which an incumbent is vying for reelection, key measures of economic performance often influence the election outcome.

### Is the Consumer Price Index (CPI) the only way to measure inflation?

No, there are a number of other measures of inflation used by policy makers and businesses to understand whether prices are increasing or decreasing. One simple measure is referred to as Core CPI. This is simply the Consumer Price Index (CPI) discussed this chapter but without adding food or energy to the market basket. Americans spend a lot of their money on food and energy, so such an exclusion may seem strange. The point of this modified statistic is that food and energy have volatile prices, and policy makers may wish to avoid making decisions about the future of the economy on short-term price swings.

The CPI gets a great deal of attention in the press. It is used to adjust Social Security payments for seniors and is the reference rate for some financial contracts. Another measure of inflation is called the personal consumption expenditure (PCE) price index. The Federal Reserve, believing

*The CPI and PCE Price Index are tools used to measure inflation.*

the PCE price index is a more accurate measure of price increases, uses it for stating its inflation goals.

The two measures, though following broadly similar trends, are not identical. In general, the CPI tends to report somewhat higher inflation. Since 2000, prices as measured by the CPI have risen by 39 percent, while those measured by the PCE have risen by 31 percent, leading to differing average annual inflation rates of 2.4 and 1.9 percent.

### Is everyone who does not have a job "unemployed"?

No. Only those that are not working but are looking for work are unemployed. Those that are retired are not unemployed, as they are not looking for work. Neither are full-time students, stay-at-home parents, or those with disabilities that making working impossible. Another statistic, called the *Labor Force Participation Rate*, measures the share of all adults that are in the labor force (working or looking for work).

### Can the unemployment rate improve while the economy is deteriorating?

Yes. The unemployment rate, due to the way it is constructed, can improve (or go down) for two reasons. First, people that were unemployed find jobs and move from being unemployed to employed. Such a result is clearly positive for the economy.

It is also possible, however, that people may stop looking for work. When that occurs, they change from being unemployed to no longer in the labor force. While this will have the effect of bringing the calculated unemployment rate down, it is not generally a good result for the U.S. economy. This typically happens when the economy is deteriorating and people give up trying to find jobs. There are more sophisticated measures of the unemployment rate that attempt to measure this phenomenon.

## QUESTIONS for DISCUSSION

1. Gross domestic product can be measured by (1) totaling all of the spending on goods and services produced in the United States or (2) by totaling all incomes received by consumers, businesses, and governments. Why should both of these add up to the same amount? (Hint: When someone spends \$2 on a soda, how much of the \$2 becomes an income to consumers, businesses, or governments?)
2. What categories are included in the Consumer Price Index's market basket?
3. How are economic indicators, such as real GDP, CPI, and unemployment rate, used by business people, elected officials, governments, and citizens?

## Whip Inflation Now

PRIMARY SOURCE

On October 8, 1974, in a speech titled "Whip Inflation Now," President Gerald Ford announced a series of proposals to directly combat the inflation the nation was experiencing at the time. President Ford took office after the resignation of Richard Nixon following the Watergate scandal. He inherited the worst U.S. economy since the 1940s, marked by high unemployment and rising inflation. Economists referred to this dire situation, a **stagnating** employment situation and **inflation**, by running the two main ills together as one word, **stagflation**.

Ford's speech sought to address the nation's economic instability brought on by an oil embargo from primarily Middle Eastern oil-producing countries that made up OPEC. This embargo, a protest against American support of Israel, was intended to stop oil shipments from reaching the United States.

In his speech, Ford referred to inflation as "public enemy number one" and endeavored to rally the nation, and Congress, behind his plans for the private and public sector to bring inflation under control. Citizens were encouraged to carpool, turn down their home thermostats, and grow their own vegetables in an effort to lessen their reliance on foreign oil.

WIN (Whip Inflation Now) buttons were worn by those in support of the policy but quickly became an object of ridicule. The plan is now considered a failure, and inflation was not brought under control until many years later when difficult monetary policy decisions were implemented by the Federal Reserve.

*A Whip Inflation Now (WIN) button from 1974.*

### QUESTIONS for DISCUSSION

1. Why would an embargo of oil have an effect on the prices of so many American products?
2. What is stagflation?
3. Why was OPEC so powerful in the 1970s and 1980s? Has anything changed to erode OPEC's power today?

Contemporary Connection

## What does Facebook "Produce"?

Gross domestic product is intended to measure all goods and services produced within the United States. While many joke about the actual value derived from social media, there is no doubt that consumers benefit substantially from all sorts of "free" online products such as Facebook, Instagram, and even a product as ubiquitous as Google Maps.

Some economists have suggested the inclusion of just Facebook would boost U.S. GDP by between 0.05 and 0.11 percentage points.[4] While those are tiny percentages, when applied to a $22 trillion economy they are more than a rounding error. The authors of the study polled a sample of U.S. users on how much they would need to be paid to give Facebook up for a month. The median response was $42.17.

Facebook is just one of many online platforms not currently considered in national statistical calculations. Many paid internet services (for example, downloading music for a monthly fee) are counted in GDP like other purchased products and services. But how can the Bureau of Economic Analysis count those that are ostensibly free to consumers? Perhaps the value of the advertising they produce is the way to measure Facebook's value, as has been applied to broadcast television.

Undercounting the value of "free" internet services doesn't only affect the overall size of the U.S. economy through our consumption-based GDP measure. It also affects the nation's measured economic growth rate and productivity (how much we can produce per worker). That said, GDP is also measured by totaling up all of the income earned by those in the United States. And, by this measure, much of the contribution of free technology services does get included.

### QUESTIONS for DISCUSSION

1. What kinds of production of goods and services are not counted by the way we measure gross domestic product (GDP)?
2. Do you think Facebook and other "free" technology services should be part of the GDP calculation?

## Web Quests

**Enter any of the links below and use the questions to get you started on your own web quest.**

### Bureau of Labor Statistics

*Visit the homepage of the Bureau of Labor Statistics.*

https://www.bls.gov/

1. What kinds of subjects does the BLS collect data on?
2. What is the current national unemployment rate? Is it up or down from last month?
3. What is the unemployment rate in the state you live in? Is it up or down from last month?
4. Find the current measure of the Consumer Price Index (CPI). Is the United States experiencing inflation or deflation? Which categories of goods and services are experiencing the most inflation today?

### Bureau of Economic Analysis

*Visit the website of the Bureau of Economic Analysis.*

https://www.bea.gov/

1. How much did real gross domestic product increase (or decrease) in the current quarter?
2. What components (consumption, investment, government spending, net exports) had the most impact on GDP?
3. Find U.S. trade data. In the current quarter, did the United States run a trade deficit or trade surplus? How big was it?

### Council of Economic Advisors (CEA)

*Visit the website of the Council of Economic Advisors.*

https://www.whitehouse.gov/cea/

1. Summarize the findings of the most recent Economic Report of the President.
2. Who currently serves on the CEA? What are their backgrounds?
3. Take a look at the open positions on this website (under "work for us"). If you aspired to work for the CEA in the White House, what kind of training and education should you pursue?

CHAPTER 7

# What Should Be the Size and Role of the Federal Government in the Economy?

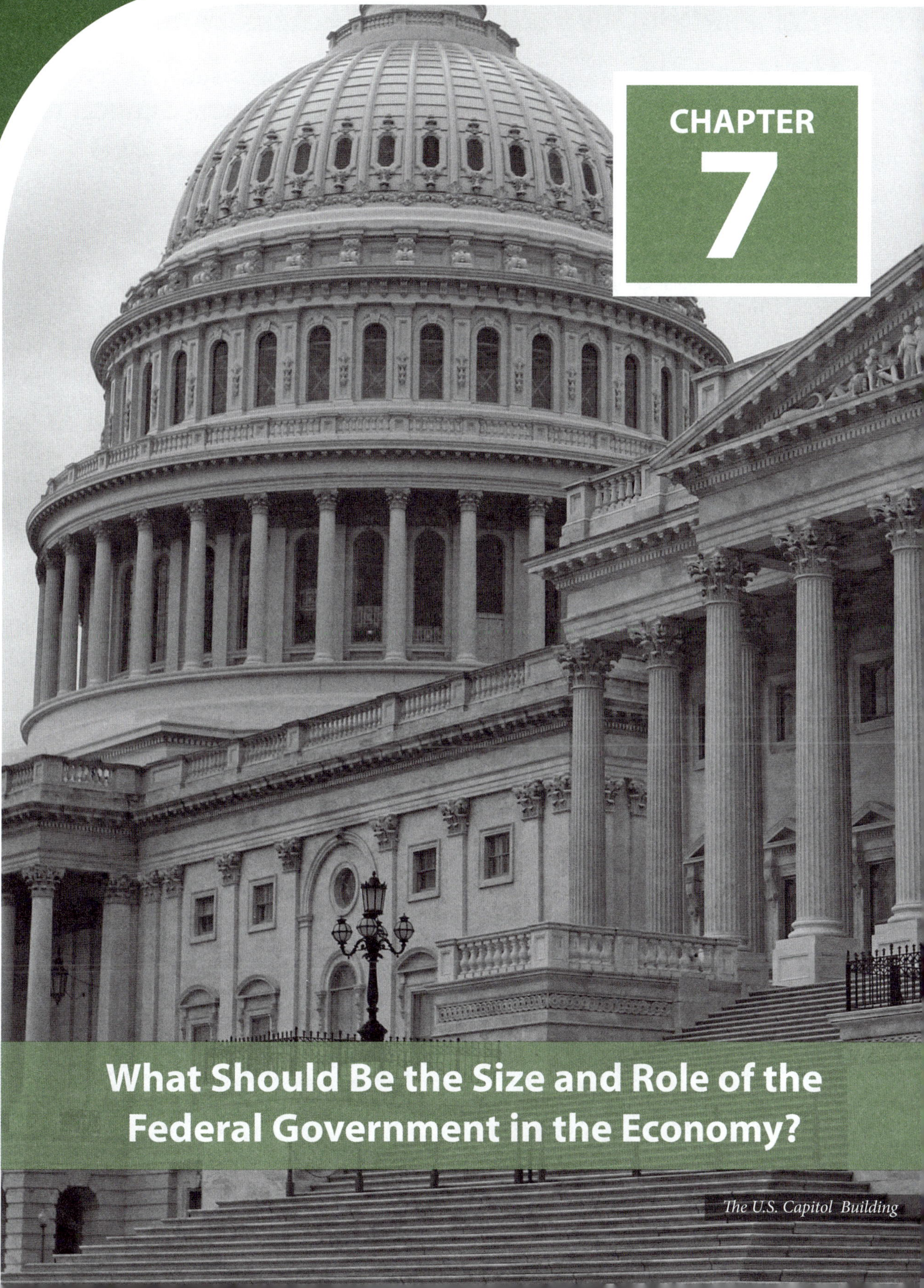

*The U.S. Capitol Building*

# Political Newcomer vs. Incumbent

**KEY ECONOMIC CONCEPTS**

gross domestic product (GDP)
national debt
national deficit
property rights
public goods

What happens when a newcomer faces a long-term incumbent in a political race? Most of the time, the incumbent will win the election. But not always!

Alexandria Ocasio-Cortez (also known as AOC) won the 2018 Democratic primary election for New York's 14th congressional district. She came to national prominence during this primary election when she defeated Democratic Caucus Chair Joe Crowley, a 10-term incumbent. Prior to running for office, she was a waitress and bartender.

Dave Brat rose to national prominence when he defeated House Majority Leader Eric Cantor in the 2014 Republican primary election for Virginia's seventh congressional district. He was an economics professor prior to running for office, then served as a U.S. representative from 2014 to 2019, and is now the dean of Liberty University's School of Business.

Both of these individuals' background and life experience led them to run for office to make our country better; they just have different visions about how to achieve that goal. AOC had been struggling financially, which likely shaped her perspective to support policies aimed at reducing income inequality to help the poor. Brat's background teaching economics to college students likely shaped his views as well. Economics shows how the most well-intentioned government policies can still lead to disastrous outcomes once we account for the unintended consequences (the secondary effects) of policies.

Is it possible that one politician could favor less government regulation and spending while another politician favors more government regulation and spending, and both believe that they are promoting what is best for the country? Certainly. It's likely rare that a politician truly has ill intentions for the country—even though that's what each political party will try to get you to believe about their opponent. What's more probable is that politicians have good intentions—even noble goals—but they don't fully understand the secondary effects of the policy at hand and

*Alexandria Ocasio-Cortez*

*Dave Brat*

therefore are simply blind to its detrimental impacts when put in practice. Or they might understand secondary effects and yet consider them worth the costs if their favored supporters gain enough.

## The Civics Context

The government serves an essential role in the protection of people and their **property rights**. This occurs through a police system, court system, and national defense.

All in our society have individual rights that protect them and their property from acts of violence and theft by others. With few and limited exceptions, all may engage in voluntary agreements as they please, as long as they don't violate the identical rights of others. Agreement must be voluntary. You can use wit and persuasion, but you cannot use physical force to get what you want, because that would be a violation of the rights of others.

In "The Nature of Government," novelist and libertarian thinker Ayn Rand describes government as a monopoly on the legal use of physical force. She explains the need for an objective code to limit that use of force. This code would have to include rules of evidence to establish a crime and identify the offender, as well as objective rules to define punishments and enforce procedures.

What does this mean? In addition to an individual's right to self-defense, a civilized society needs to have a system that penalizes anyone who violates the rights of another. In other words, to maintain order and enforce protection of each person's rights, there needs to be an entity with the exclusive right to use physical force and imprisonment.

Rand writes, "Under a proper social system, a private individual is legally free to take any action he pleases (so long as he does not violate the rights of others), while a government official is bound by law in his every official act. A private individual may do anything except that which is legally forbidden; a government official may do nothing except that which is legally permitted."[1]

*Ayn Rand, 1905–1982*

According to Rand, the proper role of government is to establish and manage a police system, court system, and national defense. Some individuals believe that the government's role extends beyond those three institutions, but nearly everyone agrees that the government's proper role includes those three institutions.

## The Economics of the Role of Government

Economists have differing views about the role of government. Some believe we should use government intervention through fiscal policy (changes in government spending and taxes) or monetary policy (changes in the money supply) to help the economy in times of unemployment or inflation, or to achieve other policy goals. Other economists believe that government intervention itself causes problems in the economy, and that the economy would be better off with limited intervention.

The British economist John Maynard Keynes believed that the total demand for goods and services in the economy (aggregate demand) could sometimes fall short. He recommended an active government role in maintaining aggregate demand. Those inspired by his work, today's Keynesian economists, believe in an expansive role for government. When the economy is experiencing a recession or depression and facing the resulting unemployment, the Keynesian fix is to boost aggregate demand by running a budget deficit. This can be achieved by increasing government spending and decreasing taxes. On the flip side, when the economy is facing an economic boom and inflation becomes a problem, the Keynesian solution is to run a budget surplus during those economic good times. This could be done by decreasing government spending and increasing taxes. Since the government would respond to the economy using its discretion, this is known as *discretionary fiscal policy*.

Keynes felt that there was no need to balance the federal budget. Using expansionary fiscal policy to run a budget deficit during economic bad times would be balanced out by using restrictive fiscal policy to run a budget surplus during the economic good times. Such a strategy is known as *countercyclical fiscal policy* because it attempts to counter the economy's cycle of expansions and recessions.

However, varied groups of economists are critics of the Keynesian approach. These groups tend to believe in a more limited role for government.

*John Maynard Keynes, 1883–1946*

First, consider what happens when a government tries to implement Keynesian fiscal policy. When the economy is weak, increasing government spending and cutting taxes is politically popular. But during an economic boom, it is not a good political strategy to propose increasing taxes and cutting the governmental programs that people have started to rely on. Hence, in real life we tend to see the Keynesian prescription for the economy implemented in an unbalanced manner. Politicians are more than eager to increase spending on governmental programs and cut taxes during times of a recession because it makes them look good. However, they don't want to cut spending or raise taxes once the economy is doing well again, because suggesting such policies could hurt their chances of winning reelection.

**FIGURE 1 Keynesian Solution to the Business Cycle**

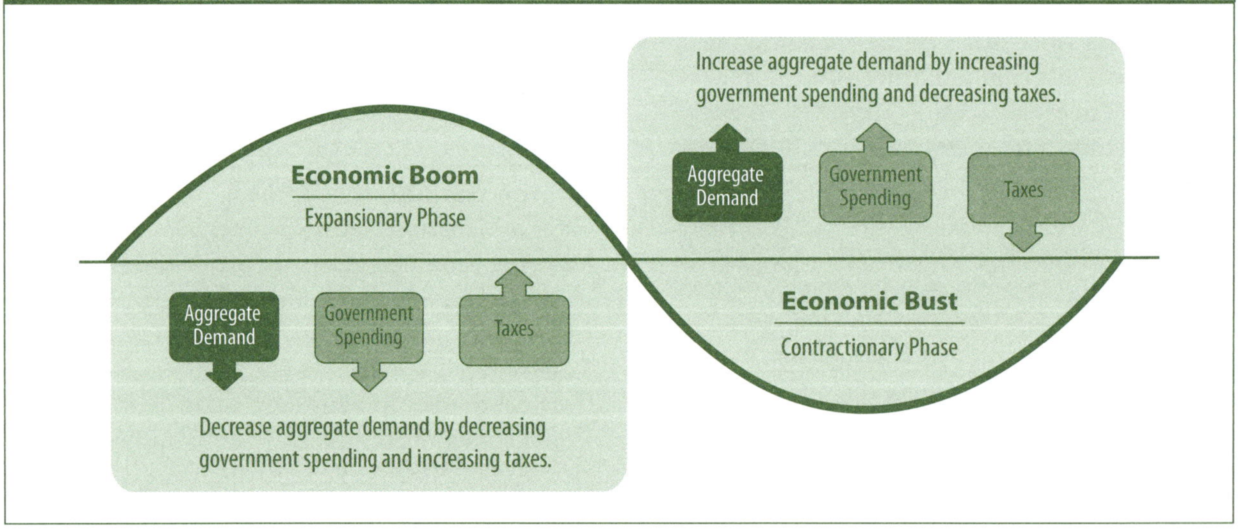

"Neoclassical economists" (also known as "new classical economists") believe that market forces will push an economy toward full employment. Therefore, they assert that using discretionary fiscal policy in an attempt to smooth the business cycle will only cause greater economic instability. Neoclassical economists believe government borrowing to finance increased government spending will change the behavior of citizens in the economy. They believe that government deficit spending will cause taxpayers to anticipate higher future taxes. Thus, taxpayers will decrease their *current* consumption to afford the future increase in tax rates. This reduction in private spending, an unintended consequence of fiscal policy, is known as *crowding out*.

Economists have closely studied possible ways in which crowding out can occur. Some point to the higher interest rates that might result from increased government borrowing, resulting in lower economic activity. Others see effects that occur when government spending affects international economic relationships. Still others see crowding out more generally, as any reduction in private spending that happens as a result of increased government spending.

Keynesian theory concentrates on aggregate demand. Another group concentrates not on what people demand, but instead on the total output an economy can produce, or *aggregate supply*. These "supply-side economists" see taxation as an important influence on aggregate supply. Supply-side economists tend to favor persistently low taxes, rather than the combination of frequent tax cuts and tax increases of Keynesian policy.

*Friedrich Hayek, 1899–1992*

## Civics Questions & Economic Answers

### Are market economies inherently stable or inherently unstable?

This is a key question underlying divergent views about the government's proper role. Keynesians believe a market economy is inherently unstable and must be managed by the government to prevent major swings. Keynes himself thought private investment was volatile, driven by business optimism and pessimism or, as he referred to it, by "animal spirits." Therefore, he believed government intervention was necessary to prevent the booms and busts of the economy.

Nobel laureate Friedrich Hayek had a different view. He saw government intervention to be the source of substantial economic instability. Hayek and his modern followers believe excessive credit expansion by the government causes artificially low interest rates, which send incorrect signals throughout the economy and lead to malinvestment. The results, they believe, are distorted investment patterns and instability coming not from an inherently unstable market economy, but from government intervention.

### Are there roles for the federal government that command wide agreement across the political spectrum?

There is wide agreement that the federal government should provide for police, courts, and national defense. These functions protect people and their property, which is a widely accepted role of government. Many also agree that the provision of roads is within government's proper role. Beyond these functions, the role of government is more controversial. Some thinkers see an extensive role of government as justified, including everything from equalization of incomes to strong and detailed environmental regulation. Others would stop at the most minimal functions of government.

## Is there something on which Keynesian economists and their critics agree?

While Keynesian and non-Keynesian economists disagree on the effectiveness of fiscal policy, they tend to agree that it is difficult to properly time legislative action for fiscal policy. This is due to several reasons: Passing legislation takes time, as it will require approval by both houses in Congress as well as the president. Once legislation is passed, it will then take months before its impact can be seen in the economy, possibly 6 to 12 months or longer. A good forecast of the economy one year in the future could offset this problem of timing, but it is incredibly difficult to accurately forecast the economy.[2] A policy that is correct for today's economic problems could be out of date and cause problems in the economy by the time it is fully implemented.

## What goods and services does government have a comparative advantage in producing (compared to the private sector)?

Government has a comparative advantage in producing what economists call **public goods**. These goods have two specific characteristics that economists call (1) non-excludability and (2) non-rivalry. Something is non-excludable if it is nearly impossible to exclude non-paying customers (or technically possible but extremely costly). Something is non-rivalrous when providing it to one person doesn't prevent another person from consuming it at the same time.

One example of a public good is national defense. It is non-excludable because it would be impossible (or near impossible) to exclude non-paying customers. It is non-rivalrous because my benefiting from a U.S. national defense system does not prevent you from benefiting from military protection at the same time.

Government tends to have a comparative advantage in producing true public goods. If the private sector attempts to produce public goods, there will be a free-rider problem. When non-paying citizens cannot be excluded, it is hard to get people to contribute "their share." They know that if the government provides it, there will be nothing stopping them from enjoying the benefits. The government has a comparative advantage in providing public goods since it can finance them with taxes.

## Does a good become a public good just because the government provides it?

No. Let's say the government decided to give out ice cream cones to every citizen once per week. Just because the ice cream cones are being paid for by the government does not mean that they are public goods. In fact, they do *not* satisfy the definition of a public good. We see ice cream shops exclude non-paying customers all the time! So ice cream is excludable (not non-excludable, as a true public good would be). Further, ice cream is not non-rivalrous (meaning, it is rivalrous!). If I eat an ice cream cone, you cannot consume that same ice cream cone at the same time. My use of the ice cream cone prevented you from being able to simultaneously use it.

Keep this in mind when you hear people refer to things like education and health care as "public goods." The government may choose to provide these—and the citizens may agree that this is proper. But remember that the sector in which something is produced does not determine whether it is a public good or not. To be classified as what economists call a "public good," the good or service must be non-excludable and non-rivalrous.

## What goods and services does the private sector have a comparative advantage in producing?

The private sector tends to have a comparative advantage in producing private goods (goods that are excludable and rivalrous in consumption). This includes most consumer goods and services. Market prices signal sellers to know how much of various items they ought to be producing for interested buyers, and the profit and loss mechanism in the private sector encourages competing sellers to keep their prices low while also encouraging innovation.

The profit and loss mechanism is not present in government. It doesn't matter how excellent a government official is at doing a job—that official is not going to be awarded with additional money the way an entrepreneur in the private sector would be rewarded. This is why we see so much innovation in the private sector when it comes to new and better products and processes. Economics teaches us that incentives matter, and the chance to earn a profit (or suffer a loss!) is a huge incentive for entrepreneurs not to waste their time or resources producing things consumers don't actually value highly relative to cost.

*Milton Friedman, 1912–2006*

### Should the government spend more to create jobs?

Creating jobs just for the sake of employment is not a wise strategy in trying to create a prosperous nation. Employment is not the end goal. An economy grows and prospers from the creation of goods and services that people value highly relative to cost. John Maynard Keynes joked about having the government pay people to dig holes and then fill them up. Even if that created jobs, it would not create output that people value.

A story about Nobel laureate Milton Friedman showcases this economic concept nicely. When Friedman was visiting China, he saw construction workers building a canal. He noticed the workers were using shovels instead of modern-day excavation machinery. When asked why excavation equipment wasn't being used (with far fewer workers), his host informed him that this was meant to be a jobs project to keep employment high. If they used modern-day machinery, fewer workers would be employed. The legend goes that Friedman then responded, "Oh, I thought you were trying to build a canal. If it's jobs you want, you should give these workers spoons, not shovels!"[3]

## QUESTIONS for DISCUSSION

1. What is the economic definition of a public good?
2. What is the relationship between public goods and the free-rider problem? How does this affect which sector has a comparative advantage in making public goods available?
3. Does the public sector currently provide goods that fall into the category of private goods? If so, provide examples and reasoning on whether these goods would be better provided by government or the private sector.
4. What are a few important goods or services that our society would have a hard time producing if we relied on private markets to provide them?

## FRED and the U.S. Debt Clock

PRIMARY SOURCE

When a government runs deficits year after year, the **national debt** grows. Note that the **national deficit** represents the amount that U.S. federal spending exceeds total federal tax revenue for the current year. The national debt represents the total accumulated deficits across time, whatever was borrowed and has not been paid off. In recent years the national debt has been growing. Is this a justifiable cause for alarm?

Clearly the national debt has grown substantially. A good source of data on the national debt, and any other U.S. economic statistic, is Federal Reserve Economic Data (FRED), maintained by the Federal Reserve Bank of St. Louis. FRED data on the federal debt divided by the population[4] confirms the impression of significant growth. In 1970, the U.S. federal debt amounted to about $1,841 per person in the United States. By 2020, the U.S. federal debt had soared to $79,050 per person.

**FIGURE 2 Total U.S. Federal Debt Divided by Population**

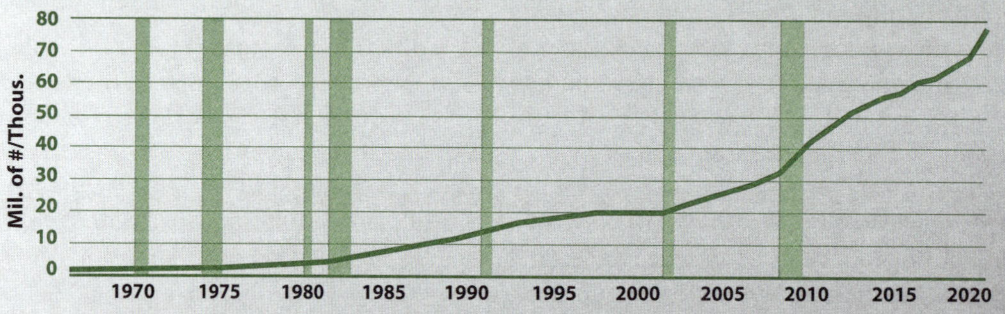


Shaded areas indicate U.S. recessions

*Source:* Federal Reserve Economic Data

That's a lot of debt! Yet in other areas we look not at total debt or debt per person, but at debt in relation to the debtor's ability to pay back—as when we look at a home mortgage as a percentage of a homebuyer's income. Using an equivalent approach for the national debt would involve calculating the national debt as a percentage of our annual output, **gross domestic product** (GDP).[5] This measure gave a more comfortable reading on the size of the debt until 2008, but then began dramatic growth.

In 1970, the federal debt was about 35.2 percent of GDP. After some ups and downs, by 2010 it had grown quite a bit, reaching about 89 percent of GDP. And in 2020, the federal debt was actually 125.2 percent of GDP! Yes, you read that right: Starting in 2013, the federal debt has been *greater* than 100 percent of our nation's GDP (this means that, for the past several years, our nation now owes more money than the value of all the goods and services our country is able to produce in a year).

**FIGURE 3** **Total U.S. Federal Debt as a Percentage of GDP**

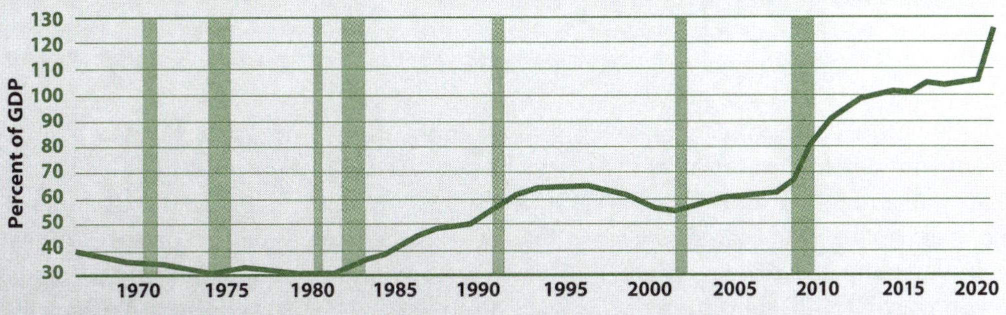


Shaded areas indicate U.S. recessions

*Source:* Federal Reserve Economic Data

Yet another way we can get a sense of how much (and how fast) our government debt is growing is to go to **www.usdebtclock.org**. This site allows you to see many statistics updating in real time. Check out the website for yourself and you'll see that all the figures are constantly updating many times *per second*! On the site, you can also hover over each statistic, and it will share a definition of the variable, along with its source.

As of December 28, 2021, the U.S. national debt was over $29.3 trillion, which is more than $88,000 per citizen and greater than $232,000 per taxpayer. By the time this book is in print, the U.S. national debt will be well over $30 trillion.

Although it is possible for any entity—household, company, or government—to have a stable yet growing debt, there may come a time when there is a debt crisis. The crisis will not occur as long as lenders, the holders of the debt, feel confident they will be repaid. If the United States brings down its national debt as a fraction of the GDP in the future, it may avoid a crisis. Crisis skeptics also point out that the U.S. government has the ability to create dollars to pay its debt. (However, the strategy to print more money comes with its own secondary effects: inflation.) If the United States comes to a day of widespread doubts about its ability to repay, it may have a shocking debt crisis just like many other nations before it.

## QUESTIONS for DISCUSSION

1. What are some of the different ways to get a sense of the size of the national debt and how it has grown across time?
2. Describe how the federal debt per person in the United States has changed over the past few decades.
3. Do you find it worrisome that our federal debt now exceeds GDP? Why or why not?
4. What are a few statistics shown by the U.S. Debt Clock that surprise you (or that you consider important)?
5. What is the difference between the national debt and a single year's deficit? (Describe the difference in terms of the meaning of each, not the difference in the dollar figures for each.)

Contemporary Connection

## What Should Be Government's Role in Health Care?

Few issues are more contentious than the role of government in health care. Our current system of public and private provision of health care, with a large role for insurance, leaves many unsatisfied. Figure 4 below shows a reason for disappointment.

Notice that the United States is far out on the horizontal axis, spending more than any other nation on health care—but decently far from having the highest life expectancy. In constant dollars on the chart, for example, Canada was spending less than half what the United States spends, but Canada achieved life expectancy six years longer. Mexico spends just a fraction of what the United States does, but since 1970 moved steadily up to 75 years of life expectancy. This compares with slightly over 78 years for the United States. Note also the achievements of Sweden, Switzerland, and the United Kingdom in achieving longer life expectancy while having lower total spending on health care.

In innovation of new drugs and techniques, the U.S. medical system leads the world. We already saw that the United States spends more per person on medical care than any other nation. And yet outcomes are disappointing. Many solutions have been proposed, most of them involving a changed role for government.

Advocates of market solutions to health care argue that the government should get out of the way and let the market work. In certain parts of health care where government has a minimal role (for example, laser vision correction), costs have come down and quality has rapidly increased. However, an inherent part of a market is excluding a product or service from non-payers. That's easy when the market is allocating big screen televisions, but it is difficult ethically when life and death are at stake. Some people believe a pure market solution would leave the poor behind and further inequality.

**FIGURE 4 Spending and Life Expectancy**

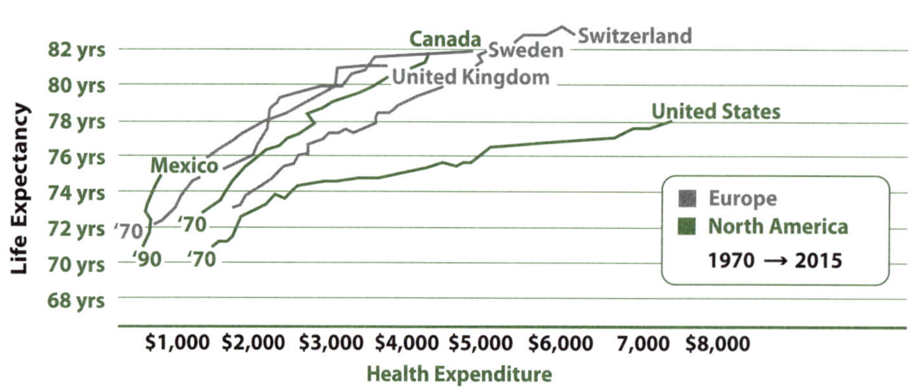


*Source:* Our World in Data[6]

*Supporters of health care reform rally in Los Angeles in 2009.*

Advocates of universal health care say the government should finance and supervise delivery of all medical services. They say that this would allow for a consistent quality of health care that could be delivered to everyone. Critics believe a totally government-run system would have low quality, and they worry that health care decisions would be politicized. Another issue that countries with a universal health care system face is long waits for appointments, surgeries, and other procedures.

That leaves us where we are right now, with a mix of market and government elements. Insurance plays a key role, paying for a wide variety of procedures and insulating consumers from high costs, but also making pricing a good deal less meaningful. If you have ever seen an original doctor or hospital bill, you will see eye-popping numbers at the top. Below that will be a number of adjustments and payments, leading finally to a line marked "pay this amount." Most patients do just that, without understanding exactly where the number came from. Most medical consumers find bills difficult to untangle. As a result, citizens have a hard time being their own advocates the way they are if they think a utility or internet bill is incorrect.

Is there some magic system that could harness the innovation and cost savings of the market while achieving the equality and security of a functioning universal care system? The first political party to find and implement that system will reap great rewards. Skeptics think no such system exists—or that, if it does, the U.S. political system cannot get us there.

## QUESTIONS for DISCUSSION

1. What are a few different perspectives when it comes to the type of health-care system the United States should have? How do these perspectives relate to our conversation about the role of government?
2. What is one benefit of a pure market health-care system? What is a downside? What is a benefit of a universal health-care system? What is a downside?
3. What do you believe to be the ideal health-care system for the United States? Why?

## Web Quests

**Enter any of the links below and use the questions to get you started on your own web quest.**

### Supply Side Economics

*Article by economist James Gwartney, published in the first edition of the* Concise Encyclopedia of Economics *in 1993.*

**https://www.econlib.org/library/Enc1/SupplySideEconomics.html**

1. Is it possible to have increased tax revenues when you lower tax rates? How?
2. Why does James Gwartney say that "the lower rates soaked the rich" in the 1980s?

### FRED (Federal Reserve Economic Data)

*Federal Reserve Economic Data (FRED) is maintained by the Federal Reserve Bank of St. Louis, and it offers a vast amount of data.*

**https://fred.stlouisfed.org**

1. Go to FRED and look up the most recent figure for the federal debt (total public debt). What does it show?
2. Explore some of the other variables available on the FRED website. You can view, graph, and download more than 800,000 time series variables from FRED.

### U.S. Debt Clock

*This website tracks the U.S. national debt and many other government statistics in real time.*

**https://www.usdebtclock.org**

1. What is the current U.S. national debt?

### Fight of the Century: Keynes vs. Hayek

*"Fight of the Century: Keynes vs. Hayek – Economics Rap Battle Round Two" by Emergent Order. This is an economics music video created by John Papola and Russ Roberts in 2011.*

**https://www.youtube.com/watch?v=GTQnarzmTOc**

1. Can war or natural disasters paradoxically be good for an economy in a recession? How would Keynes answer this question? What would be Hayek's take on the matter?
2. In the video, the actor playing Keynes says: "...The spending on war clearly goosed GDP. Unemployment was over, almost down to zero. That's why I'm the master, that's why I'm the hero." The actor playing Hayek responded, "Creating employment's a straightforward craft, when the nation's at war and there's a draft. If every worker were staffed in the army and fleet, we'd have full employment and nothing to eat. ...Jobs are a means, not the ends in themselves. People work to live better, to put food on the shelves." Analyze these lyrics using the economic way of thinking and the concepts you learned in this chapter.

# CHAPTER 8

# Public Choice Theory: Why Is Good Politics Often Bad Economics?

*An interchange on the Interstate Highway System in Austin, Texas.*

# Shelly Buys an Electric Car

Shelly is a former medical school professor who is deeply committed to environmental health. While racing between meetings in Washington, D.C., she got a ride from an Uber driver in an electric vehicle. The ride piqued her interest in electric vehicles. It didn't take long for her to take the plunge and buy one. She soon became a strong advocate of electric cars as a way to improve the environment.

People like Shelly have many reasons to prefer electric vehicles. As the cars are driven, they have no emissions. Electric cars often require less maintenance, and they come with generous tax credits.

But there are costs as well. Electric cars are expensive largely due to the new technologies involved. They have a shorter mileage range than gas-powered cars; they can usually travel around 300 miles before they need to stop for recharging. Recharging the battery takes time, and charging stations can be hard to find. Also, people who drive electric vehicles pay no gas taxes to support road maintenance.

*A woman charges her electric car.*

### KEY ECONOMIC CONCEPTS

**incentives**
**infrastructure**
**interest group effect**
**primary effects**
**productivity**
**public choice theory**
**secondary effects**
**subsidy**

The federal government in 2021 offered a tax credit of $7,500 to people who buy electric cars. This is a **subsidy**—a form of financial assistance—to nudge consumers into buying electric vehicles. But tax credits come with primary and secondary effects (see Chapter 1). The **primary effect** is to get gas guzzlers off the road to pave the way for cleaner electric cars. What might be a **secondary effect**? The $7,500 tax credit by and large goes to the wealthy. According to a 2019 Congressional Research Service report, 78 percent of the tax credits go to recipients with an adjusted income of $100,000 or more.[1] Electric vehicles account for about 3 percent of all new cars sold in the United States annually.

The electric-car subsidy might have you scratching your head. Do American taxpayers really favor using their tax dollars to help someone else buy an expensive car? Is this the proper role of government? Or should the federal government stand aside and allow the manufacturers of electric vehicles and consumers to determine what cars should be produced and at what prices?

## The Civics Context

While the debate continues on electric vehicle tax credits, there are examples of government programs that perform more or less as designed and provide more economic benefits than costs. Infrastructure spending is an example.

**Infrastructure** refers to roads, ports, bridges, airports, and railroads that support economic activity. The idea is that if government allocates resources to build infrastructure, consumers and producers both gain.

Have you ever taken a car trip on the Interstate Highway System? Maybe you use it to go to school or work or to take vacations. You probably don't think much about the roads on which you are traveling except to worry about congestion and time to your destination.

Dating back to the administration of George Washington, the federal government has encouraged road construction to bind the nation together and support trade. Today, the whole nation is connected by the interstate highways. Drivers can take Interstate 95 all the way from Florida to Maine. Interstate 80 begins in San Francisco and can take you across the country to the Big Apple, New York City.

The Interstate Highway System began when President Dwight D. Eisenhower signed the Federal Aid Highway Act in 1956. The construction was handled by the states, with an initial $25 billion in funding over 12 years. The federal government paid 90 percent of the tab while the states paid the remaining 10 percent. The cost was to be paid for by issuing government bonds (debt) and collecting gas taxes. Mostly, the program did not experience major cost overruns.

The main argument in support of construction was military, not economic. In the 1950s, the United States was in a "cold war" with the Soviet Union. It was feared that if a "hot war" broke out with the Soviets, roads would be much easier to repair after an attack than railways.

President Eisenhower and members of Congress were also aware of the possible economic benefits. With the construction of the interstates, railroad shipping and passenger travel declined, but the trucking industry exploded. The expansion paved the way for successful firms today including Federal Express, Amazon, and Walmart.

America changed in fundamental ways. A new tourist industry emerged as families hit the road for vacations. Service stations, tourist attractions, motels, and restaurants popped up

*President Eisenhower participates in the ribbon cutting ceremony opening a new extension to the George Washington Memorial Parkway, 1959.*

near countless interchanges. The interstates also reduced housing costs by allowing millions of Americans to move out of large cities and build homes in less-expensive suburbs and small towns. Finally, the Federal Highway Administration reports that fatalities have declined considerably over the past several decades.[2] Interstates were far safer than the two-lane highways they replaced because of their one-way traffic flows, carefully designed entrances and exits, and absence of stoplights.

The interstates brought overall economic benefits to businesses and consumers. Research by the U.S. Department of Transportation estimates that between 1950 and 1989, U.S. industries saved 18 cents annually for each dollar spent on the interstate roads. This reduction in costs resulted in three major benefits. First, consumers benefited from lower prices. Second, the savings enhanced profits for businesses. Finally, and most importantly, the highway system had a big impact on **productivity**. Productivity is the amount of goods and services that can be produced with a given set of resources over a period of time. Productivity gains are a key contributor to economic growth. Productivity gains from the interstate system were the highest during and immediately following construction. In the 1950s, the interstate highways' contribution to annual productivity gain was a whopping 31 percent. That dropped off to 25 percent in the 1960s and continued over time at a lower level.[2] Economists and politicians alike regard the gains as a remarkable achievement.

The Interstate Highway System had costs as well. As many people chose to leave cities for the suburbs, some large cities faced declining populations and revenues. Also, interstates sometimes cut right through minority or high-poverty neighborhoods, displacing local populations and interrupting economic activity for consumers, businesses, and workers.

## The Economics of Public Choice Theory

Economists often rely on the standard of economic efficiency to judge the economic outcomes of a government program. Efficiency suggests that government actions that generate more benefit than cost are ones that should be taken. The Interstate Highway System appears to meet this test. In contrast, actions that generate more cost than benefit should not be taken. Some government programs turn out to be inefficient. If this is true, why would members of Congress and presidents approve legislation that is economically suspect? Why is good politics sometimes bad economics?

Economists use public choice theory to answer that question. **Public choice theory** studies the behavior of elected and appointed officials in government by applying the economic way of thinking usually associated with the study of private markets.

***Individuals in Government Make Decisions.***

Public choice theory starts with the basic point that governments consist of individuals. No government thinks or acts. Government actions instead are the result of individuals making decisions in their roles as elected officials,

*Missouri claims the first interstate highway project to begin construction after the passage of the Federal-Aid Highway Act of 1956.*

appointed officials, or bureaucrats. To understand how government works, public choice theory analyzes how individuals in government make choices.

### *Decisions Are Based on Costs and Benefits.*

Individuals in government, like those in the private economy, choose options that represent the best set of costs and benefits to themselves. Their decisions are, in this sense, self-interested. This is not to say that people in government are selfish or greedy. An elected official may be devoted to expanding access to national parks for people who are physically challenged, for example. To gain support for the elected official's national-park legislation, that person may need to support a colleague's desire to build a museum as a tribute to a popular musician, bringing more jobs into the state.

### *Incentives Matter.*

Public choice theory holds that behavior in the political system is motivated by **incentives** similar to those motivating behavior in the private sector. Monetary rewards, to be sure, play an important role in the decisions of public officials. Elected officials, like other people, also consider many other incentives, including family security, recognition, travel, access to information, and satisfaction from performing community service. Because such incentives influence political leaders' decisions, we can predict actions they might take once we know what motivates them.

### *Competition Is Everywhere.*

We typically think of competition as a defining characteristic of the private economy. It is, however, a key feature of the public sector as well. Government officials face scarcity, and candidates for office compete to gain scarce nominations. This competition entails finding ways to gain the support of voters, finding volunteers, raising campaign funds, and allocating scarce time in the most effective way. Once elected, officials compete to acquire staff, resources, and the support of colleagues for policies favored in the campaign.

### *Differences Are Important.*

Important differences exist between the private economy and the political system. Two differences stand out. First, the private economy depends on voluntary exchanges between producers and consumers. Although the exchanges between voters and government officials are also voluntary, governments can in addition use force in regulating economic affairs. Governments can take property if taxes go unpaid. Ultimately, governments can put people in jail for noncompliance, though only with due process of law in our system.

Second, decisions expressed by the electorate through voting are different from the decisions expressed by "dollar voting" by consumers in the private economy. The political system adds up votes, and the majority rules. Eventually, a majority decides whether new roads will be built, which college students get government loans, or whether millions of acres of timber land will be set aside for a national park.

The private economy, however, is run by proportional rule: a minority does not need to yield to a majority. Relatively few people, for example, may be interested in spending a week fishing on a secluded lake or in purchasing the latest computer software. Yet the market does not require majority approval for anglers to seek out quiet lakes or computer buffs to buy the most sophisticated program. They may go ahead, each as a majority of one. Citizens as consumers and producers need to make far fewer compromises than citizens as policy makers. Proponents of limited government point out that people are better able to obtain just what they want as individuals rather than as members of a voting bloc.

## Civics Questions & Economic Answers

### Why do elected officials sometimes support inefficient government programs?

Public choice economists point to incentives, costs, and benefits to explain what they call the **interest group effect**. Interest groups are voluntary organizations of like-minded citizens who promote the priorities of their group. Interest groups include business owners, farmers, labor unions, consumer groups, environmental groups, and so forth.

According to the interest group effect, elected officials face incentives to support legislation that provides concentrated benefits to the members of interest groups at the expense of disorganized groups such as voters and consumers. Interest groups are likely to be successful in influencing legislation when the following happens:

- Benefits are concentrated among a few—the members of an interest group.
- Costs are spread out over many—consumers.

Here is how it works. Imagine that the City of Clovernook is deciding whether it should build a pedestrian bridge over the Clover River. Consultants estimate that the bridge will cost $250,000. They also estimate that the benefits to the citizens would be $25,000. There are 50,000 Clovernook taxpayers. So, the potential cost of the bridge is $5.00 per person. The potential benefit is 50 cents per person. This appears to be an inefficient government project. The plan should be dropped, right? Hold on. The plot thickens.

There are five contractors who would receive equal contracts of $50,000 each. The contractors have a strong incentive for the project to be approved. They might hire a public relations firm to run ads in newspapers, on TV, and in social media praising the bridge and the service it will offer to walkers and bicyclists. They are willing to make legal campaign contributions to members of the City Council.

Will voters hire a public relations firm to oppose the bridge? Will voters make campaign contributions? Probably not. They are disorganized. They are busy going to work and school and caring for their families. They might not even notice that, if approved, the bridge would increase their taxes by a paltry $5.00.

The Clover River bridge illustrates how an economically inefficient project could be approved. The benefits for the bridge are concentrated among the contractors and pedestrians served by the bridge. The costs are diffused—spread out over thousands of taxpayers who might not even notice that it is was a bad deal for most of them.

### The Clovernook example is a good illustration, but it is fictitious. Does the interest group effect work in real life?

You bet. There are countless examples. James Gwartney and his colleagues explain that there are roughly 20,000 U.S. sugar growers. The price paid by consumers for sugar is 50 percent to 100 percent higher than world sugar prices. Those 20,000 U.S. sugar growers benefit from these high prices that come from government action. Sugar growers gain thousands of dollars in income each year from government-enforced price supports and import restrictions. Most of the gains go to large, wealthy growers. Sugar growers make millions of dollars in campaign contributions to members of Congress on both sides of the aisle.[3]

This is a textbook case of the interest group effect. The benefits are concentrated among a relatively small number of sugar growers, and the costs are diffused over millions of sugar-buying consumers. Other examples of the interest group effect include most tariffs, farm subsidies, state subsidies to film makers, and so forth.

### What is "logrolling" in Congress?

Politics has a lot of colorful language. The term *logrolling* probably originated when American farmers in the early days of the republic would help a family clear land by cutting down trees and then rolling the logs away to be burned. Everyone cooperated to get a big job done.

In politics, logrolling means that elected officials make a deal to trade votes so that legislation is passed. For example, Senator A, representing a large-population urban state, might want subsidies for steel manufacturers in her state. But steel tariffs often face stiff opposition from consumer groups and firms that use steel.

Senator B, representing a rural state, wants subsidies for wheat farmers in his state. But subsidies to wheat farmers might be opposed by environmental groups concerned about increased use of chemicals in agricultural areas.

Senators A and B think they might lose if they go it alone. So, they decide to trade votes. If Senator A votes for Senator B's legislation and Senator B votes for Senator A's legislation, they will have a good chance of passing both pieces of legislation. This all makes perfect sense to Senators A and B—and to the steelworkers and wheat farmers in their states.

The subsidies might be good for these special interest groups, but the process is almost certainly economically inefficient. Note that these groups benefit at the expense of other taxpayers. Also note how the interest groups, like steel producers, received a concentrated benefit, and the costs are diffused over steel consumers who might not even notice.

### What is pork barrel spending?

The term *pork barrel legislation* or *pork barrel spending* originated in the early 19th century, when barrels were used to store pork. Over time, the term became associated with money and earning income. In politics it became associated with legislators bringing federal spending into their states or districts. Legislators who played this game well were said to be "bringing home the pork."

*A 1917 cartoon of pork barrel spending from* The Independent.

How does pork barrel spending work? It works a lot like logrolling. In this case, various federal projects to benefit special interests and bring home the pork are bundled into one piece of legislation. Separately, these projects for federally funded improvements in roads, bridges, ports, and hospitals might not be funded, but together they are nearly an irresistible incentive to incumbent politicians. Like logrolling, this all makes perfect sense to elected officials interested in being reelected.

## QUESTIONS for DISCUSSION

1. What is public choice theory?
2. In what ways do elected officials act in much the same way as do other people such as those in the private sector?
3. What is the interest group effect?
4. How would public choice theory explain federal tax credits to buy electric cars?
5. How are logrolling and pork barrel legislation similar? Different?

# The Golden Fleece Award Goes to the Bridge to Nowhere

PRIMARY SOURCE

Senator William Proxmire of Wisconsin served in the U.S. Senate for 32 years and was widely regarded as a maverick. He irritated his colleagues by crusading against logrolling and pork barrel legislation throughout his career. He was a frugal person. For example, he refused to accept campaign contributions. He spent less than $200 on his campaigns for the U.S. Senate.

*Senator William Proxmire*

Senator Proxmire drew attention to wasteful government spending through his Golden Fleece Awards. His office issued 168 Golden Fleece Awards every month from 1975 to 1988. The first Golden Fleece Award was issued in 1975 to the National Science Foundation for funding an $84,000 study on why people fall in love.

Proxmire passed the Golden Fleece Award on to a nonpartisan federal budget watchdog organization called Taxpayers for Common Sense. The Golden Fleece Award in 2003 was given to the "bridge to nowhere." The bridge was meant to connect Ketchikan, Alaska, population 8,000, with the island of Gravina, population 50. A ferry service was operating to move people back and forth. The project was finally abandoned in 2007.

On the following page are two tables published in 2005 showing research conducted by Taxpayers for Common Sense. The tables compare the costs of the Gravina Bridge in Ketchikan, Alaska, to the Big Dig in Boston, Massachusetts.

What was the Big Dig? Officially, it was known as the Central Artery/Tunnel Project (CA/T). It was the largest highway project completed in the United States. To the voters, it became known as the Big Dig. The Boston project rerouted parts of I-93 into the 1.5-mile tunnel. Thomas P. O'Neill Jr., Speaker of the House of Representatives, lobbied his colleagues to secure federal funding for the project. The project was controversial because of numerous cost overruns, delays, leaks, design flaws, and the death of one motorist. What was supposed to cost millions wound up costing billions.

Can you use public choice theory to explain the outcomes of the Bridge to Nowhere project and the Big Dig? The Questions for Discussion invite further thought.

| TABLE 1 | Comparing Per Person Costs of the Big Dig and the Gravina Bridge | |
|---|---|---|
| | Big Dig | Gravina Bridge |
| Assumed cost | $14,000,000,000 | $315,000,000 |
| Population | 5,800,000 | 13,320 |
| Cost per person | $2,414 | $23,649 |

| TABLE 2 | Comparing Usage Costs of the Big Dig and the Gravina Bridge | |
|---|---|---|
| | Big Dig | Gravina Bridge |
| Daily Usage (vehicles/day) | 500,000 | 1,000 |
| Annual cost (5% discount rate) | $700,000,000 | $15,750,000 |
| Number of trips per year | 182,500,000 | 365,000 |
| Cost per trip | $3.84 | $43.15 |
| Cost of ferry for a car | N/A | $6.00 |
| Cost of ferry for a pedestrian | N/A | $4.00 |

*Source:* These tables appeared in an article published in June 2012 by Taxpayers for Common Sense. The data was based on a report by Peter Samuel. "Alaskan pork-Ketchikan bridge vs Big Dig." April 10, 2004. TOLLROADS news.

*Boston's "Big Dig" project under construction.*

## QUESTIONS for DISCUSSION

1. What was the estimated cost per person of each project in Table 1?
2. What was the estimated cost per trip of each project in Table 2?
3. Using the concepts of public choice theory, why do you think the Big Dig was funded while the Bridge to Nowhere was not?

Contemporary Connection

## The Economics of Solar Panel Subsidies for Homes

Elected officials and environmental service businesses often argue that climate change is the biggest problem facing the nation and the world. They suggest that the government needs to actively promote renewable energy sources such as solar, wind, and geothermal. Some propose government subsidies for innovation to push the energy sector away from fossil fuels and toward renewables.

Within this context, the federal government provides a subsidy to homeowners who install solar panels on their roofs. Homeowners receive a federal tax credit. A tax credit means that a homeowner can directly reduce taxes owed by installing solar panels. Currently, homeowners can reduce their taxes by either 30, 26, or 22 percent of the cost. The price tag for home solar power systems varies by region, quality, and the size of the home. Typically, they cost between $15,000 and $25,000.

What are the benefits of subsidies for solar panels? The primary benefit is to put a dent in the amount of fossil fuels being consumed. Most U.S. energy sources today are based on fossil fuels. Solar subsidies are one way to nudge people to use more solar and depend less on fossil fuels for electricity. And the residential solar panel industry is expanding as homeowners slowly embrace renewable energy.

Homeowners receive two direct benefits. First, they receive the one-time tax credit for the purchase and installation of solar panels. Second, it helps them save on their energy bills. Using solar energy from roof solar

*Workers install solar panels on the roof of a home in Southern California.*

panels reduces the amount homeowners pay for electricity from the connected utility company. The savings can be between 10 and 30 percent on a monthly electricity bill.

Elected officials also benefit. They receive support from environmental groups who favor solar power. This support takes the form of increased campaign contributions and votes. Elected officials also receive support from solar panel companies and related industries. Solar panel companies understand that the subsidy to install solar panels increases demand for their products. They gain relative to other producers of clean energy and traditional fossil fuels.

What about the costs? Solar power itself has a long way to go. It is less than 3 percent of total U.S. energy. Not all locations in the nation have the sunshine that is necessary. Solar panels can only collect energy when the sun is shining. Although energy could be stored in the day and fed back into the system at night, the necessary storage technology is expensive. Many worry that solar is not dependable. In this context, it is unlikely that this one program—roof-installed solar panels on homes—provides a significant improvement to the environment.

Residential solar panels benefit the rich. To benefit from the subsidy, you must be a homeowner and have the cash to pay for the solar panel system. Installing solar panels is simply not within reach of many low- and moderate-income families. Setting up such systems can cost tens of thousands of dollars, which means that their use—and subsequent savings—are predominantly enjoyed by wealthy households.

While the financial benefits of solar panels go to the wealthy, it is taxpayers who bear the cost. The Joint Committee on Taxation (JCT) estimates that in 2019, foregone revenues (or tax expenditures) for all electricity production tax credits were $5.1 billion.[4]

Overall, there has been great improvement in the technology of producing solar power. The effects on the energy industry and the environment have been positive. Thus, some suggest that solar tax credits should be allowed to expire. In fact, they have been scheduled to expire several times but have been renewed by Congress each time.

Why do you think the solar panel subsidies do not expire? Is this another example of an interest group effect? A relatively small group of homeowners and solar panel businesses benefit directly. This is the concentrated benefit. The costs, however, are diffused over millions of taxpayers. While the cost is several billion dollars annually, it is likely that few taxpayers ever notice.

## Questions for Discussion

1. How does the federal government provide a subsidy for homeowners to install solar panel systems on roofs?
2. What are the benefits of subsidies for home solar panels?
3. What are the costs of subsidies for home solar panels?
4. How might the subsidies for home solar panels be an example of an interest group effect?

## Web Quests

**Enter any of the links below and use the questions to get you started on your own web quest.**

**Ike's Interstates at 50**

*This link features an article that emphasizes the role played by President Eisenhower in passing the legislation that created the Interstate Highway System.*

**https://www.archives.gov/publications/prologue/2006/summer/interstates.html**

1. Describe the event in early 1919 that first piqued the interest of Lieutenant Colonel Dwight D. Eisenhower in the establishment of a system of interstate highways.
2. How did the German autobahns further influence Eisenhower?
3. What were some of the challenges in passing highway legislation?
4. What economic changes resulted from the passage of the Interstate Highway legislation?

**James M. Buchanan on Public Choice Theory**

*James Buchanan won the Nobel Prize in Economics for his work on public choice theory. At this site, you can watch short videos and learn more about Buchanan, his life, and his ideas.*

**https://www.ubs.com/microsites/nobel-perspectives/en/laureates/james-buchanan.html**

1. How does self-interest affect politicians' decisions?
2. Are politicians motivated by the greater good?
3. Why doesn't democracy work perfectly?
4. How can constitutional rules be modified?

**Renewable Electricity Production Tax Credits**

*This is a link to a Congressional Research Service report on renewable energy tax credits. It provides a nice summary of the tax credits for renewal energy.*

**https://sgp.fas.org/crs/misc/R43453.pdf**

1. Provide a brief summary of how renewable production tax credits work.
2. What are the benefits identified in this report?
3. What are the costs?
4. What policy change is recommended? Why?

# CHAPTER 9

# How Are Taxes Incentives to Businesses and Households?

*An I.R.S. building in Washington D.C.*

# Social Security Recipient #1

How many times does the government return more than $22,000 to someone who paid in under $25? That's what happened in the case of Ida May Fuller of Ludlow, Vermont. She was the woman who in 1940 received the first monthly retirement check from the recently created U.S. Social Security system. Miss Fuller had grown up on a Vermont farm and attended school in Rutland, Vermont, where one of her schoolmates was Calvin Coolidge. Miss Fuller had worked first as a schoolteacher and later as a legal secretary, retiring in November of 1939. She began collecting benefits at the age of 65 and continued to do so until 1975 when she died at 100 years of age.

In working for three years under the new Social Security program, Miss Fuller paid $24.75 in total taxes through the program as shown in Table 1 below.[1] She collected $22,888.92 in Social Security benefits. While running an errand on November 4, 1939, Miss Fuller stopped by the Rutland Social Security office to inquire about possible benefits. Her claim was processed and transferred to the Claims Division in Washington, D.C., where her case was reviewed, approved, and sent to the Treasury Department for payment in January of 1940.

**TABLE 1 The First Social Security Recipient**

| Quarter Ending | Covered Earnings | Taxes Paid |
|---|---|---|
| June 1937 | $450 | $4.50 |
| December 1937 | $450 | $4.50 |
| March 1938 | $225 | $2.25 |
| June 1938 | $225 | $2.25 |
| September 1938 | $225 | $2.25 |
| December 1938 | $225 | $2.25 |
| March 1939 | $150 | $1.50 |
| June 1939 | $225 | $2.25 |
| October 1939 | $300 | $3.00 |
| **TOTAL** | **$2,475** | **$24.75** |

## KEY ECONOMIC CONCEPTS

**deadweight loss**
**estate taxes**
**excise taxes**
**gift taxes**
**income taxes**
**payroll taxes**
**progressive taxes**
**property taxes**
**regressive taxes**
**sales taxes**
**wealth tax**

The claims were grouped into batches of one thousand. Because Miss Fuller's was the first one on the certification list, she was issued check 00-000-001 on January 31, 1940. This happenstance of history led to Ida May Fuller being credited as the first American to receive a Social Security check. Today, more than 69 million people receive benefits under programs administered by the Social Security Administration.

The point of Social Security is not just to pay a lot for a little as in Miss Fuller's case. Over the years, there were many people who paid in and did not collect because of their early deaths. Rather, the point is social insurance—setting up a publicly financed system so that even those who come to retirement with little saved can still get by. Like any government program, it must be paid for somehow. In the case of Social Security, it is financed by taxes on current income earners to pay for current retirees. In this chapter, we explore the role of taxes more generally.

## The Civics Context

Taxes are frequently the source of heated debate in a democratic nation where the country's representatives must balance their constituents' preferences with the needs of the nation. In 1776,

*Ida May Fuller holding her social security check for $41.30.*

the anger of American colonists over British taxation was a major contributing factor to the American Revolution. And the differences among the political parties today on taxes continue to present significant divides. Taxes are, however, required to fund the government's activities. While there is significant disagreement about the proper size and role of the government, there are a number of areas where most citizens agree the government has a role. These include the following:

- Maintaining the legal and social framework. The government uses tax revenue to pay for the country's law enforcement and judicial system.
- Providing public goods and services. The government uses tax revenue to provide for national defense, one example of a public good.
- Maintaining competition. The government uses tax revenue to finance enforcement of antitrust laws.
- Redistributing income. The government uses tax revenue to provide services—health care through the Medicaid program, for example—to people who might not be able to obtain such services on their own. Government programs such as Medicaid have the effect of redistributing income from those who pay relatively more in taxes to those who receive the benefits of government programs.

Under Article I, Section 8 of the U.S.Constitution, Congress was given the power to impose taxes and levies on the general public.

> The Congress shall have power to lay and collect Taxes, Duties, Imposts and Excises to pay the Debts and provide for the common Defense and general Welfare of the United States; but all Duties, Imposts, and Excises shall be uniform throughout the United States

At the time of the nation's founding, most of these taxes were excise taxes applied to items like alcohol and tobacco. In fact, during the early years of the nation, the government was primarily funded through tariffs and land sales. Today we have a variety of taxes, including income taxes, sales taxes, excise taxes, payroll taxes, property taxes, estate taxes, and gift taxes.

Article I, Section 2 of the Constitution requires that direct taxes be apportioned among the states by population. The Founders defined "direct tax" so as to include all taxes with the exception of customs duties. The Founders expected Congress to use direct taxes and provided for the power to levy them. However, apportionment by population turned out to be an unworkable requirement. This would have called on Congress to send tax bills to the states based only on their populations. Such a system seems odd today, when everyone is accustomed to individuals being taxed on their incomes directly by the federal government.

Apportionment of taxes as originally envisioned in the Constitution eventually led to a national income tax. In 1861, the Civil War created the impetus for the country's first income tax while also leading to an early version of the Internal Revenue Service (IRS), then called the Office of the Commissioner of Internal Revenue. This bureau was responsible for collecting taxes from the states. Congress repealed this income tax in 1872 as its constitutionality was under question from the time of its inception.

In 1894, as part of a tariff bill, Congress enacted a 2 percent tax on incomes over $4,000. The tax was struck down by the Supreme Court as the constitutionality of income taxation was in doubt[2] given the Constitution's requirement that taxes be uniform throughout the country.

A national income tax therefore was impractical until the ratification of the Sixteenth Amendment to the Constitution in 1913. This amendment made it possible for Congress to pass the first national income tax in October of 1913. This new law created a 1 percent tax on net personal incomes above $3,000 and a 6 percent surtax on incomes above $500,000. In 1918 the top rate was increased to 77 percent on incomes over $1 million (equivalent to more than $19 million today) to help fund the country's World War I efforts.

During World War II, Congress introduced the modern kind of income tax we are used to today, including employer payroll withholding. Before then, employees had to pay their federal income tax in one big lump. Afterward, income tax was deducted from each paycheck—the system that is used today.

## The Economics of Taxation

How much money will a tax generate for the government? It's easy to see that when someone spends $100 in a state that has a 5 percent sales tax, the tax revenue will be $5. For any tax, the rule is:

**Tax revenue = tax base x tax rate**

The *tax base* is the dollar amount subject to the tax, and the tax rate is the percentage that goes to the government. A government sets up any tax by specifying the tax base and the tax rate. Any government will see increasing tax revenues if its economy grows, even if the tax rate is held constant. It just collects the same share of a bigger number of dollars (a larger "economic pie"). There are seven main kinds of taxes in the United States, each with a defined tax base:

- **Income taxes**: The tax base for such a tax is the money that people earn. Income taxes can be levied at the federal, state, or local level. At the federal level, the amount people are required to pay depends on factors such as their income, marital status, and number of children. There are also many tax credits that can reduce a person's tax bill. Some states, such as Florida, don't levy an income tax at all.
- **Sales taxes**: Goods and services purchased make up the base for this sort of tax. Sales tax rates vary by state and, in some cases, by municipality.
- **Excise taxes**: These taxes are similar to sales taxes. However, specific goods make up the tax base for excise taxes. Excise taxes exist on alcohol, tobacco, and gas. They are sometimes referred to as "sin taxes," as they tend to discourage the use of certain products. When a tax rate gets very high, it motivates people to avoid purchasing and can cut the tax base somewhat.
- **Payroll taxes**: For each working individual, the Social Security tax base is the amount received in paychecks, up to an annual limit. Both employees and employers pay a payroll-based Social Security tax. The tax rate for employees is 6.2 percent of wages, and employers match that amount. A similar tax exists to fund the Medicare program.
- **Property taxes**: The total value of the real estate in a local government makes up the tax base for property taxes. These taxes are typically imposed to fund local services. After determining the tax base, the local government sets a property tax rate, which then determines the amount owed by each property owner.
- **Estate taxes**: The Internal Revenue Service (IRS) defines these as "a tax on your right to transfer property at your death." Cash, securities and investments, insurance, real

*Tax forms*

estate, and businesses are all part of the tax base for estate taxes. Currently, estate taxes are not assessed for those with less than $5.3 million of assets at the time of death.

- **Gift taxes**: This is another tax on the transfer of wealth but involving two living people. Gift of more than $14,000 are included in this tax base and are paid by the recipient. This tax applies to more than just cash, including gifts like stock or cars.

These are only the taxes applied to individuals. Corporations also are charged income taxes, and some of the burden is met by reductions in the incomes of their owners, the shareholders. In 2019, about half of federal tax revenue came from income taxes. The payroll tax contributed 36 percent, the corporate income tax 7 percent, and excise, estate, and other taxes contributed the final 8 percent.[3]

## Civics Questions & Economic Answers

### Can a government always make more money by raising the tax rate?

No, not always. People respond to incentives in predictable ways (see Chapter 1). When governments raise taxes on an activity, they see less of it. A state government with a high tobacco tax, for example, might find that raising the tobacco tax rate still higher sends smokers to a nearby state with a lower tax rate. The result could actually be less tobacco tax revenue. Usually, however, when a tax rate is raised, more tax revenue comes in—just not as much as a government might expect. When a government lowers taxes on an activity, more of it takes place. Some states have reduced the taxes on companies shooting films in-state in an effort to attract more movie producers.

### What do economists mean when they say taxes cause a "deadweight loss"?

A **deadweight loss** comes from an action that causes a loss to one party without any corresponding gain to another. Taxes increase the price of products, which naturally decreases the amount people demand. In other words, taxes can contribute to deadweight loss by making consumers less likely to purchase goods and services with no corresponding benefit.

Specifically, this problem arises when taxes raise the price of a good. In practice, this means that consumers pay more, producers earn lower profits, and overall purchases of that good or service will decrease. Some consumers won't buy the product at all, though they would have been customers in the absence of the tax. The tax pushed it out of reach for them. Thus, the outcome is a deadweight loss for the economy.

Before people learn about deadweight loss, they might think that with any tax, the amount people lose will equal the amount the government gains. A tax on sports tickets might move $1 million from sports fans' pockets to the government treasury. But what if the ticket tax causes a tournament to be cancelled or moved? Then there are losses to those involved in the tournament, but without a gain to the local government. That's a deadweight loss.

### How do we know if taxes are "fair"?

While there is no definitive answer to questions about fairness, taxes can be classified as either progressive or regressive. A **progressive tax** system is one in which the tax rate paid rises as incomes rise. For example, the federal income tax is designed to be progressive and to redistribute income from those who earn more to those who earn less.

Think about someone who earns an additional dollar and pays 20 cents more tax as a result. That person has a *marginal tax rate* of 20 percent. The marginal tax rate is the percentage of an additional dollar of income taxed away. A very high marginal tax rate might cause people to slack off in earning income. Why work hard to make money if the government will get most of it? Another response to very high marginal tax rates is to hide income to avoid paying taxes on it. But with a low marginal tax rate, there's not as much gain to hiding income.

The federal income tax is made progressive by imposing higher marginal tax rates on higher incomes. Table 2 below illustrates how the federal income tax currently works.[4]

**TABLE 2 Federal Income Tax Brackets**

| Tax Bracket for Single Individuals | Marginal Tax Rate |
|---|---|
| Up to $9,950 | 10 percent |
| $9,951 to $40,525 | 12 percent |
| $40,526 to $86,375 | 22 percent |
| $86,376 to $164,925 | 24 percent |
| $164,926 to $209,425 | 32 percent |
| $209,426 to $523,600 | 35 percent |
| $523,601 or more | 37 percent |

A **regressive tax** is one for which tax rates fall as incomes rise. Sales and property taxes are considered regressive. A uniform (for example, 5 percent) sales tax is regressive because those with low incomes may spend all of their wages purchasing goods and services. That means most of their income is subject to a sales tax. In contrast, those with higher incomes are able to save more and, as a result, a smaller proportion of their income is subject to this tax.

### What is the most efficient way to levy taxes?

Most economists agree that it is most efficient to have a large tax base and a low tax rate structure. For example, taxing all income (a large tax base) enables sound enforcement of income taxes. When certain forms of income are excluded from taxation ("tax loopholes" that cut the tax base), the rest of income must be taxed at a higher rate to raise the same revenue.

This becomes important when policy makers seek to make lower-income people better off through progressive taxation. Attempts to levy taxes and redistribute the economic pie may actually shrink the total pie. The reasons for this go back to the economic way of thinking (Chapter 1) and the role of incentives. When a high marginal rate taxes away larger shares of income, that will lessen the desire to work. The incentive to produce more or invest more can also be reduced by higher marginal tax rates. The size and extent of this problem is debated among economists, but most agree that taxes function as a kind of incentive or disincentive.

Further, a high enough tax rate can lead to people taking extreme steps to avoid them. The Rolling Stones left Great Britain off their 1998–1999 world tour citing the high British marginal tax rate. The band U2 went a step further and relocated their home base from Ireland to the Netherlands to avoid paying Irish taxes. (Ireland eliminated a tax break for royalty income in 2006.) The band's lead singer, Bono, went so far as to say it would be "stupid" to pay Ireland's taxes. Businesses sometimes relocate to lower tax locations as well, lowering the tax base of the home country. The key to efficiency is designing a tax system that is able to fund the government's needs without pushing economic activity out of the tax base.

### How do taxes in the United States compare to other countries?

Marginal tax rates vary across the world.[5] For example, the highest marginal tax rate in Denmark is 52 percent. It is 50 percent in Japan but only 15 percent in Hong Kong and 13 percent in Russia. Monaco doesn't have an income tax. In terms of total taxes collected as a share of the economy (or Gross Domestic Product), the United States is quite low when compared with the other Organization of Economic Co-Operation and Development (OECD) nations.[6] In the U.S., we pay 24.3 percent of GDP in taxes. In France, Denmark, Sweden, and Belgium, this number is closer to 45 percent. Only Ireland, Chile, and Mexico have a total tax take as a smaller share of their economies.

### QUESTIONS for DISCUSSION

1. How has the U.S. Constitution evolved to accommodate an income tax?
2. What kinds of taxes are there? Which are the most important sources for funding the federal government?
3. What makes a tax progressive? Regressive? What kinds of taxes fit each category?

## The Income Tax Is Born

PRIMARY SOURCE

Ratified on February 3, 1913, the Sixteenth Amendment to the U.S. Constitution established Congress's authority to impose a federal income tax. This amendment played a central role in the creation of a powerful federal government. The official language of the amendment is as follows:

> The Congress shall have power to lay and collect taxes on incomes, from whatever source derived, without apportionment among the several States, and without regard to any census or enumeration.

Before this amendment, the Constitution required that all taxes be collected proportionally from the states based on population. In effect, this meant that a state with 10 percent of the population would have to pay 10 percent of the total income tax, regardless of whether the state earned 10 percent of the income. This requirement made a direct and national income tax cumbersome.

On passage of the new amendment, the Revenue Act of 1913 was created and imposed a 1 percent tax in incomes above $3,000 ($83,972 in today's dollars), with a top rate of 6 percent for those earning more than $500,000 (more than $13 million in today's dollars) per year. Approximately 3 percent of the U.S. population was subject to this new income tax.

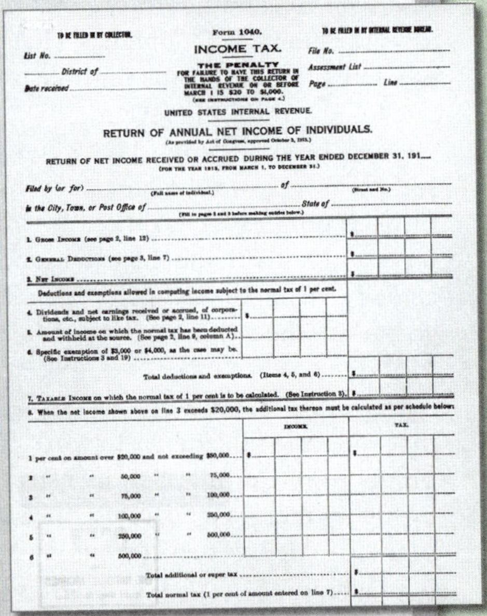

TO BE FILLED IN BY COLLECTOR. | Form 1040. | TO BE FILLED IN BY INTERNAL REVENUE BUREAU.

INCOME TAX.

List No. ..........

.......... District of ..........

Date received ..........

THE PENALTY FOR FAILURE TO HAVE THIS RETURN IN THE HANDS OF THE COLLECTOR OF INTERNAL REVENUE ON OR BEFORE MARCH 1 IS $20 TO $1,000. (SEE INSTRUCTIONS ON PAGE 4.)

File No. ..........

Assessment List ..........

Page .......... Line ..........

UNITED STATES INTERNAL REVENUE.

RETURN OF ANNUAL NET INCOME OF INDIVIDUALS.

RETURN OF NET INCOME RECEIVED OR ACCRUED DURING THE YEAR ENDED DECEMBER 31, 191...

(FOR THE YEAR 1913, FROM MARCH 1, TO DECEMBER 31.)

Filed by (or for) .......... (Full name of individual.) of .......... (Street and No.)

in the City, Town, or Post Office of .......... State of ..........

1. Gross Income (see page 2, line 12) .......... $

2. General Deductions (see page 3, line 7) .......... $

3. Net Income .......... $

Deductions and exemptions allowed in computing income subject to the normal tax of 1 per cent.

4. Dividends and net earnings received or accrued, of corporations, etc., subject to like tax. (See page 2, line 11) .......... $

5. Amount of income on which the normal tax has been deducted and withheld at the source. (See page 2, line 9, column A) ..........

6. Specific exemption of $3,000 or $4,000, as the case may be. (See Instructions 3 and 19) ..........

Total deductions and exemptions. (Items 4, 5, and 6) .......... $

7. Taxable Income on which the normal tax of 1 per cent is to be calculated. (See Instruction 3). $

8. When the net income shown above on line 3 exceeds $20,000, the additional tax thereon must be calculated as per schedule below:

| | Income | Tax |
|---|---|---|
| 1 per cent on amount over $20,000 and not exceeding $50,000 | $ | $ |
| 2 " " 50,000 " " 75,000 | | |
| 3 " " 75,000 " " 100,000 | | |
| 4 " " 100,000 " " 250,000 | | |
| 5 " " 250,000 " " 500,000 | | |
| 6 " " 500,000 | | |

Total additional or super tax .......... $

Total normal tax (1 per cent of amount entered on line 7) .......... $

*The first Income Tax form in 1913.*

### QUESTIONS for DISCUSSION

1. Why did the Constitution need to be amended to allow for a nationwide income tax?
2. How is the original income tax form of 1913 different from what taxpayers must file today?

Contemporary Connection

## Should We Establish a Wealth Tax?

Senator Elizabeth Warren in 2016.

*Wealth* refers to a person's total assets, or their net worth (assets less liabilities). Income is the amount of money received in a year. Someone like Amazon's Jeff Bezos may have a lot of wealth (in ownership of Amazon) but take only a small part of it out every year. In general, only the part taken out is subject to taxation. This occurs because we have an income tax, not a wealth tax.

Proponents of taxing wealth see Bezos's high wealth as an opportunity for taxation. He is rich, but as long as he does not take much out of Amazon in any given year, he does not owe much tax.

A significant debate has occurred in recent years over the establishment of a **wealth tax**, with U.S. Senator Elizabeth Warren of Massachusetts as a leading proponent. Supporters of such taxes see them as a way to force the wealthy (or ultra-wealthy) to pay "their fair share" of taxes. Proposals include a 2 percent per year tax on the wealth of millionaires and 3 percent on billionaires. Some claim this would generate lots of new revenue for the federal government.

Those opposed to wealth taxes make a number of points. Some argue that a wealth tax would be unconstitutional as it would represent an unportioned direct tax not covered by the Sixteenth Amendment that specifically authorizes a tax on incomes. In addition, recall that taxes are incentives and people respond to them in predictable ways. When we tax something, we tend to get less of it. Is less wealth a good national goal? In fact, such a tax may provide an incentive for the wealthy to spend their money (yachts, ski vacations, etc.) rather than save and invest the money in productive ways in the economy. Others point out that this money was already taxed when it was earned as income.

Another question is how the Internal Revenue Service (IRS) will be able to effectively value and monitor wealth collection each year, particularly as the wealthy seek to avoid this new tax. For all of these reasons, many well-known economists argue that a wealth tax would yield little revenue and distort the investment behavior of the wealthy, making it an inefficient way to increase tax collections. Given that 12 advanced economies had wealth taxes in 1990 and today only four still do, it is apparent that such a tax presents a number of challenges.

### QUESTIONS for DISCUSSION

1. How can someone have high wealth and low income?
2. What are the arguments for and against a wealth tax?
3. Which countries have a wealth tax?

## Web Quests

**Enter any of the links below and use the questions to get you started on your own web quest.**

### The Tax Foundation

*Visit the homepage of the Tax Foundation.*

**https://taxfoundation.org**

1. How much income does a married couple filing jointly need to make to be in the highest federal income tax bracket?
2. What is the Earned Income Tax Credit? What levels of income allow someone to receive it?
3. What are capital gains? How are they taxed?
4. What is Tax Freedom Day? What state reaches it first? Last?
5. What states have the highest property taxes?

### The Internal Revenue Service

*Visit the homepage of the Internal Revenue Service.*

**https://www.irs.gov**

1. What kinds of information can citizens find on this page?
2. Find three IRS tax forms. Explain what they are used for and who would use them.
3. What kinds of tax credits are available for homeowners? What about for education?

### The Social Security Administration

*Visit the homepage of the Social Security Administration.*

**https://www.ssa.gov**

1. What is a Cost-of-Living Adjustment (COLA)? How much was it this year?
2. What online services are available for citizens on this website?
3. Other than retirees, who else is eligible for benefits from the Social Security system?

# CHAPTER 10

# Can the President Really Fix the Economy?

*President Joe Biden delivers remarks on the economy during a speech at theWhite House, 2021.*

# "The Economy, Stupid"

Chester James Carville Jr. was born in October of 1944 at Fort Benning, Georgia, the oldest of eight children. Carville's father was stationed on the base during World War II. James served a two-year enlistment in the Marines from 1966 to 1968, stationed in San Diego. The Carville family hails from Louisiana where James's mom was a schoolteacher and spoke French at home. Later, in his political career, James would be given the nickname "Ragin' Cajun."

Carville, a Democrat, is an American political consultant and author who developed strategy for candidates for public office in the United States and 23 nations abroad. Carville is most famous for his help leading Bill Clinton to victory over George H. W. Bush in the 1992 presidential election. Carville's strategy for Clinton in the 1992 election had three main components: (1) change versus more of the same; (2) don't forget about health care; and (3) focus on the economy. This third plank became the slogan for Clinton's successful campaign and is often quoted by politicians and political pundits to this day.

During President Bill Clinton's successful run for the White House in 1992, Carville famously told a group of campaign staffers, "The economy, stupid"—his point being that to beat then incumbent President George H. W. Bush, they would need to focus on the problems with the economy at that time. Many years later, Carville's quote has morphed into "It's the economy, stupid," as the economy remains at the forefront of many voters' minds.

*James Carville and Mary Matalin*

**KEY ECONOMIC CONCEPTS**

**business cycles**
**fiscal policy**
**monetary policy**
**recession**
**stimulus spending**

Carville is married to political consultant Mary Matalin. Matalin, a Republican, worked for George H. W. Bush on his 1992 presidential reelection campaign. Carville and Matalin made many appearances on Sunday-morning television news programs arguing for different policies. The couple have two daughters and live in New Orleans. Carville has attention deficit hyperactivity disorder and has been an advocate for ADHD organizations.

## The Civics Context

What powers does a president have to influence the economy? It is a common quip among the media and political pundits that presidents get too much credit when the economy does well and too much blame when it slumps. This wisecrack is based on some underlying truths: The Constitution gives the president a great deal of power to set economic policy. And yet that power is restrained by the Constitution's separation of powers. Even then, setting economic policy does not guarantee economic outcomes. The economy's performance depends on actors in the private sector, and many such decisions are made independent of government policy. In this chapter we explore what all this means for the president's supposed ability to "fix the economy."

*President Donald Trump delivers a speech at the Economic Club of New York in 2019.*

Article 2 of the U.S. Constitution gives the president sweeping executive authority. Amendments, changes in the law, and the expansion of the executive branch have added to that authority. The president has the authority to appoint individuals to more than 6,000 federal positions upon taking office, including the Cabinet and executive agency heads. Perhaps most significantly, the president nominates the members of the Federal Reserve System's Board of Governors. This includes arguably the world's most powerful economic policy post, the chair of Board of Governors. (The specific structure and conduct of the Fed is detailed in Chapter 12.) The president's authority over the Fed, however, is constrained by the requirement of the U.S. Senate's confirmation of nominees. Fed appointees also serve 14-year terms, limiting the number of appointments any one president is likely to make.

Limitations on the president's power are weaker for many other appointments that influence the economy. Subject only to Senate confirmation, the president appointments include the secretaries of the Departments of Treasury and Commerce. These powerful organizations advise the president on economic and financial issues, enforce trade rules, and set employment standards, among other tasks.

The president, again with Senate approval, also chooses the leader of the Securities and Exchange Commission (SEC) who, among other tasks, is responsible for regulating America's financial markets. The president nominates the members of the National Labor Relations Board (NLRB), which acts as a quasi-judicial body deciding cases related to unions and other employment issues. Senate confirmation is not required for many government executives who work with top presidential appointees.

The president each year proposes a federal budget, kicking off the annual budget approval process. This budget may propose increasing or decreasing spending in various areas that can affect the overall economy according to the president's priorities. This document also recommends how much should be collected in tax revenues and how large a budget deficit or surplus the federal government should run. Congress then holds hearings to question administration officials about their requests as it develops its own budget plan, embodied in a "budget resolution."

There are House and Senate budget committees whose primary function is to draft and enforce the budget resolutions. These draft budget resolutions go to the House and Senate floors, where they can be amended by majority vote. A House-Senate conference then resolves any differences, and the budget resolution for the year is adopted when both houses pass the conference agreement. The president has the power to veto the budget Congress approves. Congress may override such vetoes with a two-thirds vote in both the House and Senate.

The president can unilaterally issue a variety of rules and regulations that may affect the economy. Executive orders issued by the president have the binding force of law on federal agencies but do not require approval of Congress. Executive orders have become much more numerous in recent years, affecting everything from environmental regulations to the status of federal government projects.

Although Article 1, Section 10 of the Constitution gives Congress the power to regulate international commerce, the president also has important authority including the ability to negotiate international agreements. Congress has constitutional authority to impose tariffs (taxes on imports) but, in practice, trade agreements are generally conducted by the executive branch in consultation with Congress. Tariffs were once a primary source of federal government revenue but have declined as revenue generators. In recent history they have become instruments of U.S. international trade and foreign policy.

Times of economic crisis provide still more opportunities for presidential authority over the economy. As an example, President Joe Biden ordered a federal moratorium on evictions of renters during the COVID-19 pandemic. This emergency rule was issued through the Centers for Disease Control and Prevention (CDC). It was designed both to protect renters in financial distress and to slow the spread of the virus. Reductions in evictions and moving would reduce contact between people. However, as Biden attempted to renew this order for an additional two months in 2021, the Supreme Court blocked the decision and made it clear that further extensions would require an act of Congress. Similar emergency actions occurred during the Great Depression and Great Recession housing crisis in the late 2000s, but they are always subject to constitutional checks and balances.

## The Economics of Monetary and Fiscal Policy

Many factors influence voters as they decide how they will vote. These include national security, terrorism, social issues, and climate change and the environment. Nonetheless, the economic policies advocated by candidates and political parties are important factors in voters' decisions. There are two broad types of economic policies that may be undertaken by the federal government. These are referred to as monetary policy (see Chapter 12 for more details about the Federal Reserve) and fiscal policy (see Chapter 7 for a discussion of the schools of thought related to such policies).

Monetary policy and fiscal policy are the two most widely recognized tools used to influence a nation's economic activity. **Monetary policy** is primarily concerned with the management of interest rates and the total supply of money in circulation. It is generally carried out by a central bank. **Fiscal policy** refers to the taxing and spending actions of governments. In the United States, the national fiscal policy is determined by the executive and legislative branches of the government. Monetary policy is conducted by the Federal Reserve.

Arguably, central bank actions represent the most important government policies affecting economic activity. Central bank actions are designed to control **business cycles**—the recurring patterns of economic expansions and contractions. While there is some disagreement between the Monetarist and Keynesian economic schools of thought on monetary policy priorities and tactics, there is little disagreement on its goals. As discussed earlier, the Federal Reserve is intentionally independent from the government. The president's ability to influence the bank's activities is limited to the president's appointments to its governing board.

Monetary policies are demand-side macroeconomic policies. They work by stimulating or discouraging spending on goods and services. Monetary policies attempt to dampen, or perhaps even eliminate, **recessions** (economy-wide contractions in gross domestic product). In addition to mitigating business cycles, monetary policy aims to keep price inflation low and stable and maximize employment. The primary source of disagreement between the Monetarist and Keynesian schools of thought on monetary policy stem from the question of which goal should receive priority. Monetarists emphasize controlling inflation, while Keynesians stress employment and full utilization of resources as their top goals.

Monetary policy is conducted by a central bank through control of the money supply and interest rates. Generally, central banks take steps to decrease interest rates when they are concerned about an impending recession. By expanding the money supply, they can exert downward pressure on interest rates and create incentives for business and individuals to borrow money to expand operations or purchase goods and services.

Conversely, if the economy is experiencing inflation pressures, the central bank may contract the money supply and increase interest rates. Such a move should cause firms and households to decrease their borrowing and spending on goods and services and help keep inflation at bay. There are many technical complications in the conduct monetary policy; however, all operate through the influence of interest rates and money on economic activity.

Fiscal policy refers to setting the level of government spending and taxation by government policy makers. While Congress maintains control of the level of government spending and taxation, the president plays an influential role in setting spending priorities. When the government makes decisions on the goods and services it purchases, the transfer payments it distributes, or the taxes it collects, it is engaging in fiscal policy.

Fiscal policy is said to be tight or contractionary when the government decreases its spending or increases taxes. By increasing taxes or decreasing spending, governments pull money out of the economy and slow business activity. Fiscal policy is said to be loose or expansionary when the government increases its spending or cuts taxes. If a government believes there is not enough business activity in an economy, it can increase the amount of money it spends to stimulate the economy (**stimulus spending**). If tax collections are not sufficient to pay for the spending increases, governments borrow money and accumulate debt. Governments might also lower taxes, or offer tax rebates, in an effort to encourage economic growth.

*The ideas of economist John Maynard Keynes are the basis for the school of thought known as Keynesian economics.*

The effects of fiscal policy differ across groups of citizens. Depending on the political orientations and goals of policy makers, a tax cut could apply only to a certain income group (for example, the middle class). Similarly, when a government decides to adjust its spending, its policy affects some more than others. A decision to build a new bridge, for example, will give work and more income to hundreds of construction workers. When conducting fiscal policy for expansionary purposes, efficient spending is important for achieving the maximum impact on the economy. By contrast, politically motivated spending to favor particular groups will be less effective.

## Civics Questions & Economic Answers

### If a president has so much power in setting economic policy, why is there any doubt that the president can "fix" the economy?

While the president has a huge influence on economic policy, that policy is subject to checks and balances, including Senate confirmation of appointees, Congress's control over the budget, and the Fed's independence. The president gets to propose a budget, but what Congress adopts may be very different. Even when a presidentially favored policy is adopted, there is no guarantee that the economy will respond as expected. Further, the Federal Reserve may act contrary to the president's wishes, slowing the economy when the president seeks to stimulate activity. There are even problems with the timing of presidential action. A powerful stimulus policy could fall flat if it took too long to adopt, thereby becoming obsolete or inappropriate by the time it takes effect.

### How is a new economic policy, such as an increase in the corporate income tax, implemented?

Most recommendations for new tax legislation come from the president. The Treasury Department has primary responsibility for drafting the president's tax recommendations. Advice and assistance are also solicited from other government agencies, such as the Internal Revenue Service (IRS) or people in business or professional fields. After internal reviews, the president sends a message to Congress formally submitting the proposed legislation.

Under the Constitution, all tax legislation must originate in the House of Representatives. Legislation begins in the House Ways and Means Committee, which hears testimony from government officials and representatives of private groups on how the proposal will affect the economy and specific groups. The result is the actual legislative language and a detailed report on the proposal. Once the bill and the report are completed, they get introduced in the House of Representatives for consideration.

The Senate Finance Committee begins its formal work on legislation after the House has

*The House Ways and Means Committee meets in 2019. The Committee has jurisdiction over all taxation, tariffs, and other revenue-raising measures.*

*Like the House Ways and Means Committee, the Senate Finance Committee concerns itself with matters relating to taxation and other revenue measures.*

passed its version of the bill. It holds hearings similar to those held earlier by the House Ways and Means Committee. The entire Senate debates the bill and, if the Senate passes the House version of the bill without amendments, it gets sent directly to the president. If there are differences between the House and Senate versions of the tax bill, those differences must be reconciled in a conference committee before being sent to the president.

### Why doesn't news reporting and policy discussion reflect the president's limited impact on economic results?

Consider what happens when there's good economic news, such as a reduction in unemployment from an economy's natural growth. If the president's team honestly reports that its influence was small, it gives up the opportunity to take credit. However, if an unemployment number is bad, you can bet that the opposition party will blame the president's policies. Recognizing that it will be blamed for bad news, the president's team feels it must go ahead and take credit when the news is good. This has become routine in Washington, D.C., even among reporters and officials who recognize the game being played—over-attribution of economic results to the president's actions.

## QUESTIONS for DISCUSSION

1. What powers does the president have to influence the economy?
2. How does the president work with Congress on economic policies?

## Presidents and the Economy

PRIMARY SOURCE

Below are quotes from the past five American presidents, each making various claims about their economic successes.

"We've gone from 60,000 jobs per month to 60,000 jobs every three days—more than 600,000 jobs per month since I took office. More than 3 million new jobs all told. That's the fastest growth, I'm told, at this point in any administration's history."

—Joe Biden in 2021

"Barack Obama talked a lot about hope, but Donald Trump delivered the American Dream. All the economic indicators, what's happening overseas, Donald Trump has proven to be far more successful than Barack Obama."

"In many ways this is the greatest economy in the HISTORY of America."

—Donald Trump tweets in 2018

"Since I have come into office, there's almost no economic metric by which you couldn't say that the U.S. economy is better and that corporate bottom lines are better. None."

—Barack Obama in 2014

"Look at what the economy has done. It's strong. We've created a lot of jobs. I'd be reminding people that tax cuts have worked in terms of stimulating the economy."

—George W. Bush in 2006

"We passed the bill which reversed trickle-down economics by one vote. (It was) close like the health care bill (this year). And it led to an enormous flowering of the economy in America."

—Bill Clinton in 2010

## QUESTIONS for DISCUSSION

1. What are some similarities between these presidential statements related to the economy?
2. Presidents often talk about strong employment growth during their administrations. What are some examples of steps a president might take to encourage employment?
3. Why would it not be smart politically for a presidential administration to admit it had little to do with good economic news?

Contemporary Connection

## Fiscal Policy in a Pandemic

In addition to an unpresented health crisis, the COVID-19 pandemic also ushered in an economic crisis. The pandemic-induced shutdown was initially the worst hit to the U.S. economy since the Great Depression. Employment and output declined more during the pandemic than in 2008 in the depths of the financial crisis—but then rebounded strongly. In contrast, after the 2007–2009 recession, economic output took three years to return to its prerecession level and never returned to the growth trajectory it had been on.

While the reopening after the government-imposed economic shutdowns made a rebound inevitable, a number of factors account for the fast recovery from the initial shock of the pandemic. The Federal Reserve rapidly slashed interest rates to near zero and stabilized financial markets to prevent the economic crisis from becoming a financial crisis. Strong fiscal policies were also adopted. Congress approved a $5.9 trillion emergency measure that included forgivable loans for small businesses that kept their employees (Paycheck Protection Program or PPP) and stimulus checks to almost everyone. Other fiscal measures expanded unemployment insurance to included gig workers and supplemented state

*The U.S. government instituted massive government programs in response to the economic crisis caused by the COVID-19 pandemic.*

unemployment benefits with an extra $300 to $600 per week. Low-cost loans were made to larger businesses and state and local governments.

Many of these tools were experimental and the government learned a few lessons as they were implemented. With Congress' approval, the Treasury delivered stimulus directly into household bank accounts quickly. The PPP program demonstrated a novel way to preserve employment during an economic shock that many economists consider to be a success.

It cannot be determined how the economy would have recovered without these massive government programs. And the money had to be borrowed, causing the publicly held federal debt to balloon from 79 percent of gross domestic product (GDP) in 2019 to almost 100 percent today. With future interest rates almost certain to be higher than today, future administrations may struggle to implement their policy agendas while also making large interest payments on the national debt.

## QUESTIONS for DISCUSSION

1. What steps did the federal government take to soften the economic impact of the COVID-19 pandemic?
2. What are some of the costs of these policies?

## Web Quests

**Enter any of the links below and use the questions to get you started on your own web quest.**

### Office of Management and Budget

*Visit the homepage of the White House Office of Management and Budget.*

https://www.whitehouse.gov/omb

1. What are the primary functions of this department?
2. Examine the current president's budget. What are the main priorities of this budget?
3. In the historical documents section of the website, open the "Summary of receipts, outlays, and surpluses or deficits: 1789–2026" spreadsheet. At what times in the nation's history did the federal government run surpluses? What about large deficits?

### Keynes and Hayek Rap Battle

*Watch "Fear the Boom: Keynes vs. Hayek" rap battle.*

https://www.youtube.com/watch?v=d0nERTFo-Sk

1. Describe the differences between Keynes's and Hayek's views on fiscal policy.
2. Which of the two philosophies does the current president subscribe to? Explain your reasoning.

# CHAPTER 11

# How Does the Supreme Court Shape the Rules of the Game?

*Members of the media gather in front of the U.S. Supreme Court building in 2015.*

# Let's Play Monopoly Baseball!

Baseball occupies a unique place in the American economy, and Judge Kenesaw Mountain Landis has much to do with it. Unlike all other industries, baseball has long enjoyed an absolute exemption from federal **antitrust** laws. These laws are designed to encourage **competition** by limiting the market power of any particular firm.

This legal oddity came about during the last serious challenge to baseball's monopoly power. A **monopoly** is a market that is difficult to enter and typically dominated by one producer. The Federal League, a six-team organization of baseball clubs, attempted to form a third major league in 1914 and 1915. The arrival of the American League, as a new and successful challenger to the National League in 1901, suggested that a rival league could succeed.

*Kenesaw Mountain Landis's plaque in the National Baseball Hall of Fame and Museum.*

## KEY ECONOMIC CONCEPTS

**antitrust**
**competition**
**eminent domain**
**holding company**
**monopoly**
**predatory pricing**
**regulation**
**rules of the game**
**trust**

The Federal League filed a lawsuit against the owners that oversaw the American and National Leagues. Its lawsuit was based on the Sherman Act of 1890, the United States' first antitrust law. The term *antitrust* emphasizes the goal of countering that era's **trusts**, combinations of businesses that teamed up to form a monopoly to attempt to raise prices. Opponents of those monopolies were known as "trust busters."

This is where Judge Landis enters the story. The Federal League filed its lawsuit in a Northern Illinois U.S. District Court specifically because Landis was known as a trust buster. He also proved to be a rabid baseball fan, scolding the Federal League's lawyers that attacks on baseball "would be regarded by this court as a blow to a national institution."[1] After hearing arguments, Landis refused to issue a ruling for more than a year. Over that time, the Major Leagues secured an agreement with all but one Federal League owner, driving the league out of business.

The sole holdout, Ned Hanlon, was the owner of the Baltimore Terrapins. He was offended both by the buyout offer of $50,000 he received and by comments by the owner of the Chicago White Sox, Charles Comiskey, about the city of Baltimore. Hanlon's antitrust lawsuit against the Major Leagues made it to the Supreme Court.

In 1922, the Supreme Court ruled unanimously that baseball was not subject to

*The Second Bank of the United States building, now a National Historic Landmark, in Philadelphia, Pennsylvania.*

antitrust laws. Justice Oliver Wendell Holmes Jr. wrote in the decision that baseball was "public exhibition, not commerce"[2] and therefore exempt from antitrust scrutiny. Subsequent lawsuits, including those by the other professional sports leagues, have been denied by the Supreme Court. The court has been unwilling to use the baseball ruling as precedent, thus giving baseball a legal advantage enjoyed by no other sport.

## The Civics Context

The judicial branch, a co-equal unit alongside the legislative and executive branches, occupies a unique place in our government. When Congress or the president wants to initiate a change, either can start the process. The judicial branch, in contrast, makes its policies by ruling on disputes that are brought before it. After these disputes work their way up from lower courts, the judicial branch's final ruling comes from the Supreme Court. Therefore, each Supreme Court decision contains the names of real-life opponents separated by "v" for "versus," as in *Marbury v Madison*. Supreme Court rulings have defined the legal environment of the economy. (See Chapter 1 for more about how the rules of the economic system influence behavior.) The following are three landmark cases that established economic **rules of the game**.

### *McCulloch v Maryland*

This 1819 case centered on the future of the Second Bank of the United States (for more on central banking and the Federal Reserve System, see Chapter 12), but its decision had wide-ranging impacts related to the implied powers clause of the Constitution. The case went a long way in settling a simmering debate over how far Congress could go in carrying out its expressed powers.

In 1791, Alexander Hamilton, the first secretary of the treasury, assisted in the creation of the Bank of the United States. After a controversial 20-year life, the bank's charter expired in 1811. But in 1816 a second national bank was established, headquartered in Philadelphia, with 18 branches in other states. In 1818, Maryland passed a law that taxed the Baltimore branch and levied a $15,000 per year franchise fee. The bank branch ignored this Maryland law and, as a result, the state of Maryland brought a suit against the Baltimore bank's cashier, James W. McCulloch.

The Baltimore County Court upheld the state's position, and the Maryland Court of Appeals confirmed the findings. The Bank of the United States appealed to the Supreme Court, and the case was argued in February of 1819. The lawyers for the state of Maryland argued that the state had the right to tax any business within its borders. They further argued that the bank's creation was unconstitutional. The federal lawyers argued that the Constitution gave Congress the authority to carry out its expressed powers and to regulate money. They insisted that the bank was a reasonable means of accomplishing these expressed powers.

The court delivered a unanimous decision in favor of the bank. The decision had two significant implications. First, it confirmed that Congress has the power to carry out its constitutional implied powers derived from Article I, Section 8 of the Constitution using reasonable actions. This decision by the court enhanced the power of the federal government. Second, the court rejected the argument that one level of government can tax another level of government. The federal government may not tax the income of the states, and the states may not tax the income of cities, counties, or schools.

*Chief Justice John Marshall*

### *Gibbons v Ogden*

In the early 1800s, Aaron Ogden and Thomas Gibbons were in business together, running a steamboat service in the Hudson River area of New York and New Jersey. Eventually, Gibbons separated from Ogden. They became bitter rivals, with Ogden asserting exclusive rights to serve routes authorized by the state of New York and Gibbons contending that he too could operate New York passenger service because of a federal license he had been issued in 1793.

In October of 1819, the New York Court of Chancery ruled in favor of Ogden, upholding the concept of states' rights in interstate commerce on waterways. The New York finding would have given states the ability to set up monopoly rights over waterway routes, even when they ran between states.

The case went to the U.S. Supreme Court in February of 1824. Daniel Webster and General William Wirt represented Gibbons and argued that New York's laws conflicted with federal law and must be struck down. They argued that Congress had the power to regulate commerce, on water or land, of any kind between the states, including goods or people.

Chief Justice John Marshall delivered the Supreme Court's unanimous opinion. The court ruled that interstate commerce referred to any type of trade between the states, not just the buying and selling of goods. The operations of Gibbons's steamboat clearly met this definition and could not be forbidden by New York. Marshall's ruling freed steamboats from state laws that granted monopoly powers to a chosen few.

### *Northern Securities Company et al. v United States*

Does the government have the power to regulate the growth of huge interstate trusts? That was the question this attention-grabbing trial of 1903 settled. It occurred against the background of the early 1900s, known as a time of growth and rivalry featuring clashes of flamboyant owners.

One such quickly growing industry was railroads. The Northern Pacific, owned by J.P. Morgan, and the Great Northern, owned

*"The Bosses of the Senate," an anti trust political cartoon by Joseph Keppler, 1889.*

by James Hill, had tracks that ran in parallel from Minnesota to the Pacific Ocean. The Union Pacific, owned by E. H. Harriman, had a competing east to west route located farther south. All three of these railroads terminated in Chicago, where they linked up with the Chicago, Burlington, & Quincy Railroad (commonly referred to as the Burlington).

The three railroad tycoons understood that whoever controlled the Chicago, Burlington, & Quincy would have an advantage in this cutthroat business. For years they fought over ownership of the Burlington. Morgan found himself outmaneuvered, with his railroad almost taken over by rivals, and vowed to strengthen his position.

To protect himself against future takeover attempts, Morgan decided to create a corporation so large it could not be taken over by anyone. He created a **holding company**—a corporation that exists only to own stock in other companies—called Northern Securities Company and capitalized it at $400 million (the equivalent of more than $11 billion in today's dollars). This new holding corporation controlled the assets of the Northern Pacific, Great Northern, and Burlington railroads.

This new concentration of wealth and power attracted the attention of politicians in Washington, D.C., including the new president, Theodore Roosevelt. In 1902, Roosevelt ordered an investigation of the Northern Securities Company, and, in March of that year, the government filed a federal lawsuit in St. Paul, Minnesota, charging the company with violating the Sherman Antitrust Act of 1890.

The Sherman Act had rarely been used since its inception 12 years earlier. The law's primary purpose was to prevent illegal combinations of businesses that would cause a restraint of trade. That is, the government was given the power to prevent monopolies from restricting the free flow of interstate commerce by eliminating or reducing competition. The crux of the question in *Northern Securities Company et al. v United States* was whether Northern Securities was a monopoly under the meaning of the Sherman Act.

Eventually, the case made its way to the Supreme Court. Morgan and his lawyers argued that their trust had not restrained trade, but rather only had the potential to do so. They contended that a company cannot be penalized for actions that have not occurred. The federal government argued that Northern Securities controlled nearly all transportation across a large segment of the country.

In 1904, the Supreme Court in a 5–4 decision ruled against the Northern Securities Company. Justice John Marshall Harlan wrote that no scheme or organization of a company could more obviously come under the purview of the Sherman Antitrust Act. In this case, the government established its right to regulate business against abuses of competition, and President Roosevelt now had a tool to use to exert control over other big corporations.

## The Economics of the Supreme Court

The Supreme Court sits at the top of the entire federal court system. It is the final judge regarding the legal rules of the economic game. This court is the guardian of rule of law, which is critical to the success of a market economy. The Supreme Court makes the final decisions regarding the economic **rules of the game** in two key areas: **regulation**, which includes interstate commerce, and competition.

Taken together, the Supreme Court rulings in *McCulloch v Maryland* and *Gibbons v Ogden* set the stage for greatly expanding the power of the federal government to regulate the U.S. economy. Today federal agencies enforce the rules of the game by issuing regulations to implement legislation passed by Congress. The result each year is thousands of pages of regulations that influence many parts of the economy. The economic question for regulation is simple: Are the potential benefits of a proposed regulation worth the potential costs?

Some regulations have achieved real economic benefits far beyond the costs. For example, the constitutional basis of the 1964 Civil Rights Act was, in part, the Commerce Clause. Few would disagree that the benefits were well worth the

*Justices of the U.S. Supreme Court in 1899.*

costs. Others point to the benefits regulations may have in protecting the environment, safeguarding workers' rights, and providing for public safety.

But some regulations may have adverse effects on businesses and consumers. For decades, airline travel was regulated by the federal government. The Civil Aeronautics Board (CAB) controlled which routes airlines flew and set airfares. Economists and reformers argued that regulation by the CAB added to costs and harmed consumers. President Jimmy Carter agreed, and he appointed Cornell economics professor Alfred Kahn to head the CAB. With Kahn leading the way, legislation was approved to deregulate the airlines. The result was dramatically lower airfares and more competition in the airline industry. And it did not stop there. Deregulation also took place in trucking, cable television, railroads, and telecommunications.

Each year, some businesses come under scrutiny by the U.S. government to see if they are operating in violation of antitrust laws. These laws are intended to preserve competition, which benefits consumers by keeping prices low and quality of goods and services high.

Adam Smith warned his readers about business practices that can harm consumers. In *The Wealth of Nations*, he wrote:

> People of the same trade seldom meet together, even for merriment and diversion, but the conversation ends in a conspiracy against the public, or in some contrivance to raise prices. (page 145)[3]

Supporters believe that aggressive antitrust enforcement can increase competition and provide benefits to consumers. This includes maintaining competitive prices, spurring improved quality for goods and serves, and increasing innovation. The breakup of Bell System in the 1980s, for example, is regarded as an economic success. Until then, the Bell System held a monopoly on telephone services. Breaking up the monopoly resulted in creating seven regional companies known as the Baby Bells. Following the breakup was a wave of increased competition, creating several new companies such as Sprint and MCI. It also set the stage for the development of the internet and cable television, among other innovations.

## Civics Questions & Economic Answers

### In the absence of antitrust action, would monopolies persist?

Perhaps not. Unless they have the regulatory support of the government, monopolies may be fragile. Consider this scenario: A firm breaks through with an innovation. It becomes highly profitable and dominates the industry. Potential competitors take notice of what the lead producer is doing. They imitate the same business practices and then improve on them. Eventually, they break out with their own innovations and leave the leader in the dust. This may happen without antitrust action at all. Short-term monopolies, for example, due to patent protection, can exist in industries like pharmaceuticals and lead to high drug prices until the patent period expires.

Critics of antitrust point to the example of IBM, which was the leading producer in the early days of the computer industry. The U.S. Justice Department accused IBM of being a monopoly by controlling a large share of the market. For over 10 years, from 1969 to 1982, the U.S. Department of Justice pursued IBM. Finally, after thousands of court hours and millions of dollars in legal fees, the case was dropped. Market events ended IBM's monopoly power before the government could, as more agile competitors used service and innovation to expand at IBM's expense. No one today imagines that IBM is a monopoly.

### Is "predatory pricing" a threat to consumer?

Probably not. **Predatory pricing** means a company is charging prices below its costs to gain control of a market. But economists have been skeptical of the narrative that says predatory pricing hurts consumers. They point to three problems with this thinking. First, lower prices benefit consumers, so how are they harmed? The usual story is that after driving out all competitors, a monopoly raises prices, but this has turned out to be difficult to accomplish. Second, a company may be charging less than its competitors but not be operating at a loss. The company may just be a more efficient producer. Finally, a potential monopolist cannot indefinitely charge prices below its costs. As some point it will need to raise prices or face bankruptcy. It is simple arithmetic.

The Supreme Court has often expressed skepticism regarding claims of predatory pricing. In the 1986 case of *Matsushita Electric Industrial Corp. v Zenith Radio Corp.*, the American television producer Zenith failed to persuade the court that Matsushita was charging predatory prices to drive Zenith out of the market. The court noted that "there is a consensus among commentators that predatory pricing schemes are rarely tried, and even more rarely successful."[4]

## Should we worry about having too many federal regulations?

Clyde Wayne Crews Jr. of the Competitive Enterprise Institute (CEI) thinks so. Each year he publishes a report cleverly titled, *Ten Thousand Commandments: An Annual Snapshot of the Federal Regulatory State*. Among other things, the report tracks of the level of federal regulation by reporting the number of pages in the *Federal Register*. The *Federal Register* is an index that lists new and proposed federal regulations. In the decade of the 1950s, the *Federal Register* had 107,030 pages. In the decade of the 2020s, it has 836,560. Regulations have increased in all recent administrations including Presidents Bill Clinton, George W. Bush, Barack Obama, Donald Trump, and Joe Biden. Crews's report estimates that regulations cost businesses and consumers nearly $2 trillion in 2021, about 9 percent of GDP.[5]

*The* Federal Register *is a daily journal that contains government agency rules, proposed rules, and public notices.*

Defenders of the expansion of regulation stress that the benefits to the environment, workers, health, and safety of the nation outweigh these costs. And, while business leaders often complain that regulations increase costs, hurt profits, and harm job creation, some actually prefer federal regulation over state regulation. Businesses that operate in more than one state, for example, find it economically efficient to follow a uniform set of rules.

## What is the administrative state? Is it constitutional?

The administrative state refers to the idea that federal agencies, controlled by the executive branch, have vast powers when it comes to interpreting legislation passed by Congress. The agencies often write the actual regulations that businesses will be asked to follow. In 1984, the Supreme Court in *Chevron v National Resources Defense Council* created the rule known as "Chevron deference." That means that a federal agency, such as the Environmental Protection Agency, can develop regulations when legislation itself is silent or vague regarding its provisions.

In practice, Chevron deference means that lawmakers adopt legislation that sets out broad goals and then allow the federal agencies to fill in the blanks of what regulations are actually developed. Chevron deference means that the federal courts generally allow the regulations written by federal agencies to stand up against legal challenges.

*Justices of the U.S. Supreme Court in 2021.*

Defenders of Chevron deference say it is completely reasonable that federal agencies fill the gaps when Congress writes vague legislation. Opponents argue that this practice delegates what amounts to legislative authority to unelected staff who work in federal agencies. The Constitution provides that Congress establishes the "rules of the game" through passing legislation. Opponents say that Chevron deference gives too much legislative authority to the executive branch.

## QUESTIONS for DISCUSSION

1. Do you think monopolies can maintain their power by charging high prices to consumers? Why or why not?
2. Why are economists skeptical of claims that predatory pricing harms consumers?
3. Do you think citizens should be concerned about the expansion of federal regulations? Why or why not?
4. What is the administrative state?
5. What is the constitutional issue involved in the administrative state?
6. Do you think the administrative state places too much authority in the executive branch?

## *Kelo v City of New London*

PRIMARY SOURCE

In 2000, the City of New London, Connecticut, wanted to acquire a block of homes for new development. Suzette Kelo and several of her neighbors did not wish to sell to the city. The issue involved the city's use of **eminent domain**—the right of a government to take over private property for public use, with payment of compensation. The Takings Clause of the Fifth Amendment says, "nor shall private property be taken for public use without just compensation." The key is what is meant by "public use." If the purpose had been building a road, the city would clearly have had the right to take over the property. But in this case, the city wished to acquire the land and turn it over to a private developer.

The case went to the Supreme Court in *Kelo v City of New London*. In a controversial 5–4 decision in 2005, the court ruled in favor of the city. It found that the city's plan qualified as a permissible "public use" under the Takings Clause of the Fifth Amendment.[6]

Justice Stevens delivered the opinion of the court (June 23, 2005), recognizing the conflicting interested involved:

> In affirming the City's authority to take petitioners' properties, we do not minimize the hardship that condemnations may entail, notwithstanding the payment of just compensation. We emphasize that nothing in our opinion precludes any State from placing further restrictions on its exercise of the takings power. Indeed, many States already impose "public use" requirements that are stricter than the federal baseline. ...

But Justice Stevens went on to say that the Supreme Court was not deciding among those interests, but instead just interpreting the Fifth Amendment:

> This Court's authority, however, extends only to determining whether the City's proposed condemnations are for a "public use" within the meaning of the Fifth Amendment to the Federal Constitution. Because over a century of our case law interpreting that provision dictates an affirmative answer to that question, we may not grant petitioners the relief that they seek. The judgment of the Supreme Court of Connecticut is affirmed. It is so ordered.

Justice O'Connor, writing for the four dissenting justices, cited classic legal reasoning as forbidding the city's use of eminent domain in this case:

> Over two centuries ago, just after the Bill of Rights was ratified, Justice Chase wrote:
>
> "An act of the Legislature (for I cannot call it a law) contrary to the great first principles of the social compact, cannot be considered a rightful exercise of legislative authority .... A few instances will suffice to explain what I mean.... [A] law that takes property from A. and gives it to B: It is against all reason and justice, for a people to entrust a Legislature with such powers; and, therefore, it cannot be presumed that they have done it."

Justice O'Connor saw the upholding of eminent domain in this case as a major weakening of the Fifth Amendment:

> Today the Court abandons this long-held, basic limitation on government power. Under the banner of economic development, all private property is now vulnerable to being taken and transferred to another private owner, so long as it might be upgraded—i.e., given to an owner who will use it in a way that the legislature deems more beneficial to the public—in the process. To reason, as the Court does, that the incidental public benefits resulting from the subsequent ordinary use of private property render economic development takings "for public use" is to wash out any distinction between private and public use of property—and thereby effectively to delete the words "for public use" from the Takings Clause of the Fifth Amendment. Accordingly, I respectfully dissent.

## QUESTIONS for DISCUSSION

1. What is eminent domain?
2. What does the Takings Clause of the Fifth Amendment say about taking private property?
3. What is the primary argument set forth by Justice Stevens?
4. What is the primary agreement set forth by Justice O'Connor and the other dissenters?
5. Do you think the Supreme Court made a constitutionally correct decision in its ruling in *Kelo v City of New London*? Please explain your answer.

## Contemporary Connection

## Is Big Tech Too Powerful?

Are the big tech firms of today too powerful? Many Democrats and Republicans alike are concerned about online privacy and children's safety, the transparency of tech companies' data-collection practices, accountability for content posted on social media, and the market dominance of a few large tech firms.

At the center of many of these debates is Section 230 of the 1996 Communications Decency Act. This foundational law, as applied to the internet, assigns responsibility for publicly posted content. It provides a shield from prosecution for online companies such as Facebook and Twitter. It assures that these companies are not liable for harmful content a user posts on their sites. Further, it provides big tech companies with the power to remove content they deem objectionable, without liability, so long as they can show they are acting in good faith.

This law applies to any "provider or user of an interactive computer service." This includes big social media platforms. In addition, any website, mobile app, or online service qualifies for protection too. Many policy makers are concerned that Section 230 gives large technology companies too much power to decide what information Americans can see. Some argue that this law allows too much negative and unproven content

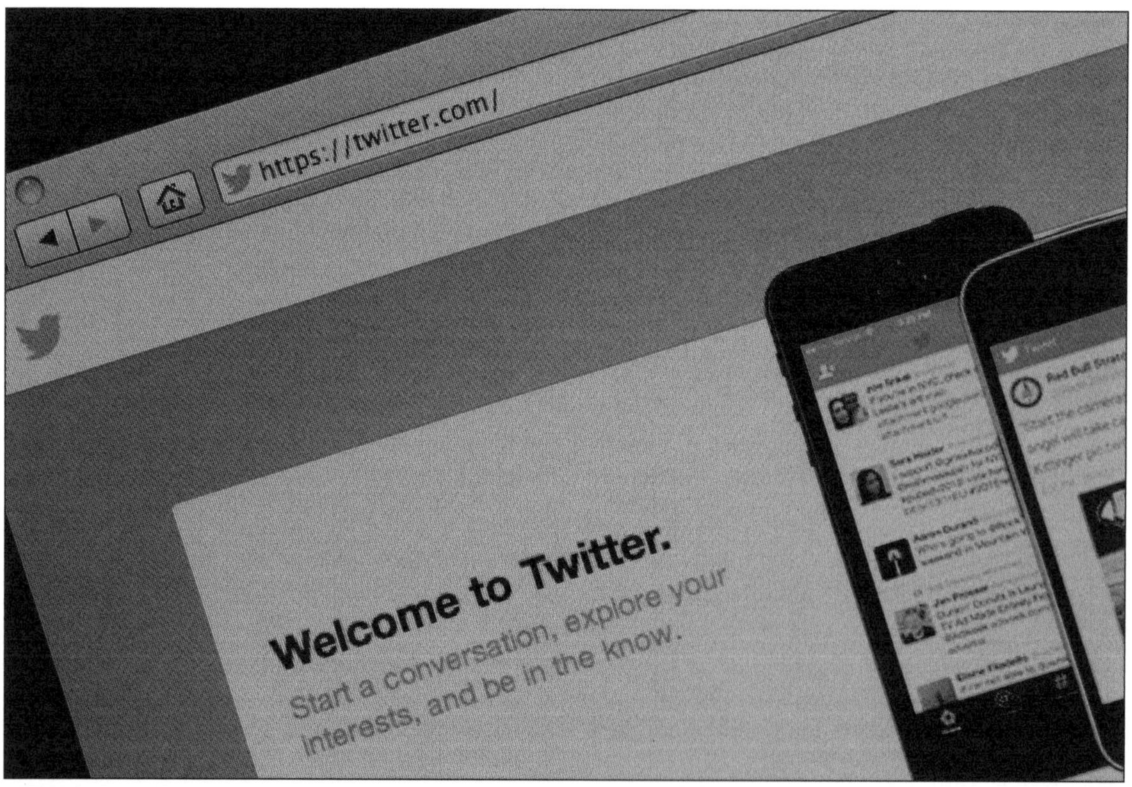

to spread, while others worry that the platforms censor content, sometimes with a particular political viewpoint.

The ramifications of this law were on full display when Facebook and Twitter took the unprecedented step of locking former president Donald Trump out of his accounts after his supporters stormed the U.S. Capitol on January 6, 2021. While some welcomed this step as a needed clampdown, others saw it as unwarranted censorship and an infringement on the former president's freedom of speech.

Those who defend Section 230 say that tech companies own their own websites and have the right to determine what content appears on them. This argument is based on the First Amendment and protects the rights of citizens and companies from government restricting their speech. Others argue that without Section 230, the internet would look very different. For example, travel or restaurant websites may be unwilling to post consumer reviews for fear of being held liable for any inaccurate statements. Some have called for revoking Section 230, while others have called for reforming it. In either case, changes seem likely to this law and the court system is sure to be involved.

## QUESTIONS for DISCUSSION

1. What is Section 230 in the 1996 Communications Decency Act?
2. What is the main argument for keeping Section 230 just as it is?
3. What is the main argument for reforming Section 230?
4. What do you think should be done regarding Section 230? Please explain your answer.

## Web Quests

**Enter any of the links below and use the questions to get you started on your own web quest.**

### Welcome to the *Federal Register*

*Take a deep dive into federal regulations by visiting the* Federal Register.

**https://www.federalregister.gov/index/2021.**

1. Develop a list of the areas of the economy where the federal government plays a significant role.

### Update on Regulation

*The Mercatus Center at George Mason University does economic research in several areas, including regulation.*

**https://www.mercatus.org/tags/regulation.**

1. Click on Regulatory Analysis. What are one or two of the latest reports?
2. Click on Regulatory Accumulation. What are one or two of the latest reports?
3. Click on Regulatory Process Reform. What are one or two of the latest reports?

### Learn More about the *Kelo* Case

*The* Kelo v New London *ruling of 2005 was and remains controversial.*

**https://www.oyez.org/cases/2004/04-108**

1. What are the main points made in the oral argument in *Kelo v New London*?
2. What were the main points made in the opinion of the court by Justice Stevens?
3. What were the main points made in the dissenting opinion made by Justice Thomas?

### Dig Deeper into Section 230

*Cornell Law School has a site that shows the full text for Section 230 in the 1996 Communications Decency Act.*

**https://www.law.cornell.edu/uscode/text/47/230.**

1. What subjects are addressed in Section 230?
2. What is the section that has become most controversial?
3. In your own words, explain why this section causes so much debate.

CHAPTER 12

# Monetary Policy and the Federal Reserve

*Senator Robert L. Owen, an early architect of the Federal Reserve System, in 1914.*

# Robert Latham Owen: Architect of the Fed

How did it happen that a friend of the Cherokee peoples, himself part Cherokee, became an architect of the central bank of the United States? That's the story of Robert Latham Owen, who was born in Virginia but moved west to the Indian Territory at an early age after family misfortune. There, in what became Oklahoma, he built a life as a schoolteacher of Cherokee orphans, lawyer, journalist, federal Indian agent, and community banker. In 1906 he gained attention by winning a court case on behalf of the Eastern Cherokee, providing compensation to the tribe from the federal government for lost Cherokee lands. The publicity from this case helped him win election to the Senate in 1907. He was one of the first two senators from the new state of Oklahoma.

Owen served three terms in the U.S. Senate. While in the Senate, Owen focused on national banking issues. He was the first chairperson of the Senate Committee on Banking and Currency. Owen cosponsored the Glass-Owen Federal Reserve Act of 1913, the legislation that created the present-day **Federal Reserve System**. Owen was an influential architect of the Fed, arguing for a central Federal Reserve Board along with 12 regional Federal Reserve banks. He argued against a movement at the time to put the new central bank under the control of the banking industry.

### KEY ECONOMIC CONCEPTS

**cryptocurrency**
**currency**
**deflation**
**discount loans**
**Federal Funds Rate**
**Federal Open Market Committee**
**Federal Reserve System**
**inflation**
**interest rates**
**monetary policy**

*Senator Robert L. Owen, posing for a marble bust by Moses Dykaar, noted Russian sculptor, 1926.*

In the 1920s and 1930s, Owen was highly critical of the Federal Reserve's deflationary policy. **Deflation** is a sustained *decrease* in the average level of prices. He believed this policy stemmed from the influence of the nation's largest banks on the Fed. He blamed Federal Reserve policies as the primary cause of the Great Depression, but this was a minority view at the time. However, it has since gained widespread acceptance and is now the consensus view of most economic historians.

## The Civics Context

Every economically developed nation has a central bank. While the exact structures and particulars of these institutions vary, they all serve as their government's bank. Most perform functions for their nation's commercial banks, issue **currency**, clear payments between financial institutions, regulate the banking sector, and act as a "lender of last resort" in a financial crisis.

Every central bank's structure is shaped by its nation's history and politics. In the Fed's case, this includes the determination of how a central bank fits within the nation's Constitution and the initial struggle for independence.

To finance the Revolutionary War, the Continental Congress printed the new nation's first paper money, known as "continentals," and the states took on significant debts. After the war, the new nation lacked a common national currency, and many states had printed their own money. As the Constitution was drafted, both of these issues were on the minds of the document's framers. Alexander Hamilton argued for the federal government to take over war debts issued by the states and to have the federal government establish the power to print and coin a common currency.

Article I, Section 8 of the Constitution specifically gives Congress the power to "borrow money" and also to "coin money and regulate the value." It does not specifically grant Congress the power to print paper money or to charter a bank. However, the Constitution leaves it up to Congress to determine the appropriate means by which powers should be exercised (unless specifically prohibited). The Constitution also grants Congress the power to adopt "all Laws which shall be necessary and proper for carrying into Execution the foregoing Powers and all other powers vested by this Constitution in the Government of the United States or in any Department or Officer thereof" (Article I, Section 8, Clause 18).

Pointing to these powers, Hamilton proposed The Bank of the United States in 1790 to assume the war debt and get the new nation off on a solid financial footing. It was designed by Hamilton with a structure similar to the Bank of England. Foremost among its functions, it would issue currency.

Hamilton imagined that the new bank would assist with government finances and also create a source of capital that would help with the development of new businesses. There were few banks in the new country because Britain had sought to protect London's banking sector from rivals during the colonial period.

From the beginning, many argued the bank was unconstitutional.[1] Critics contended the Constitution only allowed Congress to print money and not to establish a bank with so much authority. Further, with the war debt reduced, many saw no need for a national bank, and Congress did not renew its charter in 1811.

After the War of 1812, federal debt was once again an issue. With the elimination of The Bank of the United States in 1811, banking had shifted to a system of state-chartered banks, each issuing its own currency. With public opinion becoming supportive of a new national bank, The Second Bank of the United States was chartered in 1816. The Second Bank became one of the most powerful institutions in the country. President Andrew Jackson was concerned that this power was susceptible to corruption. Jackson opposed the bank during his campaign for president and, when elected, refused to renew the bank's charter, pulling all federal deposits from its vaults. This action crippled the bank, and its charter expired in 1836.

For the next 77 years, the United States operated without a national central bank. From 1837 to 1862, the nation relied on a "free banking" system in which state-chartered banks were again the primary source of credit and banking services. The "free banking" system worked reasonably well until the country experienced a series of financial panics in 1873, 1893, and 1907. While each panic had unique elements, the 1893 panic brought on the worst depression the country had ever experienced, and the banking system was only stabilized after the intervention of banking mogul J. P. Morgan. After another panic in 1907, bankers and Congress again considered a centralized national bank.

A National Monetary Commission was established in 1908 to develop a response to the nation's financial and banking needs. Under the administration of President Woodrow Wilson, Virginia Representative Carter Glass, the chair of the House Committee on Banking and Finance, and adviser H. Parker Willis, a former economics professor, worked to design a new central bank for the nation. With input from Oklahoma Senator Robert Latham Owen, the Glass-Owen bill, officially titled the Federal Reserve Act of 1913, was approved, and the modern Federal Reserve System was born. Today it often is simply called "the Fed."

**TABLE 1** Chairs of the Board of Governors of the Federal Reserve System

| Name | Term | Initially appointed by |
|---|---|---|
| William Gibbs McAdoo | Dec 1913 to Aug 1914 | Ex officio |
| Charles Sumner Hamlin | Aug 1914 to Aug 1916 | Woodrow Wilson |
| William Harding | Aug 1916 to Aug 1922 | Woodrow Wilson |
| Daniel Richard Crissinger | May 1923 to Sep 1927 | Warren G. Harding |
| Roy A. Young | Oct 1927 to Aug 1930 | Calvin Coolidge |
| Eugene Meyer | Sep 1930 to May 1933 | Herbert Hoover |
| Eugene Robert Black | May 1933 to Aug 1934 | Franklin D. Roosevelt |
| Marriner S. Eccles | Nov 1934 to Jan 1948 | Franklin D. Roosevelt |
| Thomas B. McCabe | Apr 1948 to Mar 1951 | Harry S. Truman |
| William McChesney Martin | Apr 1951 to Jan 1970 | Harry S. Truman |
| Arthur F. Burns | Feb 1970 to Jan 1978 | Richard Nixon |
| G. William Miller | Mar 1978 to Aug 1979 | Jimmy Carter |
| Paul Volcker | Aug 1979 to Aug 1987 | Jimmy Carter |
| Alan Greenspan | Aug 1987 to Jan 2006 | Ronald Reagan |
| Ben Bernanke | Feb 2006 to Jan 2014 | George W. Bush |
| Janet Yellen | Feb 2014 to Feb 2018 | Barack Obama |
| Jerome Powell | Feb 2018 to present | Donald Trump |

## The Economics of Money and Monetary Policy

The Federal Reserve's unique structure, the result of years of study and legislative compromises, created a quasi-government central bank. As a result, the Fed is both centralized within the federal government and decentralized with its reserve banks around the country.

The Fed serves as the fiscal agent for the U.S. government. It maintains the Department of Treasury's accounts. The Fed also acts as a "banker's bank." In this role, it provides banking services including electronic payments between banks, replacing damaged currency, and making loans to banks, if required.

More importantly from a governmental point of view, the Fed sets the nation's monetary policy. In support of this mission, the Fed sets a target range for a key **interest rate** and then uses policy tools to keep the rate within the target. This interest rate affects the decisions of consumers and producers. The Fed also serves as the banking system's "lender of last resort." The Fed stands behind the banking system and has the authority to help banks navigate short-term funding crises.

In 1978 Congress added to the Fed's monetary policy functions. The Humphrey-Hawkins Act established a "dual mandate" for the Fed. This role specifically requires the Fed both to maintain price stability in the economy (that is, keep **inflation** low and stable) and work for maximum employment of the country's citizens. These two distinct goals are at times in conflict, making this dual mandate challenging to successfully navigate

MAP 1 **Federal Reserve Regional Banks**

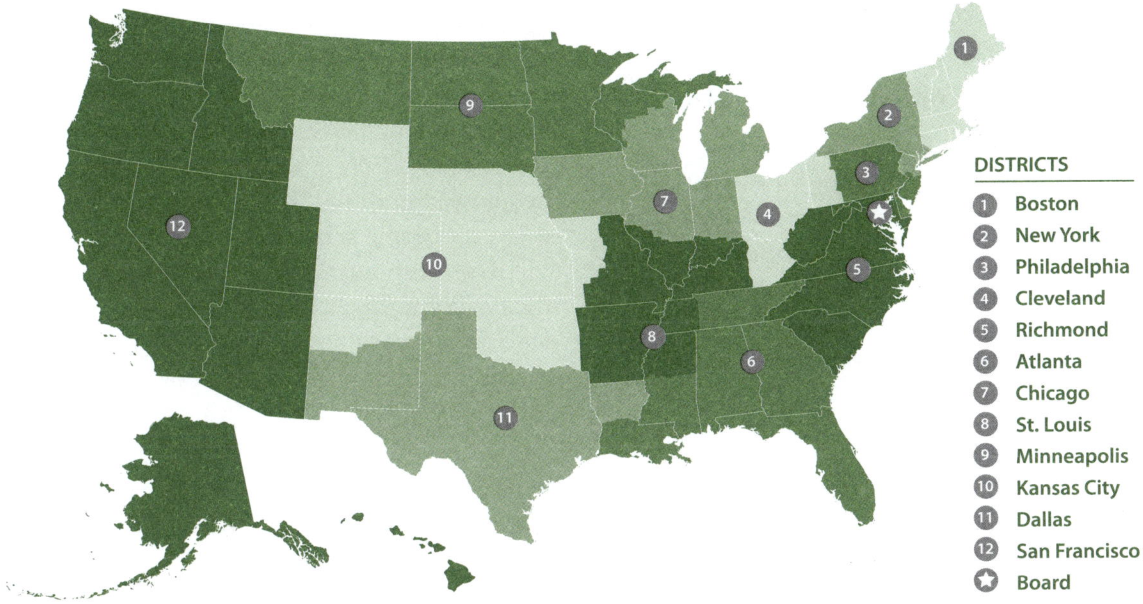


*Source:* Federal Reserve

for the Fed's leadership.

The Fed has three parts that, while separate, also work together to achieve the central bank's goals. Located in Washington, D.C., the Fed's Board of Governors is made up of seven members. These members are appointed by the president of the United States and confirmed by the Senate. They serve 14-year nonrenewable terms, and one of the governors serves as the chair for a four-year term that may be renewed and frequently is renewed, even by presidents of a different political party. These individuals are charged with overseeing the Federal Reserve System and setting and implementing the nation's monetary policy.

There are 12 Federal Reserve Banks. Each serves a specific district of the country. These banks are located in Atlanta, Boston, Chicago, Cleveland, Dallas, Kansas City, Minneapolis, New York, Philadelphia, Richmond, San Francisco, and St. Louis. These regional reserve banks perform banking services for the banks in their regions (for example, check clearing or damaged currency replacement). They also supervise and regulate most of the banks in their regions and provide community and educational outreach programs. These banks have teams of economists that study the economies of their regions and the nation and prepare their bank's president to represent their district at national Federal Reserve meetings. Regional Federal Reserve banks also lend funds to banks in their districts to provide short-term liquidity through their "discount window" lending facility when needed. *Liquidity* is the ability to convert assets to money quickly, and even a well-run bank with sound assets can run short of liquidity temporarily.

The final component of the Federal Reserve is the Federal Open Market Committee (FOMC). This group is made up of the seven Board of Governors' members and five of the regional Federal Reserve Bank presidents. One of the five voting members on this committee is always the president of the New York Federal Reserve Bank, and the others rotate as voting members. All bank presidents and governors meet eight times per year, and these meetings garner international attention. This is the policy group that determines whether the Fed should raise, lower, or maintain interest rates to meet the dual mandate as required by law.

## Civics Questions & Economic Answers

### Is the Federal Reserve undemocratic?

It's clear that the Fed is not quickly or easily directed by elected officials. Instead, the Fed was deliberately set up with a measure of political independence. Most economists believe that central bank independence (or autonomy from the government) is critical to a strong economy. The Federal Reserve is likely the most independent government agency in the United States; this is also true of central banks in other countries. Independent central banks are not beholden to elected officials or political pressure. Countries with independent central banks tend to have lower rates of inflation, and they rarely experience extreme inflation (referred to as *hyperinflation*). In the view of some observers, politicians in a democratic society may neglect the long term as they are driven by the need to win their next election. With reelection as the primary goal, politicians are unlikely to focus on long-term objectives, such as a stable inflation rate. Instead, they may seek short-term solutions to problems such as high unemployment and high interest rates, even if such short-term solutions will have undesirable long-term consequences. Still, the Federal Reserve is subject to long-term control through appointments of the chair and new governors.

### How does the Federal Reserve influence the economy?

The Federal Reserve can nudge economic activity to speed it up or slow it down. The Fed's control over an interest rate called the **Federal Funds Rate** is the primary policy used by the Fed to accomplish its goals. When the economy seems to be running too fast and generating dangers of inflation, the Fed through the Federal Open Market Committee (FOMC) may raise the Federal Funds Rate target range—which influences other interest rates on things like business loans and personal loans—and is likely to slow the economy down and lower inflation.

Conversely, if the Fed would like to see more economic activity (perhaps in an effort to lower the unemployment rate), it can push interest rates down. Lower interest rates act as an incentive to individuals and companies to make large purchases (maybe a new home or car) or expand business operations. These loans should lead to more economic activity and hopefully more jobs.

The mechanisms used by the Fed to influence the economy have changed in recent years. In fact, if you are taking an economics course, it is almost certain that your textbook is out of date on this topic.[2]

### Why are Federal Reserve governors appointed for such long terms?

These 14-year terms are directly related to the Fed's independence. Those designing the Fed's structure wanted the new central bank to be stable and removed from politics. With such long terms, the Board of Governors members will be in office longer than most presidents and members of Congress. Further, the extended terms make it highly unlikely that any one president can quickly appoint a majority of the bank's board. Lastly, nonrenewable terms make the governors less likely to need to be popular or cater to politicians. Thus, they are free to make long-term decisions that are best for the nation's economy.

### Why does the Federal Reserve have regional districts, unlike other powerful parts of the government?

These districts represent a compromise among the legislative founders of the Federal Reserve System. Some were concerned about having the bank, and therefore all of the country's monetary policy decisions, centralized in Washington, D.C. The United States is a large and diverse nation. The goal was to assure that the bank would represent all of the economy's interests. At the time, the welfare of both rural farmers and urban banks and businesses needed

*A $10,000 Federal Reserve Note from 1918.*

to be balanced. With regional banks throughout the country having representation on the national monetary policy setting board, these groups were convinced they would not be left out.

### Is the Fed the only government agency that deals with the economy?

No. There are a number of federal and state agencies that deal with the economy. The U.S. Department of the Treasury is tasked with maintaining a strong economy, job opportunities for Americans, and economic conditions that foster growth. Specifically, this agency manages the federal government's finances, collects money owed to the government, and deals with currency and coinage. The Treasury also manages the government's accounts and its public debt, supervises some banks and thrifts, and enforces federal finance and tax laws. Separately, the Department of Commerce also promotes economic growth and employment in the United States. It is tasked with ensuring fair international trade and collecting economic data to support decision making. This department helps to negotiate bilateral trade agreements with other countries and enforces laws designed to level the playing field for U.S. businesses and workers.

## QUESTIONS for DISCUSSION

1. Describe the structure of the Federal Reserve System.
2. How is the Fed independent from the Federal government?
3. What are the Fed's primary tools to influence the economy?

## Alexander Hamilton Visits Broadway

PRIMARY SOURCE

As we saw earlier, at the end of the Revolutionary War the new nation had accumulated significant debts. It might not seem like a big deal today, but in 1790, there was a serious debate about whether the federal government should fund all of the national and state debt. An excerpt from the *Hamilton: An American Musical* soundtrack song "Cabinet Battle #1"[3] illustrates the debate in President George Washington's cabinet between his secretary of state, Thomas Jefferson, and Treasury Secretary Alexander Hamilton. As the lyrics reveal, Hamilton was a proponent of a national bank that would assume the debts from the states that built up during the Revolution. Jefferson was opposed to a national bank; he was concerned that such an institution would create a financial monopoly that would hurt plantation owners and family farmers.

*Ladies and gentlemen, you could have been anywhere in the world tonight*

*But you're here with us in New York City*

*Are you ready for a cabinet meeting, huh?*

*The issue on the table, Secretary Hamilton's plan to assume state debt and establish a national bank*

*Secretary Jefferson, you have the floor, sir*

*Life, liberty and the pursuit of happiness*

*We fought for these ideals, we shouldn't settle for less*

*These are wise words, enterprising men quote 'em*

*Don't act surprised, you guys, 'cause I wrote 'em (ow)*

*But Hamilton forgets*

*His plan would have the government assume state's debts*

*Now, place your bets as to who that benefits*

*The very seat of government where Hamilton sits*

*Oh, if the shoe fits, wear it*

*If New York's in debt, why should Virginia bear it?*

*Uh, our debts are paid, I'm afraid*

*Don't tax the South 'cause we got it made in the shade*

*In Virginia, we plant seeds in the ground*

*We create, you just wanna move our money around*

*This financial plan is an outrageous demand*

*And it's too many damn pages for any man to understand*

*Stand with me in the land of the free and pray to God we never see Hamilton's candidacy*

*Look, when Britain taxed our tea, we got frisky*

*Imagine what gon' happen when you try to tax our whisky*

*Thank you, Secretary Jefferson*

*Secretary Hamilton, your response*

*Thomas, that was a real nice declaration*

*Welcome to the present, we're running a real nation*

*Would you like to join us, or stay mellow*

*Doin' whatever the hell it is you do in Monticello?*

*If we assume the debts, the union gets new line of credit, a financial diuretic*

*How do you not get it, if we're aggressive and competitive*

*The union gets a boost, you'd rather give it a sedative?*

*A civics lesson from a slaver, hey neighbor*

*Your debts are paid 'cause you don't pay for labor*

*"We plant seeds in the South. We create." Yeah, keep ranting*

*We know who's really doing the planting*

## QUESTIONS for DISCUSSION

1. How do the lyrics of this song summarize Thomas Jefferson's objections to a national bank?
2. What event is this song line meant to foreshadow? *Imagine what gon' happen when you try to tax our whisky*

## Contemporary Connection: Cryptocurrencies

Today, central banks such as the Fed control monetary policy. But central banks may have new rivals in the form of cryptocurrencies in the future. Is there a digital dollar in your future? Let's look more deeply.

The best-known **cryptocurrency** is called bitcoin. Bitcoin, like all cryptocurrencies, is a decentralized virtual currency that uses a computer network—called a blockchain—to approve and validate transactions. Working anonymously under the name "Satoshi Nakamoto," a programmer (or group of programmers) launched bitcoin in 2009. Bitcoin is independent from any government, central bank, or financial institution. Bitcoin allows individuals and firms to engage in financial transactions with complete anonymity while assuring that payments are properly sent and received.

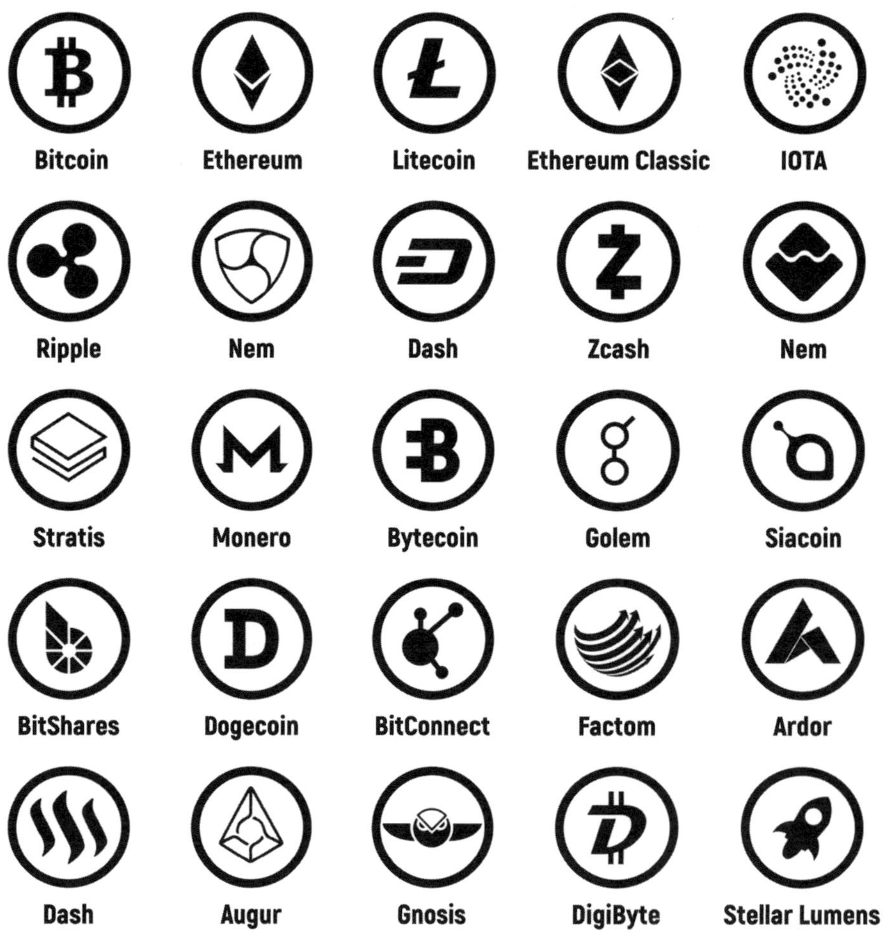


*Cryptocurrency logos*

Transactions made via bitcoin are verified by a system of network consensus. Potential transactions are broadcast over the network publicly in blocks of data. Individuals in the network then devote computing power to decode these encrypted blocks of transactions. These individuals are referred to as "miners," and they are compensated in new bitcoin whenever they decode and approve a transaction. This process will continue until 21 million bitcoins have been created, and at that time no further bitcoin will be created. For many, this serves as a kind of "gold standard" or check on a central authority that may choose to print excessive amounts of currency and deflate its value. The anonymous feature of bitcoin has caused it to become popular with online criminal websites that engage in illegal drug sales or even prostitution.

There are many other popular cryptocurrencies including ethereum, binance coin, tether, and dogecoin. They work in a similar manner. In 2021, bitcoin became legal tender in El Salvador. A number of nations, sometimes in an effort to evade international sanctions, have been working on developing their own central bank digital currencies. These include Cuba, Iran, and Venezuela. There is much debate among U.S. politicians and within the Federal Reserve System about how to properly regulate cryptocurrencies and whether the Fed should issue its own version of digital money.

*A woman uses a bitcoin ATM.*

The Federal Reserve is currently analyzing the pros and cons of a U.S. central bank digital currency. A digital dollar would represent a third version of money that uses digitally tokenized "dollars" to instantly settle transactions between people and businesses—and across borders. A master ledger, governed centrally by the Fed or in a more distributed, rules-based model like a blockchain network, would track the history of every transaction and verify the unique ID of each digital dollar to ensure legitimacy and instantly transfer funds from wallet to wallet. Just like the dollar, the supply of digital dollars would be controlled and backed by the Federal Reserve.

## QUESTIONS for DISCUSSION

1. What are the advantages and disadvantages of cryptocurrency?
2. Are there platforms that already exist and allow for digital dollar payments? Give examples. Why are they popular?

## Web Quests

**Enter any of the links below and use the questions to get you started on your own web quest.**

### The Federal Reserve System

*Visit the homepage of the Federal Reserve System.*

**https://www.federalreserve.gov**

1. Who are the current members of the Board of Governors? What are their backgrounds?
2. View the minutes of the last Federal Open Market Committee (FOMC) meeting. What were the main topics the members discussed? Did they take any actions to change interest rates?
3. Find the Beige Book for the district where you live. Summarize the key findings from this document about the economic conditions in the district.

### Federal Reserve Economic Data

*Visit the Federal Reserve Economic Data (FRED) website.*

**https://fred.stlouisfed.org**

1. Create a graph of the Federal Funds Effective Rate from 1960 to today. What trends do you see? When did it increase and decrease?
2. Create a graph of **discount loans** (Monetary Authority; Loans to Domestic Banks Through the Discount Window). When have banks taken out loans from the Federal Reserve District banks? What explains this activity?

### A Rap Song About Janet Yellen

*Listen to this song about former Fed chair Janet Yellen.*

**https://www.youtube.com/watch?v=12NEKj9Z3hA**

1. What do you know about Yellen's background from this song?
2. What kinds of policies does the song suggest Yellen was interested in?
3. What led to the end of Yellen's Fed chair position?

CHAPTER 13

# How Do the 50 State Governments Encourage Innovation?

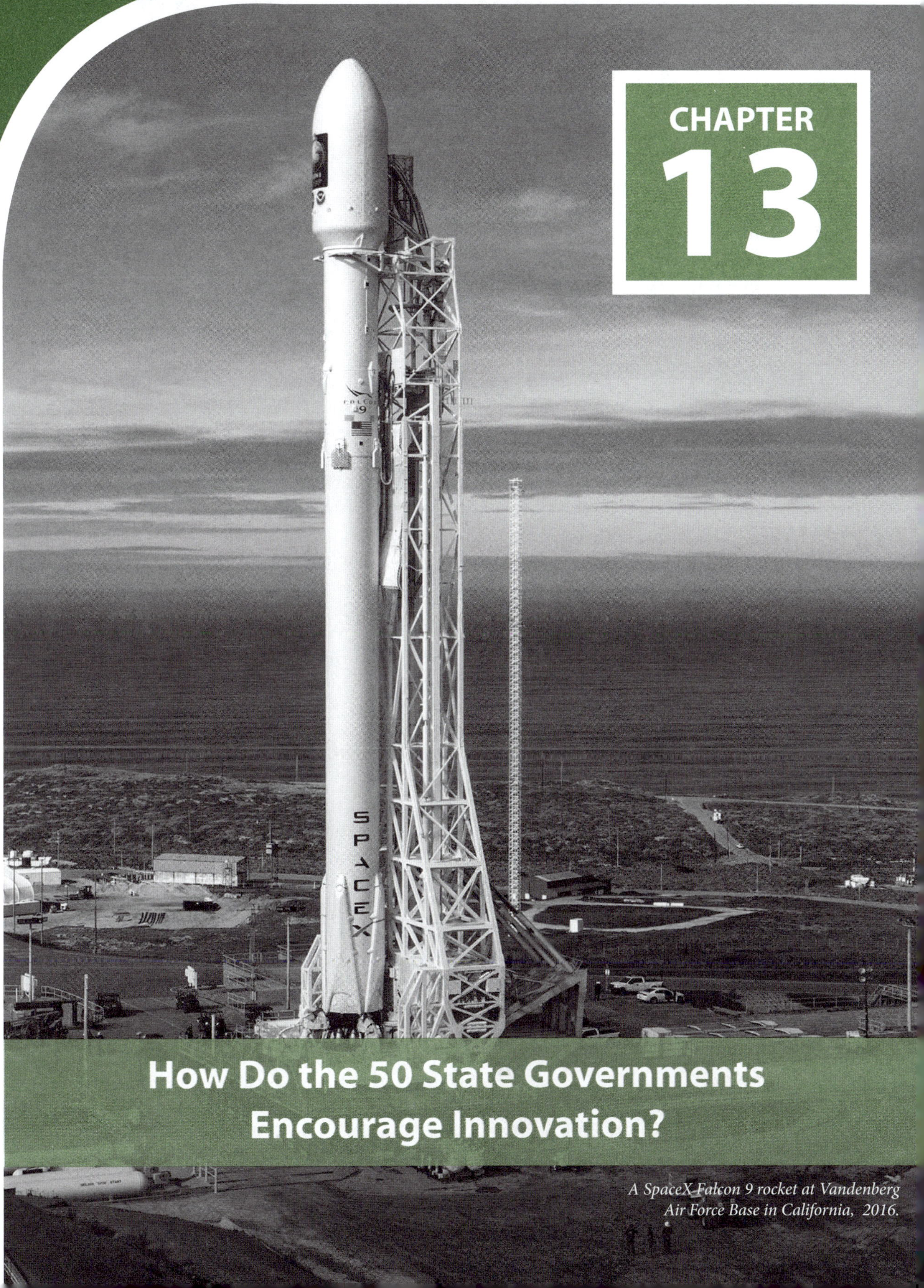


*A SpaceX Falcon 9 rocket at Vandenberg Air Force Base in California, 2016.*

# A Billionaire on the Run

Why is Elon Musk a billionaire on the run? Musk, an American entrepreneur and business leader, has always been a wanderer. He was born to a Canadian mother and South African father and raised in Pretoria, South Africa. After graduating from the University of Pennsylvania with degrees in economics and physics, Musk moved to California and cofounded the software company Zip2 with his brother Kimbal. Zip2 was eventually acquired by the computer maker Compaq. Musk then cofounded an online banking company that eventually became PayPal.

More recently, Musk founded SpaceX, an aerospace manufacturer and space transportation company, where he currently serves as chief executive officer. Musk has also served Tesla, Inc. in a number of functions, all the way up to CEO. An avid user of social media, Musk has stirred up controversies on topics such as cryptocurrencies and new **taxes** on billionaires. From his success in technology-related business ventures, Musk today is one of the wealthiest people in the world.

*Elon Musk in 2019.*

**KEY ECONOMIC CONCEPTS**

**competition**
**economic freedom**
**recession**
**taxes**

In 2021, Musk announced that he was planning to leave California for Texas, taking some of Tesla's operations with him. Musk has cited California's high taxes and regulations on business as the primary reasons for moving. Musk does not draw a salary from his businesses but rather takes his compensation in stock, frequently borrowing against his vast wealth for living expenses. Had Musk remained in California, his gains on stock sales would have been subject to a tax of more than 13 percent. Texas does not charge state taxes on gains in stock values (capital gains). Thus, by moving, Musk may have saved billions in capital gains taxes, given the size of his ownership stake in Tesla.

## The Civics Context

The Constitution lays out a system of federalism in which power is shared between the federal government and the 50 state governments. The Tenth Amendment to the Constitution states, "The powers not delegated to the United States by the Constitution, nor prohibited by it to the States, are reserved to the States respectively, or to the people." This clause in the Bill of Rights set the stage for what is referred to as federalism. Federalism refers to a system in which the powers of government are divided into federal powers, shared powers, and state powers. The laws of the national government apply to all citizens regardless of the state they live in, but states have their own laws and constitutions too. The principle, as laid out by James Madison in an October 24, 1787, letter to Thomas Jefferson, was to draw a line. This line, Madison wrote, "would give to the General Government every power requisite for general purposes, and leave to the States every power which might be most beneficially administered by them."

At the time the U.S. Constitution was adopted, most citizens felt their first loyalty was to the state and not the new nation. Madison and Alexander Hamilton and John Jay understood fears of an overly powerful federal government and wrote *The Federalist Papers* in part to argue against those fears.

As the federal system developed, all state constitutions established the role of a governor (executive branch), legislature, and judicial system. Today, with the exception of Nebraska's unicameral state legislature, all states employ a two-house (bicameral) system. Table 1 describes the powers that most state governments control and those they share with the federal government.

Most state constitutions are significantly longer than the federal equivalent. The state documents are more detailed and are designed to address the everyday relationships between the state and the citizens. Unlike the federal constitution, most state constitutions are relatively easy to amend. Many such amendments have been passed to enshrine rights in a manner such that future governors, legislatures, or courts may not alter. Alabama has the longest state constitution at almost 390,000 words and 950 amendments.

## The Economics of Federalism

Economist Barry Weingast notes, "For the last 300 years the richest nation in the world has had a federal structure."[2] He is referring to the Netherlands in the 16th and 17th centuries, England in the 18th and 19th centuries, and the United States in the 20th century. There may be many reasons for the correlation between a federal system and a wealthy nation. However, one important factor is likely to be that the lower levels of government (state and local) have to compete with one another, leading to innovations and efficiencies.

As can be seen in Table 1, most state powers concern three areas: public safety, regulation of state businesses, and establishing political subdivisions within the state. Examples of the

**TABLE 1 Shared and State Powers of Government[1]**

| Shared Powers (with Federal Government) | Powers of State Governments |
|---|---|
| To levy and collect taxes | To regulate trade within the state |
| To borrow money | To establish local governments |
| To establish superior and inferior courts | To protect public health, safety, and morals |
| To enforce laws | To ratify constitutional amendments |
| To apprehend and punish lawbreakers | To determine qualifications of voters |
| To charter banks and other corporations | To conduct elections |
| To take land for public use | To change state constitutions |
| To provide for the general welfare | To establish and support public schools |
| | To license occupational specialties |
| | To exercise the "reserved powers" not granted to the federal government not prohibited to the states |

specific responsibilities of state governments in these three areas include the following:

### Public Safety

- Patrolling highways
- Aiding local law enforcement agencies
- Training national guard units
- Operating state court and prison systems

### Regulation of State Businesses

- Issuing state banking charters and examinations
- Developing agricultural rules and practices
- Licensing doctors, nurses, teachers, and other professionals
- Regulating the state's insurance industry

### Establishing Political Subdivisions

- Overseeing a system of local school boards and state universities
- Establishing boundaries for legislative districts and regulating local, state, and national elections
- Approving boundaries for new towns and assisting with local government finance

Chapter 10 described how the federal government constructs a budget. In a similar way, each state passes a budget that specifies how funds will be raised and spent. Unlike the federal government, most state governments are required to balance their budgets. This means that state spending each year must not exceed the revenue the state raises through taxes. During times of **recession**, a sustained period of a weak economy,

*State governments have the power to license medical and other professionals.*

this feature of the state budgeting process can lead to difficult decisions.

The states depend on their individual income taxes (35.9 percent) and sales taxes (31.3 percent) for most of their revenue.[3] Other state taxes include license taxes, corporate income taxes, and property taxes. The vast majority of property tax collections, however, go to support counties, cities, and towns. Unlike federal taxes, the rates states charge for income and sales taxes vary widely. In fact, nine states do not charge any income tax on their residents, and five states don't charge a state sales tax.

These differences in tax rates represent another way states may compete with each other to attract residents and businesses. Associate Justice of the Supreme Court Louis Brandeis popularized the saying that states "are laboratories of democracy."[4] Justice Brandeis meant that the federal system of government allows states to experiment with new policies that may turn out to be a model for others to copy and adopt. Such a system also recognizes that what is good for California may not be good for Alaska, so laws and policies may be designed to reflect these differences.

Elections are a well-established method for voters to express their preferences. As economists and political scientists have long noted, people can also express preferences through their location choices. They "vote with their feet" by moving away from state or local governments they dislike. Or they may cast positive votes by moving to state or local governments that they prefer. The outcome is less precise than an election. People may move for many reasons, not just the governments involved. Still, governors certainly notice when large numbers of people are leaving their state.

## Civics Questions & Economic Answers

### How does federalism encourage people and businesses to "vote with their feet"?

Federalism allows states to differ in their policies in any number of ways. This system also allows individuals and businesses to move if they perceive another state provides better opportunities. The San Francisco Bay area, with its expensive housing costs, has lost population to places like Sacramento, California, Seattle, Washington, Phoenix, Arizona, and Austin, Texas. New York City has seen a similar pattern. In many cases the moves are driven by people leaving the city for suburbs, but an almost equally large number of New Yorkers moved to Florida as well. The 2020 Census revealed that Texas gained the most population since the 2010 Census and Utah grew the fastest over the time period followed by Idaho, Texas, North Dakota, and Nevada.[5] Three states saw their populations shrink: West Virginia, Mississippi, and Illinois.

### Does the federal government try to influence state decisions?

Yes. The Constitution established a federal system in which the national government's powers are limited, and the states retain political powers as enumerated in the Tenth Amendment. Still, there are a number of ways the federal government can influence the states. As an example, Medicaid, a federal health care program for eligible low-income adults and children, is technically voluntary for the states to join. However, if a state rejected Medicaid and established its own program for the needy, it would lose its share of federal Medicaid funds even as its citizens would have to pay Medicaid taxes. In practice, all 50 states have decided to operate Medicaid programs.

Control of the Highway Trust Fund is another tool the federal government has wielded to put

*President Ronald Reagan signs the National Minimum Drinking Age Act of 1984.*

pressure on the states. This account, established in 1956 along with President Eisenhower's interstate highway project, is funded largely by gas taxes and controlled by the U.S. Congress. This money is allocated to states using rules Congress establishes. Using the threat of withholding funds, Congress forced states to comply with a national drinking age of 21 in 1984, a national speed limit of 55 miles per hour in 1974 (since repealed), and a national motorcycle helmet requirement in 1975 (since repealed). As Chapter 1 made clear, people respond to incentives in predictable ways. The people who run state governments are no exception.

## Do states differ in their business and economic climates?

Yes. A number of independent research organizations rank states based on their economic policies. For example, the Vancouver, Canada, based Fraser Institute publishes an annual *Economic Freedom of North America* report ranking U.S. and Mexican states and Canadian provinces by their levels of economic freedom (see Contemporary Connection for more information). The Tax Foundation does an annual ranking of each state's business climate, based primarily on the differences in state tax policy. *U.S. News and World Report* provides an annual ranking of the 50 states' economies using measures of employment, economic growth, and the business environment based on new business creation rates, tax burdens, company headquarters, and venture capital investment. Finally, a number of studies have ranked states based on the climate for entrepreneurs.

## Is it better for governments to compete or cooperate?

Many economists believe **competition** among governments leads to better governance. In choosing where to live, people can compare the public services offered and taxes levied. They are attracted to towns that use tax dollars wisely. Competition keeps political leaders alert and responsive to their citizens. If people feel that their taxes exceed the value of their public services, they can go elsewhere. They can, as already noted, vote with their feet. The argument applies not only to individuals but also to businesses and capital. Businesses benefit from various government services, including infrastructure, the protection of property rights, and the enforcement of contracts. But if taxes vastly exceed these benefits, businesses may move to places offering a better mix of taxes and services.

### Are there some things state governments can't practically do?

Yes. When national uniformity is important, state-by-state approaches will not work. National defense is one example. If left to the states, military readiness might be lower in some states, resulting in a loss of security to neighboring states that valued defense more. Environmental pollution does not respect state lines, and therefore a lenient state might impose pollution on its neighbors. Interestingly, views on federalism in both national defense and environmental regulation have changed over time. Early in our history, state-governed militia were an important part of our defense, and there was little or no environmental regulation at any level. Today, major defense decisions are entirely national, while some states and groups of states have more aggressive environmental regulation than others.

### QUESTIONS for DISCUSSION

1. What does federalism mean?
2. Explain some ways state policies differ.
3. What are some benefits from a federal system where states compete with each other?

## Economic Freedom in the States

PRIMARY SOURCE

*Economic Freedom of North America* is an annual publication of the Fraser Institute. It measures the extent to which the policies of individual American and Mexican states and Canadian provinces are supportive of **economic freedom**, or the ability of individuals to act in the economic sphere free of undue restrictions. There are two indices: one that examines provincial/state and municipal/local governments only and another that includes the influence of the federal governments' policies as well.

The subnational index employs 10 variables for the 92 provincial/state governments in Canada, the United States, and Mexico in three areas: (1) government spending, (2) taxes, and (3) labor market freedom.

In the 2020 report (using 2018 data), the most economically free state was New Hampshire, followed by Florida, Virginia, Texas, and Tennessee. The least-free state was New York, followed by West Virginia, Alaska, California, and Vermont. The most economically free Canadian province was Alberta and the least free Quebec. In Mexico, Jalisco led the index while Tabasco was least free.

*New Hampshire is the most economically free state, according to the Fraser Institute's 2020 report.*

Why does economic freedom matter at the state and provincial levels? The jurisdictions in the least economically free quartile (one-fourth) from this study had an average per-capita income of just $2,277, compared to $50,645 for the most economically free quartile. In addition, economic freedom at the subnational level has generally been found to be positively associated with a per capita income, economic growth, as well as various measures of entrepreneurial activity.

**MAP 1 Economic Freedom in the United States**

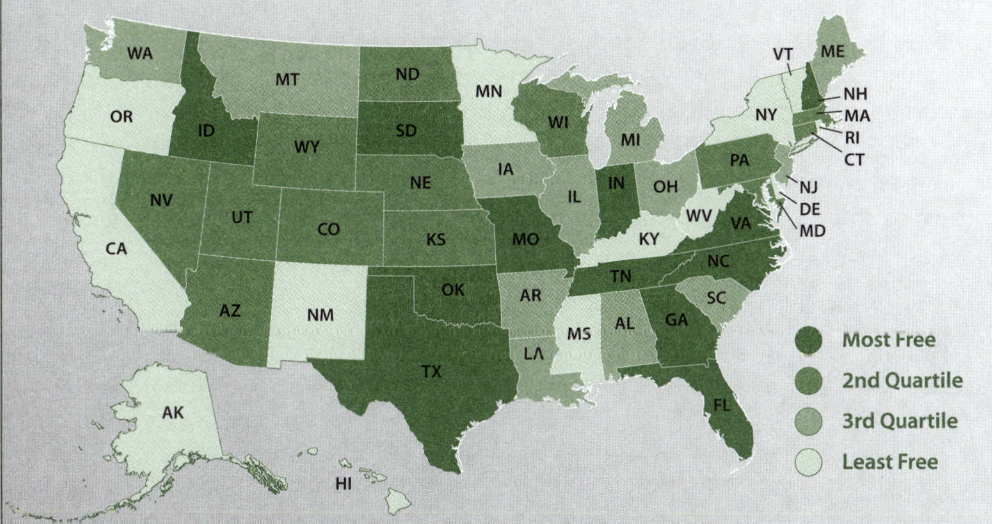


*Source:* The Fraser Institute's *Economic Freedom of North America: 2020 Annual Report*

## QUESTIONS for DISCUSSION

1. What is the definition of economic freedom?
2. How do states differ in their levels of economic freedom? What causes these differences?
3. What goals might a state be seeking when it decides to limit economic freedom? Name several possibilities.

Contemporary Connection

## Publicly Financed Sports Stadiums

The former owner of the Baltimore Ravens, Art Modell, said, "The pride and the presence of a professional football team is far more important than 30 libraries."[6] This quote summarizes what many state and local officials hope to gain by attracting or keeping a professional sports team. They view sports stadiums as the anchors around which cities can develop new entertainment and shopping areas. Others clamor to be a "big league" city and to receive all the local pride and attention that comes with hosting a professional sports team.

With a new stadium, a team generally attracts more fans and increases revenue through upgrades such as luxury suites. Since the teams experience substantial benefits, why would taxpayers build sports stadiums for millionaire athletes to play for multimillionaire sports team owners?

Part of the answer is the monopoly power that professional sports leagues hold over their franchises. The owners tightly control the number and location of the teams in their leagues. This monopoly power allows the leagues to take advantage of our federal system and encourage states and cities to compete against each other to host their teams. Frequently, this competition involves renovating a current stadium or building a new stadium that is heavily subsidized

*The Los Angeles Memorial Coliseum was built with public funds and is jointly owned by city, county, and state governments.*

by the local taxpayers. Further, interest groups, particularly in the construction and hospitality industries, stand to gain a lot from these new stadiums. They lobby their city's politicians to approve such taxpayer subsidized projects (see Chapter 8 for more examples of interest groups and their influence over public policy).

Interestingly, this monopoly power that exists in the North American sports leagues does not occur in the European soccer leagues. These soccer leagues use a "promotion and relegation" system that takes away owners' control of league structure. (There are currently seven English Premier League soccer teams located in London.) Under promotion and relegation, teams with good performance are promoted to a higher league. Teams with poor performance are relegated to a lower league. Thus, the owners do not directly control which teams can play in the highest league. This removes their ability to exert influence over local officials in an effort to subsidize their stadiums.

## QUESTIONS for DISCUSSION

1. What are the direct and indirect benefits to a city from hosting a professional sports team?
2. Which groups in a community are likely to support the construction of a new sports stadium at taxpayer expense?
3. Which groups in a community are unlikely to support the construction of a new sports stadium at taxpayer expense?

## Web Quests

**Enter any of the links below and use the questions to get you started on your own web quest.**

### Fraser Institute *Economic Freedom of North America*

*Visit the Fraser Institute's* Economic Freedom of North America*'s latest report.*

**https://www.fraserinstitute.org/economicfreedom/map?geozone=na&page=map&year=2019&selectedCountry=USA**

1. Where does the state that you live in rank in this study?
2. Which state is the most economically free? The least?
3. When all of North America is considered, which country has the most states or provinces in the "most free" quartile? The "least free"?

### Your State Government

*Visit the homepage for the state government where you live.*

1. Who is the current governor of your state? What is their background?
2. What kinds of services does your state's government provide to citizens?
3. What kinds of services does your state's government provide to businesses?

### State Constitutions

*Find a current copy of your state's constitution online.*

1. How long is this document?
2. What are the major categories that it covers?
3. Is there a preamble and declaration of rights section? How are these sections similar to or different from the U.S. Constitution?

### Free to Choose Network

*Watch the movie* Corporate Welfare: Where's the Outrage? *(55 minutes long)*

**https://www.freetochoosenetwork.org/programs/corporate_welfare/**

1. Are there examples where federalism, and the pressure to compete with other cities and states, might lead to unfair tactics to attract businesses?
2. How can you ensure your city uses fair practices in attracting new business so it doesn't harm the city's current businesses?
3. If legislatures are going to subsidize farmers, should it be family farms or large farming corporations?

# CHAPTER 14

## Why Do Citizens Vote? The Economics of Voting and Elections

# It's a Tie!

David Yancey and Shelly Simonds were in a tight 2017 race for a seat in the Virginia House of Delegates. Yancey was the Republican incumbent. Simonds was a late entry as the Democratic candidate. Simonds, a local school board member, had lost to Yancey by more than 2,000 votes in 2015.

On Election Day, November 8, 2017, it appeared that Simonds had lost by 10 votes. She demanded a recount and got one. Weeks later, after the recount, it appeared that Simonds had won by one vote: Yancey: 11,607, Simonds: 11,608.

But there's more to the story. The Yancey campaign challenged an uncounted ballot. It had been marked for both candidates but had a slash mark through Simonds's name. A three-judge panel examined the ballot and decided that it should be counted for Yancey. That resulted in a tie: 11,608 for each candidate.

The final decision, according to Virginia state law, was made by a drawing of lots. Both candidates' names were printed out and cut into identically sized pieces of paper. The papers were placed in old film canisters, stirred around in a bowl, and then one was drawn by an official of the Virginia State Board of Elections. Yancey won!

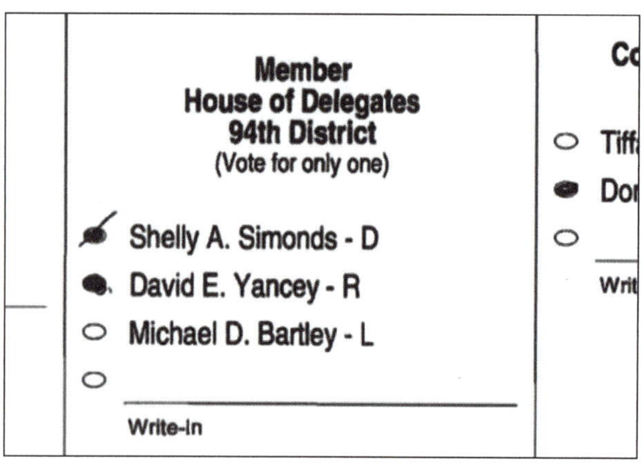


*The deciding ballot in the 2017 race for the Virginia House of Delegates. Judges counted the vote for Yancey, resulting in a tie.*

**KEY ECONOMIC CONCEPTS**

- benefits of voting
- costs of voting
- Electoral College
- incentives to vote
- information costs
- rational ignorance

This is a cautionary tale regarding the importance of voting. If Simonds had won, the Virginia House of Delegates would have been tied at 50 Democrats and 50 Republicans. Instead, the Republicans retained the majority by a slim 51 to 49 seats. And then the tables turned again. Simonds won the seat from Yancey in 2019.

## The Civics Context

### Responsibilities of American Citizens

U.S. Citizenship and Immigration Services state:

> Citizenship is the common thread that connects all Americans. We are a nation bound not by race or religion, but by the shared values of freedom, liberty, and equality.[1]

Having a shared set of values is part of what is sometimes called being a patriotic citizen. Being a patriotic citizen is viewed with suspicion in some quarters. For some, it is associated with unthinking loyalty to a country. Others see it as a reasoned, sometimes critical, but overall respectful view of the nation. The founding economist Adam Smith viewed patriotism as part of human nature. Here is a quote from his book *The Theory of Moral Sentiments*:

> The love of our country seems, in ordinary cases, to involve in it two different principles; first, a certain respect and reverence for that constitution or forms of government which is

actually established; and secondly an earnest desire to render the condition of our fellow-citizens as safe, respectable, and happy as we can.[2] (page 231)

Regardless of differing views of patriotism, being an American citizen comes with certain rights and responsibilities. Inalienable rights, the natural rights we possess because we are part of humanity, are protected by the U.S. Constitution. These rights include freedom of speech, freedom of religion, trial by jury, the right to vote, and so forth. Also protected are rights proclaimed in the Declaration of Independence, including "life, liberty, and the pursuit of happiness."

Let's examine four areas of responsibilities. The first is obeying the law. This is a fundamental responsibility. It includes respecting local, state, and national laws. Second, citizens are to voluntarily pay local, state, and national taxes. Government provides certain vital functions such as protecting the life, liberty, and property of citizens. Without revenue from taxes, the government could not provide its most basic functions. Third, citizens participate in the judicial system. The U.S. Constitution guarantees a person accused of a crime to a trial by a jury, where a group of citizens will hear the evidence and decide the case. Finally, citizens have the responsibility to participate in the democratic process. The most common way most citizens participate is by voting. In 2020, a total of 155 million Americans voted in the presidential election.

Many people consider voting to be their most important duty as a citizen. Well-informed voters know the candidates and the issues and cast their ballots accordingly. Voting is a way for citizens to express their wishes to elected officials, and it is a way for elected officials to gain consent for their policies. Voting helps make sure that elected officials are listening to the will of the voters. Perhaps this is what Thomas Jefferson had in mind when he said, "The government you elect is the government you deserve."

## The Economics of Voting

Most economists would certainly agree that voting is one of the best methods for citizens to communicate their wishes to elected officials. How many citizens actually turn out to vote?

The U.S. Census Bureau tracks how many people report that they voted. Historically, voter turnout for presidential elections is higher than for the congressional midterm elections held between presidential election years. As you can see in Figure 1, voter turnout in presidential elections hovers in the range of 60 percent to nearly 70 percent.

The 2020 presidential election had the highest voter turnout in recent years. Figure 1 shows that the only higher voter turnout was in 1992. In 2020, former vice president Joe Biden was running as the Democrat against Donald J. Trump, the incumbent Republican president. Biden defeated Trump. In 1992, much as in 2020, the incumbent president George H. W. Bush, a Republican, was defeated for a second term by Democratic nominee Bill Clinton, the former governor of Arkansas.

Voting patterns shifted somewhat in the 2020 race. The incentive to get out and vote increased for some groups. For example, compared with the 2016 race, there was higher turnout of young people, people without college degrees, African Americans, Asian Americans, and Latino and Hispanic voters. But according to the U.S. Census

**FIGURE 1** **Voter Turnout in Presidential Elections, 1980 to 2020**

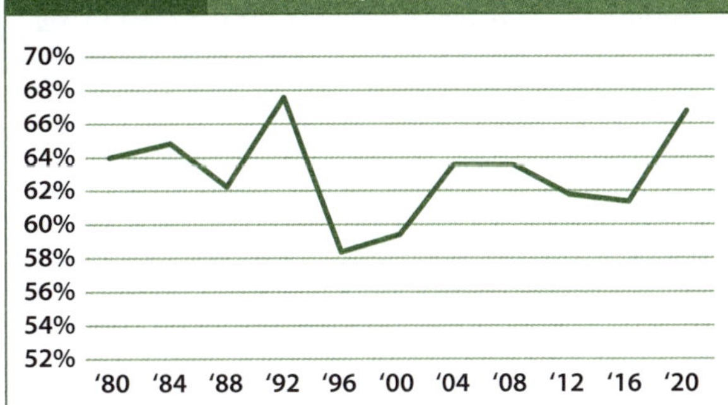


*Source:* U.S. Census Bureau[3]

Bureau,[4] other historical patterns remained in place:

- Voter turnout was highest among older adults. People aged 65 to 74 had a 76.0 percent turnout.
- Voter turnout was lowest among younger voters. People aged 18 to 24 had a 51.4 percent turnout.
- Women voted more than men (68.4 percent compared to 65 percent).
- Nonwhite citizens voted less than whites, but the gap narrowed in 2020. African American turnout was 62 percent, Hispanic turnout was 53.7 percent, and Asian American turnout was 57.9 percent. White turnout was 68 percent.
- Voter turnout also increased with higher levels of educational attainment. High school graduate turnout was 55.5 percent, while turnout for those with a bachelor's degree was 77.9 percent.
- People with higher income voted more than people of lower income. For people whose income was \$100,000–\$149,999, turnout was 81.0 percent. For people whose income was \$30,000–\$39,999, turnout was 63.6 percent.

Individuals and groups face differing **incentives to vote**. Older adults, for example, have relatively strong incentives to vote. They are more likely to be longtime residents of their communities and feel a need to be involved. They may feel more connected to the local, state, and national political scenes. Older voters also face incentives to support candidates who say they will protect retirement benefits such as Social Security and Medicare.

Younger voters face weaker incentives. They are less likely to have deep community roots. They are just getting started in careers. They are more mobile. Younger voters have less firsthand experience with the political system and might lack knowledge about the basics, such as how to register and where to show up for in-person voting. These and other factors may reduce their incentive to vote.

Let's dig a little deeper into voter behavior by considering the benefits and costs of voting. **The benefits of voting** might include the following:

- The satisfaction people gain from fulfilling their duty as a citizen. Voters conveying their opinions about politicians and policies is the essence of a democratic republic—one that many Americans have fought to protect. This is how citizens hold elected officials accountable.
- Some people feel better about themselves when they vote. They might put on "I Voted" stickers that are distributed at polling places to encourage others to do the same.
- The benefits people feel when cheering on their favored candidates and issues with their votes. These are folks who derive satisfaction from voting to save the planet, reduce poverty, or lower taxes.
- The chance that your vote alone might make a difference in the outcome, which happened in the 2017 Virginia House of Delegates race. Especially in local races and special elections, when voter turnout can be low, a handful of votes can significantly influence the outcome.
- Sheer political pleasure. Some people love politics. Voting just adds to the fun for them.

What are the **costs of voting**? Cost might include the following:

- Time! People are busy. They don't wish to take the time to vote. In presidential elections, in-person voting may involve waiting in long lines.
- Frequent trips to the polls. People are asked to vote often. There are primary elections, springtime elections, and special elections.
- Interference with work. Elections are held on weekdays. For some people it is inconvenient to break away from work.
- Voters have to be registered. The process of registering to vote varies from state to state. Some states make it more convenient than others.

*Election workers check in voters at a polling place in Arlington, Virginia, in 2018.*

More costs come from the time and effort it takes to cast an informed vote. These are called **information costs**. No doubt, our government would reflect the wishes of voters more closely if the voters themselves were well informed. But seeking political information takes time. Listening to campaign slogans and talking points isn't nearly enough. An informed voter needs to study voting records and pore through detailed position papers, attend campaign events, and watch debates.

And there is still more for an informed voter to know. Ballots often include more than just casting votes for, say, a presidential candidate. Voters are asked to vote on state and local candidates as well. States often include referendum issues on the ballot. A referendum is legislation upon which voters are asked to vote directly. A referendum might involve a decision on raising taxes or approving a state constitutional amendment. Being informed on the entire ballot takes time.

Article I, Section 4, Clause 1 of the U.S. Constitution makes it clear that voting is largely governed by state legislatures. Several states, some in response to the COVID-19 pandemic, have taken steps to increase voter turnout by reducing the costs of voting. The changes include making voting easier by mailing ballots to registered voters or expanding opportunities for early voting. Other states have made it easier to cast absentee ballots. To reduce information costs to voters, Colorado provides voters with a nonpartisan explanation of all ballot issues. Other nations have tried different alternatives. Elections in Australia, for example, are held on a weekend day in the hopes that fewer people are at work.

## Civics Questions & Economic Answers

### What are the chances that my vote will make a difference in the election?

Despite the tie vote in the 2017 Virginia House of Delegates race, the chances that a single vote would change the outcome of an election are low. Millions of people vote in national presidential elections. Voters have more influence in local and special elections because turnout is much less. Nonetheless, it is rare that one vote changes an election outcome. In this sense, it is sort of surprising that voter turnout is as high as it is. Clearly, people are not voting *only* because of the chance of changing the outcome—any more than sports fans cheer *only* in hopes of making their team win. In both voting and sports, it's about expressing support for your side.

### How are incentives for voters different from incentives to consumers—people who use "dollar votes" to buy goods and services?

Public choice economists (see Chapter 8 for more on public choice theory) suggest that the weak incentive for voters to become well informed results in **rational ignorance**. This means that it makes some sense for voters not to obtain information about political issues or candidates. According to the idea of rational ignorance, the cost of seeking out all of that information is not worth the benefit, because one vote has little effect on the outcome of an election. The opposite is true for consumers in the private sector. When an individual is buying a car or new computer, there is a strong incentive to do research to make sure it is the right purchase. Buying a car or a computer has a direct and immediate result. You get what you purchase. When you vote? Not so much.

### If the costs are high to be an informed voter and the benefits are low, what do voters tend to do?

Voters tend to use shortcuts or rules of thumb. Party affiliation is one example. Members of the Republican Party are widely regarded as conservatives. Conservatives tend to support traditional values and institutions. The members of the Democratic Party are widely regarded as liberals. Liberals are associated with desiring change in traditional values and institutions. So, voters who favor change over tradition might favor Democratic Party candidates. Voters who favor tradition over change might favor Republican Party candidates. For some voters, knowing party affiliation is a low-cost way of casting a modestly well-informed vote.

### Questions for Discussion

1. How was the outcome of the 2017 race for a seat in the Virginia House of Delegates decided?
2. What are some differing views regarding patriotism?
3. What are the rights of citizens?
4. What are the responsibilities of citizens?
5. Who tends to vote more: a 19-year-old recent high school graduate or a grandparent who has lived in the same community for the past 50 years? Why do you think that might that be the case?
6. What are the benefits of voting?
7. What are the costs of voting?
8. What does it mean to be rationally ignorant?

# The Case of the Hanging Chads

PRIMARY SOURCE

It was a cliffhanger. Late in the evening of November 7, 2000, the presidential race in Florida was still undecided. George W. Bush, the Republican former governor of Texas, was running for president against Al Gore, the Democrat and former vice president under Bill Clinton. The attention of the nation shifted to Florida where the race was very close, almost a tie. The tightness of the vote triggered an automatic machine recount according to Florida law. The ballots were run through the ballot machines a second time.

What happened next was controversy regarding the ballots themselves. Some Florida counties used a card-punch ballot like the one pictured. Known as a "butterfly ballot," it displayed candidates' names on both sides of a middle column of punch holes. Voters would use a small card puncher to punch a hole next to the name of their favored candidate.

The little square that was pushed out was called a "chad." When hand recounts were conducted in some Florida counties, election officials squinted at ballots trying to figure out what the voter intended. For example, the chad might not have been pushed all the way out. These were called "hanging chads." As the recount continued, it was clear that different recount standards were being applied in different Florida counties.

Ultimately, the U.S. Supreme Court in *Bush v Gore* ruled in a complicated decision that the hand recount was unconstitutional and could not proceed. The original close results stood and Bush became president after collecting Florida's 25 electoral votes. The national electoral vote was 271 for Bush and 266 for Gore.

This close outcome may have provided Florida voters with a stronger incentive to vote in subsequent elections. It also provided a strong incentive for the Florida legislature to change its voting process. The hanging chads controversy was a national embarrassment.

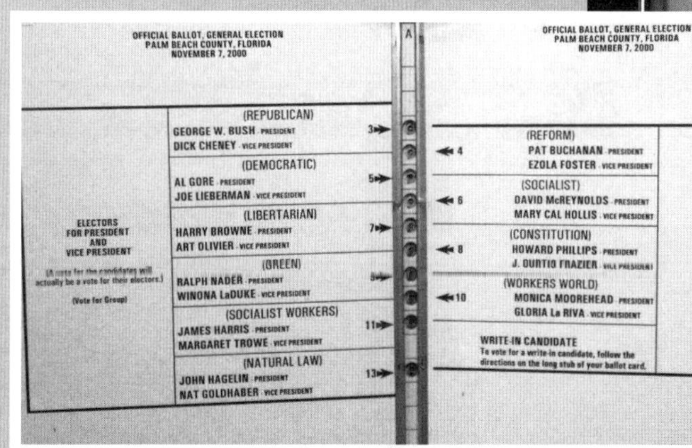


*Palm Beach County's "butterfly ballot" in the 2000 presidential race.*

## QUESTIONS for DISCUSSION

1. In what way was the 2000 presidential election in Florida a cliffhanger?
2. What were chads? Why were they controversial?
3. How was the final decision made in the Florida election?

Contemporary Connection

# The Costs and Benefits of the Electoral College

The **Electoral College** establishes the rules of the game regarding presidential elections. These rules provide important incentives to candidates seeking the presidency. And, like other institutions, the Electoral College comes with costs and benefits.

In nearly all elections, voters vote for the candidate whose name appears on the ballot. But in a presidential election, voters are actually voting for a set of state electors. The electors, in turn, cast their ballots for the president based on the state results.

This probably strikes you as a strange system because, well, it is. Let's think back to the Constitutional Convention of 1787. When it came to figuring out how to select a president, the Founders faced some difficult choices. At the time, no nation elected its national leader. At the time, no national leader operated in a system of checks and balances. None of this had been tried before.

Some Founders favored a direct election of the president by the voters. Another camp favored having members of Congress pick the president. Many wished to provide an essential role for the states. After all, it was a big nation. States in different regions had different concerns. Faced with these clashing views, the Founders came up with a compromise.

Under this compromise, each state had electoral votes equal to the number of its members of the House of Representatives plus two for its two Senate seats.

**MAP 1 State Electoral Votes: Republican Party, Democratic Party, and Swing States**

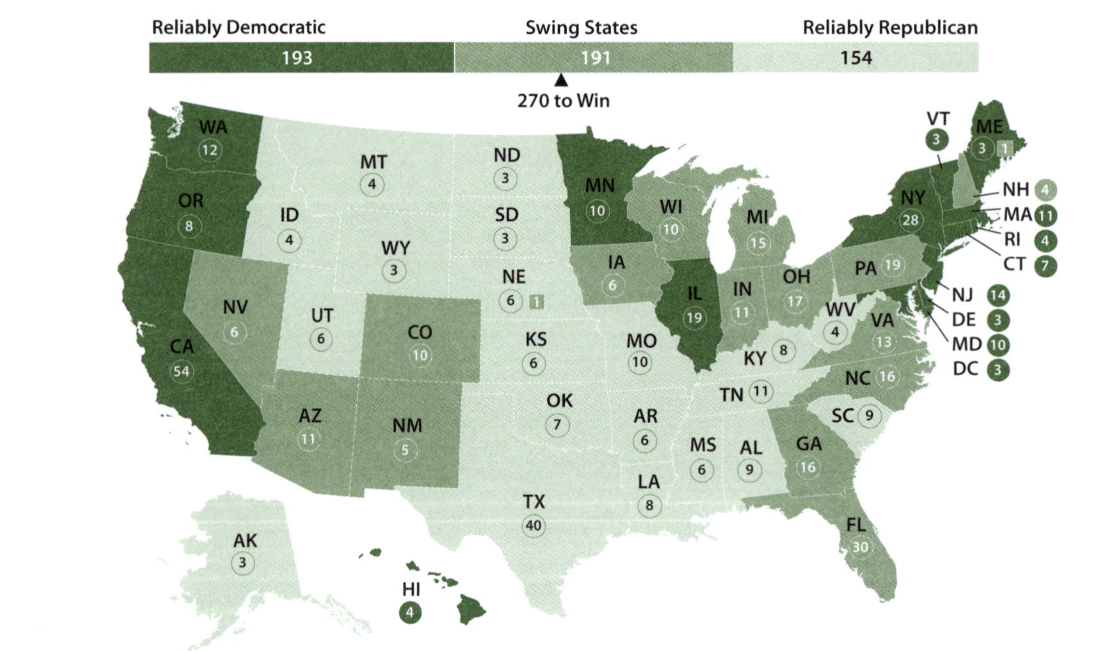

How does the system function today? Today there is a total of 538 electoral votes. To win, a candidate must get a majority—at least 270. States still have a number of votes equal to their House of Representatives plus Senate seats.

The Constitution leaves it to the state legislatures to decide how to distribute their votes. Today, every state gives its votes to the winner of the popular vote in that state. The winner of the popular votes receives all of the electoral votes in most states.

Voters probably imagine the modern presidential election as one national race. But the candidates know better. Every four years, candidates face 51 state elections (including Washington, D.C.) for president.

Let's now turn to the costs and benefits.

Perhaps the biggest benefit is that the Electoral College provides an incentive for candidates to campaign across many regions of the country. Without the Electoral College, there would be an incentive for candidates to campaign only in large metropolitan areas, ignoring small towns and rural areas.

The Electoral College was intended to reduce the influence of the majority. The fear of the Founders was the election of a tyrant who would dominate the other branches of the government.

Finally, the Electoral College tends to magnify the victory margin of the winner, providing a greater mandate. It requires the winner to obtain a majority of electoral votes. The Electoral College also puts a brake on endless recounts or demands for run-off elections.

What about the costs? The biggest criticism of the Electoral College is that it is possible for a candidate to win a majority in the Electoral College but lose the national popular vote. This seems undemocratic. This outcome has happened five times in U.S. history, and it always generates controversy.

A primary fear of the Founders was that poorly informed voters would pick candidates who would abuse the office. This still could happen, but today's modern communications make it possible for voters to be well informed.

Finally, under the Electoral College, most of the candidates' time and money is spent campaigning in swing states. In the colorful language of U.S. politics, there are blue states, red states, and swing states. Voters in red states vote reliably for Republican Party candidates. Texas and South Dakota are examples. Voters in blue states reliably vote for Democratic Party candidates. New York and California are examples. And then there are the swing states. In other words, they are competitive and have gone either way in recent elections. Florida went red or Republican in 2016 and 2020. However, it went blue in 2008 and again in 2012.

## QUESTIONS for DISCUSSION

1. Why did the Founders design the Electoral College the way they did?
2. How does the Electoral College operate today?
3. What are the benefits of the Electoral College?
4. What are the costs of the Electoral College?
5. Do you think the benefits outweigh the costs? Explain.

## Web Quests

**Enter any of the links below and use the questions to get you started on your own web quest.**

### Rights and Responsibilities of Citizens

*Check out this Khan Academy set of videos on citizens' rights and responsibilities.*

**https://www.khanacademy.org/humanities/us-government-and-civics/x231f0f4241b58f49:citizens-us-gov-civics/x231f0f4241b58f49:what-are-the-rights-and-responsibilities-of-citizenship/v/personal-rights**

1. Compare and contrast the personal rights of citizens with political rights.
2. What are the economic rights of citizens? How are they related to personal and political rights?
3. What are the responsibilities and obligations of citizens?

### U.S. Census Voter Turnout Data

*Want to take a deep dive on voter turnout in the 2020 election?*

**https://www.census.gov/data/tables/time-series/demo/voting-and-registration/p20-585.html**

1. What trends do you see in voter turnout by various demographics such as race and age?
2. What trends do you see in voter turnout by education attainment?
3. Use economic reasoning—costs and benefits—to voters to help explain the trends you observed.

### How the Electoral College Works

*The National Archives offers more details on the Electoral College.*

**https://www.archives.gov/electoral-college/about**

1. What is the Electoral College?
2. Who are the electors?
3. What happens after the general election?
4. What are the restrictions on who electors can vote for?
5. What flaws do you see in this process? What benefits do you see?
6. Do you think the costs of maintaining the Electoral College outweigh the benefits?

# CHAPTER 15

## How Do Mass Media and Social Media Affect What You Know about Government and the Economy?

*Presidential candidate Barack Obama addresses a crowd of supporters in Charlotte, North Carolina, in 2008.*

# The Historic Candidacy and the Tech Whiz

Then-senator Barack Obama had a problem: Young people were inclined to support his upstart candidacy for president in large numbers, but they were hard to reach. It was 2007, and most of Obama's young supporters did not read newspapers or watch conventional television. Young voters traditionally did not give money to political campaigns and had low turnout on Election Day. Could Obama's inspirational candidacy change that?

Enter Joe Rospars. At 25 years old, Rospars was a tech whiz who knew technology and politics from his work at startup Blue State Digital. Obama appointed Rospars as his campaign's new media director (a title that had not even existed in traditional presidential campaigns).

From today's vantage point, it may seem odd, but **social media** platforms Facebook, Twitter, and YouTube were new and untested at the time. Rospars used these platforms to connect with Obama supporters, build interest, and collect donations. Rospars even established a new social network at MyBarackObama.com, where registered users could find each other. They were able to create in-person events in their local areas, raise funds, and seek out other local events. Emails and texts kept up interest throughout the campaign.

On Election Day, young voters joined the broad coalition that made Obama the first African American president, delivering a margin of 200 electoral votes. No candidate has since won the presidency without a strong social media strategy.

## KEY ECONOMIC CONCEPTS

**mass media**
**media bias**
**narrative**
**objectivity**
**social media**

*The website MyBarackObama.com in 2008.*

## The Civics Context

### The Town Meeting and the Media

Imagine a town so small that, when it comes to information and government, you can do everything directly. You find out for yourself what's going on, and people make decisions in a town meeting where everyone votes. That would be one small town!

Even in our small nation in 1788, the framers of our Constitution knew things could not be done directly. Rather than making decisions directly, people would elect representatives. And rather than gathering information for themselves, people would rely on newspapers to collect and report information.

In short, people would act through go-betweens, or "intermediaries." Representative government would be one form of intermediary, and newspapers would be another. Today we use the term *media* for information intermediaries between us and current events. Media platforms today include many forms of **mass media** that go for large audiences, such as television, newspapers, and websites. New since 2000 are widespread social media that tailor each user's experience. No one's Instagram feed is identical to anyone else's!

If representative government and media platforms work well, well-informed media consumers cast intelligent votes at the polls. Elected officials are then held accountable by the public, acting on information obtained through the media. All of this is imperfect, however, as we'll see in this chapter.

## Big Differences Between Government and Media

Government and the media are both based on voting, but in very different ways. "One person, one vote" in politics means that anyone has a vote equal to that of anyone else. Even a billionaire or rock star only gets one vote. Majority winners are then declared, and they are called on to govern until the next election. In New York City in 2021, Eric Adams was elected mayor and took office promising to fight crime. If voters do not like how Mayor Adams governs, they can vote him out next time.

The media, like all profit-making businesses, are based on "dollar voting." People cast votes with their dollars. The voting never stops. There is no formal process to sum up the votes. But products and services that do not get enough dollar votes go out of business. That is, if they do not bring in enough dollars to cover their costs and then return a profit, somebody pulls the plug.

Nobody elects the media. But every day, by tuning in to some media outlets and neglecting others, consumers shape the direction of the media.

## The Economics of Media Coverage

All organizations face scarcity, including media organizations. They have limited time and attention. Therefore, media organizations cannot just try to collect every fact and then make sense of it all. Instead they are guided by models of how to do their jobs. The **objective** model of news coverage says that media platforms try to report fairly on current events without showing favoritism, or **media bias**, in their coverage. A news report in the objective style takes a detached viewpoint. It passes along the claims of contending parties and leaves the reader to form opinions.

One traditional form of the objective model is "he said, she said" journalism. Under this form, when a political figure makes a claim, the reporter goes to the opposition for its reaction. In the final news story, the reporter presents both sides without trying to make one look better. All claims are treated skeptically. In crime coverage, even someone caught in the act of a bank robbery is referred to as the "alleged" robber.

The objective model has been criticized because, it is argued, no one can truly report news without favoring one side or the other. Another criticism is that "he said, she said" gives equal weight to both sides when one side may be clearly in the wrong. Thus, denying any wrongdoing gives the guilty party more credit than is due.

*Social media platforms have changed the way many Americans consume news.*

The **narrative** model of news coverage says that media platforms decide in advance on an overall story that they plan to push and then fit news events into that story. For example, a news outlet may decide that government intervention into the economy is generally good and then look for stories that fit the narrative. Stories about the success of a program, complete with video and pictures, advance the narrative. Stories about the costs or unintended side effects are not reported.

Much news coverage cannot be labeled as purely objective or purely narrative. Even seemingly objective accounts can make a non-favored person or position look bad. On the other hand, media platforms looking for a narrative will sometimes question the narrative and reverse course.

In American history there have been waves of objective and narrative coverage. Early in our history, newspapers were fiercely partisan and made no attempt at objectivity. In the mid-20th century, the objective model ruled. Newspapers were careful not to slant their news coverage. TV stations interviewed both sides of contentious stories. This was a time of limited numbers of media outlets, all seeking the largest possible audiences to sell to advertisers. Offending any segment of media consumers was bad business.

Sometime before 2000, the objective model was deserted in large numbers and media platforms turned again to narrative coverage. This coincided with an explosion in the number of outlets available to media consumers. Cable news offered increasingly partisan coverage. It started with a largely objective model, but competition pushed every cable outlet to please its viewers. Talk radio came onto the scene and was especially popular with political conservatives. Apparently, many media consumers like their favorite narrative better than objective coverage.

The fragmentation that began with cable television accelerated after 2000 as social media outlets became prominent. Outlets such as Facebook, Twitter, and Instagram succeeded by rapidly adding followers. These social media platforms make money with "clicks" on stories and advertisements. Early in their history, social media companies discovered that they made more money by delighting and by enraging audiences, not with even-handed coverage of the events of the day. Social media platforms tend to show people viewpoints that they already agree with rather than exposing them to differing ideas.

## A Major "Rule of the Game": The First Amendment

The entire media landscape of the United States has been shaped by a major "rule of the game": the First Amendment. The text of the amendment itself is brief:

> *Congress shall make no law respecting an establishment of religion, or prohibiting the free exercise thereof; or abridging the freedom of speech, or of the press; or the right of the people peaceably to assemble, and to petition the Government for a redress of grievances.*

In short, Congress cannot abridge the freedom of speech or of the press. The idea behind the First Amendment was not that media outlets would individually be fair and objective. At the time, there were many highly partisan outlets. Rather, the hope was that freedom to report and make political statements would result in a "marketplace of ideas" where good ideas win out and bad ideas are discarded. The First Amendment counted on a thriving media market to work, even if individual outlets were highly partisan or even dishonest. With few and limited exceptions, the government would not get to control what is said in the media.

Courts and policymakers are still determining just how the First Amendment will apply to the Internet. At first, the Internet was hailed as a way that anyone could start a blog and become a publisher, thereby guaranteeing freedom of expression. More recently, the Internet has produced giants like Facebook and Twitter that have gained the ability to shape political debate. Media mergers have dramatically reduced the number of truly independent voices.

## Civics Questions & Economic Answers

### Does our system of law and government require media outlets to be fair and objective?

No. They have broad freedom to publish whatever they want, fair or unfair, biased or unbiased. Ideally, informed media consumers will limit misbehavior by media outlets by turning away from those that do not uphold basic standards of fairness. However, consumers are free to reward unfair and biased media outlets with their continued attention.

### Do media platforms seek to maximize profits like many other businesses?

Yes, in a way. As explained in Chapter 1, people respond to incentives in predictable ways. For most media organizations, profits, the money left over after costs have been subtracted from income, are important incentives. Most media organizations are then organized as profit-making businesses. When they see an opportunity to increase profits, they take it, usually by trying to increase their audiences. But the source of revenue makes a big difference in media behavior. When revenue comes mostly from subscribers, content and coverage are arranged to keep those subscribers paying. A common strategy is to emphasize the news and content that subscribers want to hear, shielding them from other opinions or unwelcome content. But when revenue comes mostly from advertisers, media outlets try to maximize their audiences. Outlets going for big numbers of readers understand that slanted coverage may turn some readers away. For these outlets, more balanced coverage is a smart strategy.

Once a media platform has achieved reliable profits, its owners are then free to pursue goals other than profit maximization, such as working for what they see as the public interest or promoting particular political viewpoints. Many successful media outlets would therefore deny that they are profit-maximizing firms, pointing instead to their public service missions.

## How do "network effects" work in mass media and social media?

Network effects occur when you get some benefit out of using a product just because many other people use the same product. Network effects are small for, say, apples. Why do you care if a lot of other people also like Red Delicious apples? Network effects are medium-sized for newspapers and news websites. If your friend happened to read the same article, the two of you can talk about it. But network effects are huge for social media. You get a lot of benefit from being on Instagram if all of your friends are, too. And the more of your friends that join, the more valuable the site is to you. Network effects mean that big, popular social media sites may get bigger and more popular *just because of their size.*

## Why does the government regulate print, broadcast, and web media differently?

Print media are specifically mentioned in the First Amendment ("freedom of the press") and so there is little legal room for Congress to regulate the press. When broadcasting originated in the 20th century, things were less clear. A scarcity of broadcast channels led Congress to establish the Federal Communications Commission with far more power over content than anything similar in the press. When the internet burst onto the scene in the late 20th century, it was not clear that the government could regulate web content even if it wanted to. At the same time, new video technologies greatly reduced the scarcity of broadcast channels. Today, conventional broadcast radio and television is still subject to FCC regulation, but there is little regulation of the content of other media.

## What is political polarization, and how does it affect the media coverage that we see?

Political polarization occurs when attitudes about government diverge, with those on the right moving rightward and those on the left moving leftward. Terminology can differ, but those favoring limited government (on the right) are often referred to as "conservatives," and those favoring more powerful government (on the left) are referred to as "liberals." Whatever the terms used, political polarization has increased sharply, meaning there are fewer voters and media consumers who consider themselves "in the middle." When there were many consumers in the middle, media outlets found it profitable to offer moderate news and opinions to attract the largest audience. Polarization means that there

**FIGURE 1** Increasing Polarization Among Voters

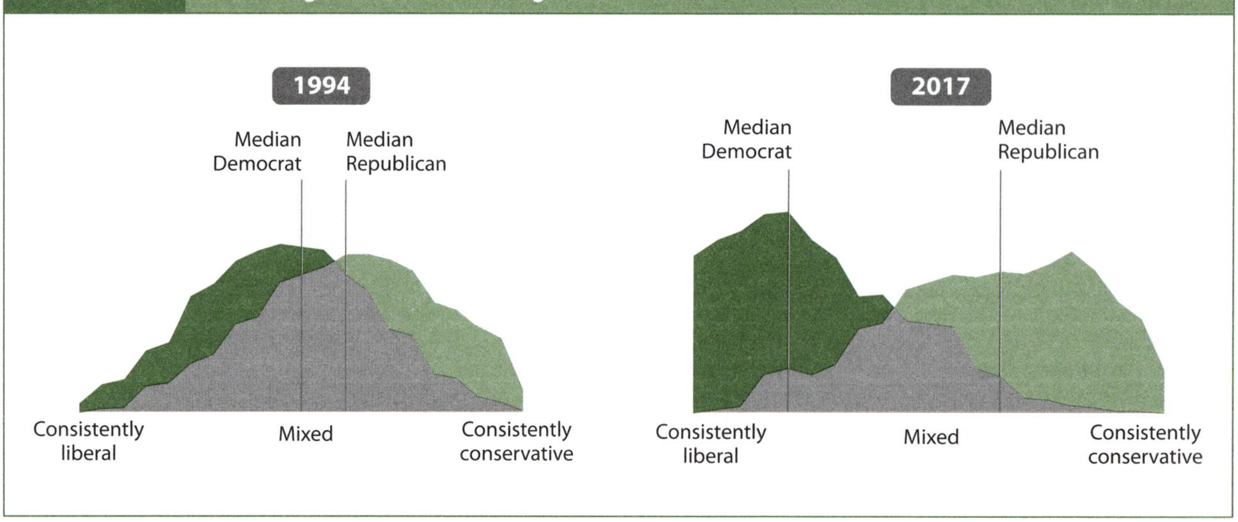


*Source:* Pew Research Center

are more media consumers now who are highly conservative and highly liberal. Many of these consumers prefer not to hear other viewpoints presented fairly. Thus, profits are higher for media outlets that favor extreme views, specifically foregoing the (now shrinking) audiences of moderates.

Although in modern times Democrats have been consistently "left" of Republicans ("more liberal"), in 1994 they were not that far apart. There were large media audiences in the middle of the road politically. By 2017, Republicans had shifted "right" and Democrats had shifted "left." The middle audience was much smaller, and media outlets sought viewers by moving away from the political center.

### Why are people—particularly younger media consumers—increasingly getting their news from comedy talk shows and social media?

Younger media consumers find comedy and social media outlets more pleasant and entertaining than conventional news. They may place a lower value on objectivity and exposure to careful analysis or conflicting viewpoints. Comedy and social media work in part by creating heroes to be praised and villains to be mocked. Difficult policy choices do not make for good comedy material. (When was the last time you heard a good joke about taxation of passive income?)

### What "blind spots" will people have about government and the economy if they only see media accounts they already agree with?

Media consumers who see mostly pro-government narratives will have "blind spots" about the unintended consequences of government policies. Consider rent control, which limits or forbids increases in rent for existing tenants. This helps keep rents affordable but reduces the supply of rental housing. Most economists, liberal and conservative, believe rent controls are bad policy. They point out that rent controls lead to shortages, reduced construction of new units, and poorer maintenance. A pro-government narrative will concentrate on the benefits to the tenants who do get into rent-controlled housing units: their rent is cheaper. The narrative will ignore resulting rental shortages, or it will blame landlords for maintenance issues that they can't afford to fix due to the controls placed on the rent they're legally allowed to charge.

Media consumers who see mostly antigovernment narratives will have "blind spots" about inequality and related subjects. If pro-growth policies such as investment tax credits or free trade increase economic prosperity, coverage will concentrate on the prosperity and say nothing about those who do not gain as much. Emphasis on favorable economic statistics will neglect the state of low-income consumers.

The common element in these "blind spots" is the use of individual case stories. Stories about people make for good reading and interested audiences. Yet all it takes is one nontypical personal story to support a nonfactual narrative.

## QUESTIONS for DISCUSSION

1. Suppose an individual is dissatisfied with a business and a local government. What actions can this individual take in response to these two sources of dissatisfaction? How do these actions differ from each other?
2. Do you tend to prefer objective or narrative coverage? Choose and explain your answer.
3. Why don't elected officials just ignore the media when they believe they are being covered unfairly?

## Dewey Defeats Truman

PRIMARY SOURCE

The election of 1948 did not seem especially close. The sitting president, Harry S. Truman, had taken over with the death of Franklin Roosevelt and was regarded as a temporary caretaker. New York governor Thomas E. Dewey, the Republican nominee, was popular and well qualified. Public opinion polling showed Governor Dewey with a comfortable national lead.

So large was Dewey's lead that pollster Elmo Roper stopped taking surveys in September 1948 and said that unless something changed, there would be no further survey results from him. Dewey ran a low-key campaign with little sense of urgency because of the widespread belief that he would win easily. Truman's campaign gained strength late in the fall, after Roper stopped polling.

In 1948, newspapers worked hard to put an edition on the street with the latest news, and more rapidly than their competitors. They would make up pages in advance using the cumbersome mechanical technology then available. By writing the most likely outcomes into their stories and headlines, they would be ready to start the presses when confirmation came.

On November 4, 1948, *The Chicago Daily Tribune* jumped the gun by declaring Dewey the winner. About 150,000 copies of the newspaper were printed based on opinion polling and the *Tribune*'s veteran political correspondent. As election night wore on, the *Tribune* eventually admitted the error and corrected the story.

A key error in the *Tribune*'s coverage was relying on polls conducted by telephone. At that time, telephone service was not widespread and more likely to be present in Republican households. The sample covered by the polls was therefore much more likely to vote for Dewey.

Two days after the election, Truman was happy to hold up a copy of the incorrect newspaper for gathered photographers. The result was the famous "Dewey Defeats Truman" photo.

## QUESTIONS for DISCUSSION

1. What mistake did pollsters make in the 1948 election?
2. Why wouldn't a newspaper in the 1940s simply wait until the outcome of an election was definite and then compose and print the newspaper?
3. Will a pollster using telephone surveys today get an unrepresentative sample of voters? Why or why not?

Contemporary Connection

## Coverage of Minimum Wage Legislation

The minimum wage is a continuing subject of news coverage. The policy itself is simple: Anyone hired must be paid at least a government-mandated minimum per hour. Standard economic analysis shows that an increase in the minimum wage has benefits and costs. The benefits are the higher incomes earned by those who continue to be employed at the higher wage. The costs result from a reduced incentive for employers to provide jobs at the higher wage.

Employers react to a higher minimum wage in a variety of ways. Some with strong businesses and plentiful cash flow simply raise wages. Others cut back on workers' hours or lay off some workers. Still others may invest in labor-saving technology so that they can hire fewer people in the future.

Responsible coverage of the minimum wage would include all of these elements and the tradeoffs involved. Unfortunately for voters seeking balanced information, coverage is mostly narrative-driven. There are good points to be made in favor of both major competing narratives.

The pro–minimum wage narrative emphasizes the benefits to low-income workers who receive an increase in pay. The benefit is real and important to its recipients, and this positive impact is visible when such employees are interviewed. Some economic studies on the minimum wage show small or nonexistent reductions of unemployment, and these studies may be mentioned in this narrative's coverage. But more often, the pro–minimum wage narrative simply omits discussion of employment effects.

*Fast food workers and their supporters march for an increase in the minimum wage in New York City, 2014.*

The anti–minimum wage narrative concentrates on lost employment among the intended beneficiaries. Coverage may include pictures and interviews showing small businesses struggling to pay the higher minimum wage, but some secondary effects are less visible to the public eye. For example, it's hard to measure or interview all the individuals not getting hired when they otherwise would have been. Some economic studies show significant reductions in employment from a higher minimum wage, and these studies may be mentioned as part of this narrative's coverage.

Media consumers should beware of the phrase "there's no evidence" in the minimum wage debate, as in "There's no evidence that the minimum wage reduces employment" or "There's no evidence that the minimum wage helps poor people." There is in fact evidence for both propositions, and that's what makes coming to a fully reasoned judgment on the minimum wage hard.

## QUESTIONS for DISCUSSION

1. How would an objective approach to an increased minimum wage differ from a narrative approach?
2. If an economic study shows that raising the minimum wage in California during an economic boom had no observable effect on employment, does that guarantee that raising the minimum wage nationally will have no observable effect on employment nationally?
3. Why might someone concerned about employment losses from a minimum wage law remain quiet rather than raising objections?

## Web Quests

**Enter any of the links below and use the questions to get you started on your own web quest.**

### Media Matters

*A left-leaning site with updates and criticism of conservative media.*

**http://mediamatters.org**

1. Have a look at Media Matters' homepage and click a "show more" button if you see one. What source of news is being most frequently criticized by Media Matters? What narrative do you find Media Matters advancing in this criticism?
2. Take a headline from Media Matters that seems biased and write two new versions: one that is neutral and one that is biased in the opposite direction. For example, "Right-Wing Media Undermine Police Reform" might be rewritten as "Conservative Media Stand Up for Police." Which of your headlines do you prefer and why?
3. Which is more common at Media Matters: praise of left-leaning news personalities or criticism of right-leaning news personalities?

### Media Research Center

*A right-leaning site with updates and criticism of liberal media.*

**http://mrc.org**

1. Have a look at the Media Research Center's homepage and click a "show more" button if you see one. Is there a single source of news being most frequently criticized by Media Matters, or are many outlets criticized? Support your answer.
2. Take a headline from Media Research Center that seems biased and write two new versions: one that is neutral and one that is biased in the opposite direction. For example, "Exposing the Media's Blatant Partisanship on Election Laws" might be rewritten as "Coverage Calls Out Vote Suppression Efforts". Which of your headlines do you prefer and why?
3. Which is more common at the Media Research Center: praise of right-leaning news personalities or criticism of left-leaning news personalities?

### News Habits and Media from Pew

*The Pew Research Center's compilation of information on news and news consumers.*

**https://www.pewresearch.org/topic/news-habits-media**

1. Are advertising revenues growing or falling as a source of dollars for newspapers? Other than advertising, how do newspapers get revenue? Is that source increasing or decreasing?
2. Will students your age be avid cable news viewers in the future?
3. How has the split between digital (online) and nondigital (radio, TV, and newspaper) advertising revenue been changing in recent years? Will that trend continue?

# CHAPTER 16

# What Is Free about Free Trade Agreements?

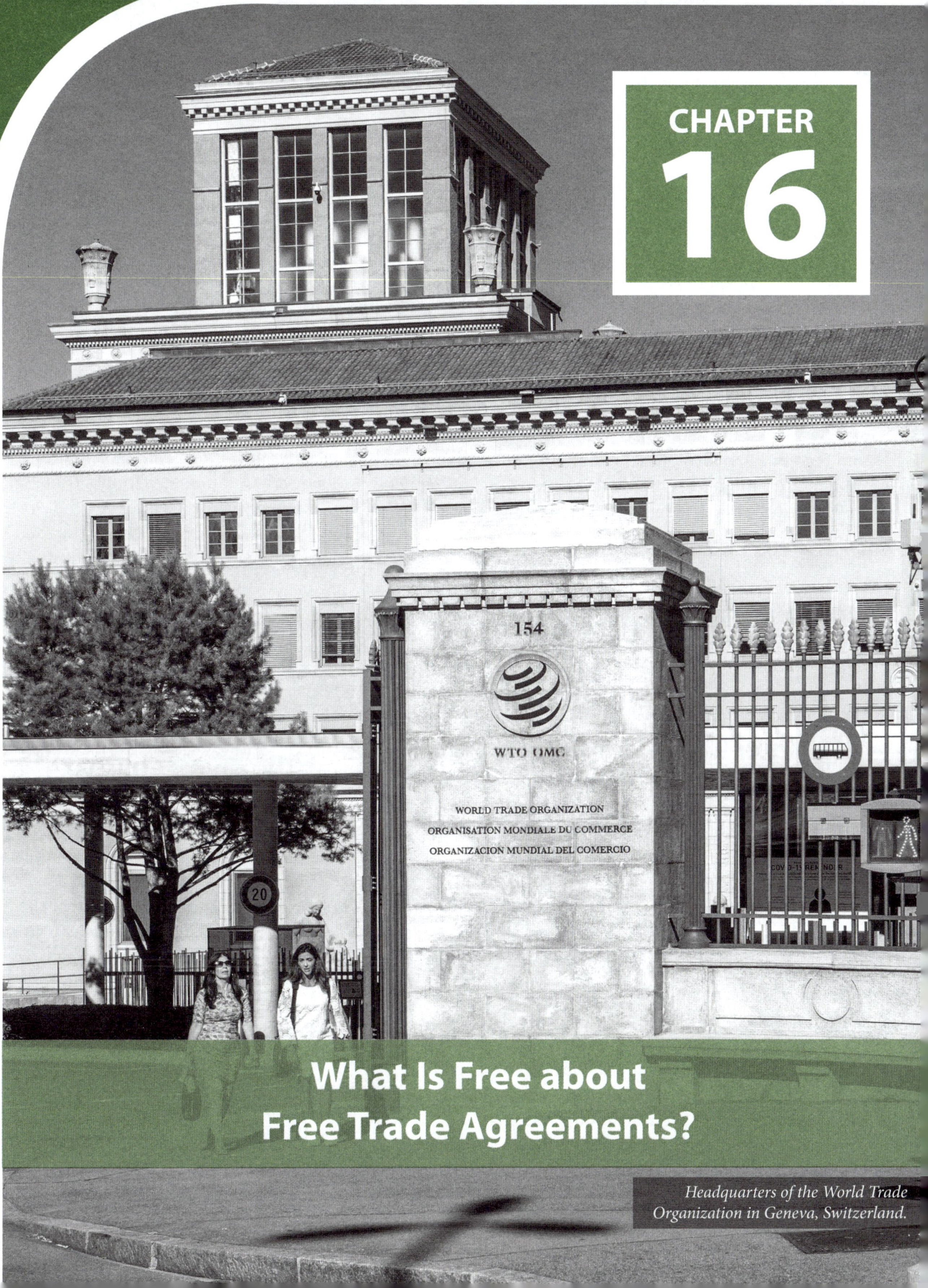


*Headquarters of the World Trade Organization in Geneva, Switzerland.*

# David Ricardo's Long-Standing Trade Ideas

While economists are frequently chastised for not being able to agree on important issues, one area of near unanimity is the benefits of free trade. Economists on the political left (like Paul Krugman) and on the right (like Milton Friedman) have strongly favored free trade in their professional writing and speaking. Recent surveys of well-known economists put support for free trade at near 90 percent.[1]

Beginning with Adam Smith, the first economist, free trade has been viewed as a central contributor to a nation's economic prosperity. David Ricardo, who expanded on Smith's ideas and developed the idea of free trade in its modern and recognizable form, has a continuing influence on today's economic thinkers.

Ricardo was a British political economist and member of Parliament. Born in 1772, the third surviving child of his parents' 17 offspring, Ricardo was close friends with other famous philosophers of his time, including James Mill, Jeremy Bentham, and Thomas Malthus. In Parliament, Ricardo was an adamant supporter of free trade in opposing British laws to establish sugar and timber duties. Most famously, he made a strong case against Britain's Corn Laws. The Corn Laws, with their roots in England going back to the 1400s, were established to encourage exports, restrict imports, and support a mercantilist philosophy of economic prosperity. Largely discredited today, **mercantilism** was the dominant economic idea of the 17th and 18th centuries. It favored using trade to accumulate as much gold and silver as possible.

In fighting mercantilism, Ricardo established a theory on international trade that is still considered generally accurate today. He expanded on the concept of absolute advantage and emphasized a new idea he illustrated called *comparative advantage*. Many mercantilists believed that in international trade one country gained while the other lost. Ricardo countered with the then-novel idea that trade is mutually beneficial to both participants. Ricardo made the point that even if Portugal could produce cloth and wine with less labor, the country would still benefit from trade with England.

David Ricardo

### KEY ECONOMIC CONCEPTS

- **comparative advantage**
- **dumping**
- **embargo**
- **exports**
- **free trade**
- **imports**
- **mercantilism**
- **protectionism**
- **quota**
- **subsidies**
- **tariff**

## The Civics Context

Article I, Section 8 of the Constitution gives Congress the power "To regulate commerce with foreign nations, and among the several states, and with the Indian tribes." This is known as the Commerce Clause of the Constitution. The states regulate trade within their borders, as with any other commercial activity. In practice, Congress' role is to advise, monitor, and legislate on U.S. trade policy issues. The House Ways and Means Committee and the Senate Finance Committee have primary responsibility for trade policy issues. Each of these committees has a subcommittee on trade.

Article II, Section 2 of the Constitution gives the president the "Power, by and with the Advice

*Vice President Kamala Harris Swears in Katherine Tai as U.S. Trade Representative in 2021.*

and Consent of the Senate, to make Treaties, provided two thirds of the Senators present concur." In practice, Congress and the president work together to negotiate and implement U.S. trade agreements. Beginning with the Reciprocal Trade Agreements Act of 1934, Congress delegated limited **tariff** authority to the president to enter into reciprocal trade agreements to reduce tariffs within preapproved levels.

Congress adopted "fast track," or Trade Promotion Authority (TPA), in the Trade Act of 1974. The object was to provide U.S. trade negotiating objectives and quick action on bills implementing future trade agreements while preserving constitutional oversight by Congress. Under TPA, legislators establish trade negotiation objectives and set consultation or reporting requirements for the executive branch. The agreements then negotiated by the president receive an "up or down" vote in Congress. "Fast track" means that no amendments to these agreements are permitted. Without "fast track," deals that have been struck with foreign governments, often over many rounds of negotiations, could be endangered by special interests.

For most of U.S. history, the State Department was responsible for negotiating all trade agreements. In 1962, Congress created the Office of the United States Trade Representative to separate the commercial interests of trade from U.S. foreign policy goals. By statute, the U.S. Trade Representative (USTR) is the lead U.S. trade negotiator. Key trade policy components pursued by the USTR include the following:

- Bilateral, regional, and multilateral trade and investment issues and agreements;
- Expansion of market access for American goods and services;
- Negotiations affecting U.S. import policies;
- Oversight of complaints against foreign unfair trade practices and import relief cases;
- Trade-related intellectual property protection issues; and
- World Trade Organization (WTO) issues.

More than a dozen government agencies, commissions, and international courts have jurisdiction over some aspect of U.S. international trade policy. Many of these agencies work closely with USTR. Several government agencies collect detailed trade-related economic data used by the public and private sector. Others deal with enforcement of international trade laws and the distribution of U.S. aid to developing nations.

### Department of Commerce

The Commerce Department has several offices devoted to trade. Various Commerce Department offices assist U.S. businesses with practical advice on trade and country-specific resources. They also investigate potential violations of fair-trade agreements and help American firms overcome foreign barriers to trade to gain market access. The U.S. Commercial Service, another office within the Commerce Department, promotes U.S. exports abroad and lobbies for market access and protection of U.S. exports abroad. The Commerce Department also maintains a web portal called Export.gov, which offers a wide array of information for exporting firms geared toward first-time exporters.

Other Commerce agencies that focus on trade include:

- Census Bureau: Maintains foreign trade statistics that track and categorize U.S. exporters by state, product, and destination country.
- Industry and Security Bureau: Regulates the export of sensitive goods and technologies, and cooperates with other countries on export control and strategic trade issues. Also assists U.S. industry in complying with international arms control agreements.
- Patent and Trademark Office: Enforces U.S. trademarks and intellectual property in international jurisdictions. Acts as an advisor to the Department of Commerce and the president in matters of patent and trademark law.

### Department of Labor

The Department of Labor coordinates international economic trade, immigration, and labor policies with other government agencies. The agency focuses on international child labor standards and implements labor accords in international agreements. The agency also researches the impact of U.S. and international trade and immigration policies on U.S. workers.

### The Department of Health and Human Services

The Department of Health and Human Services (HHS) enforces the Federal Food, Drug and Cosmetics Act, which protects the health, safety, and commercial interests of consumers. HHS also coordinates with U.S. Customs to oversee regulations on imports. The agency alerts retailers, brokers, wholesalers, and consumers of imports that have been detained. HHS also coordinates safety aspects of trade in U.S. and foreign markets.

### Department of Agriculture

The Department of Agriculture oversees market development, international trade agreements, and negotiations related to U.S. agricultural exports. The department collects and analyzes statistics and market information on agricultural trade and international markets. Another of the department's functions is to administer food aid programs. It helps increase income and food availability in developing nations by mobilizing expertise for agriculturally led economic growth.

### Department of the Treasury

The Treasury Department patrols U.S. borders to intercept illegal drug shipments and other illegal goods, enforces U.S. tariffs, and provides advice to firms or people that want to import goods into the United States. Treasury also administers and enforces economic and trade sanctions against targeted foreign countries, terrorism-sponsoring organizations, and international narcotics traffickers based on U.S. foreign policy and national security goals.

### Department of Justice

The Department of Justice coordinates international efforts to combat computer crime, such as hacking, piracy, and violation of

*The U.S. Food and Drug Administration (FDA) is a federal agency of the Department of Health and Human Services.*

intellectual property violations. The agency also enforces the Economic Espionage Act, deterring and punishing the theft of trade secrets.

## Department of Transportation

The United States actively promotes the flow of commerce over the world's oceans and waterways. Over 95 percent of American imports and exports are carried by ship, and the majority of these ships are foreign-flagged. The Coast Guard is the lead agency for developing uniform international standards that apply to ships worldwide. The Coast Guard also assists U.S. Customs in enforcing U.S. laws and treaties, through multi-agency counter-drug operations and seizure of illegal contraband.

The Federal Highway Administration maintains and administers America's network of highways and other federal roads. The administration creates and enforces regulations governing the size and weight of trucks and other commercial vehicles on U.S. roads. These regulations, along with others, are important in cross-border trade with Canada and Mexico.

## Department of State

The State Department's Bureau of Economic and Business Affairs promotes U.S. business interests overseas. The Bureau's Trade Policy and Programs Division works to increase trade by opening overseas markets and freeing the flow of goods, services, and capital. The division works closely with USTR and other government agencies to expand open market approaches to trade. Its mission includes everything from reducing foreign trade barriers to promoting U.S. interests within the World Trade Organization.

### U.S. Court of International Trade

Congress, with the Customs Courts Act of 1980, equipped the federal judicial system to handle the increasingly complex problems arising from international trade disputes. The court reviews civil actions arising out of import transactions under federal law. The president, with the advice and consent of the Senate, appoints the nine judges of the U.S. Court of International Trade. The judges are appointed for life. The court, located in New York, has national as well as international jurisdiction.

### The Export-Import Bank of the United States

The Export-Import Bank is an independent federal agency aimed at helping exporters become more competitive in the global marketplace through export finance programs. The Export-Import Bank provides guarantees of working capital loans for U.S. exporters and guarantees the repayment of loans. It may also directly make loans to foreign purchasers of U.S. goods and services and provides credit insurance against nonpayment by foreign buyers for political or commercial risk. The Bank focuses on exports to developing countries.

## The Economics of Trade

The United States is the world's largest economy and international trader. In recent years, U.S. markets and production have become more integrated, especially with emerging economies. The 2020 top U.S. trading partners were Canada, Mexico, China, Japan, and the United Kingdom (UK) and, as a bloc, the European Union.

From thc vicwpoint of the United States, imports are goods and services bought from people in another country. Exports are then goods and services produced in the United States and sold elsewhere. The United States has a long-running trade deficit, meaning U.S. imports exceed U.S. exports. Conversely, countries such as China and Germany run a persistent trade surplus, a condition in which their exports exceed their imports. In popular commentary, trade deficits are considered to be bad. Politicians tend to attribute trade deficits to unfair trade practices or bad trade agreements. Most economists, on the other hand, are not particularly concerned with trade deficits. They also point out that macroeconomic variables (aggregate savings and investment, valuation of the dollar) play a larger role in determining the U.S. trade deficit than trade practices or agreements.

Economic reasoning shows how international trade can be beneficial at the national level, but

**FIGURE 1 U.S. Exports and Imports—2000 to Present**

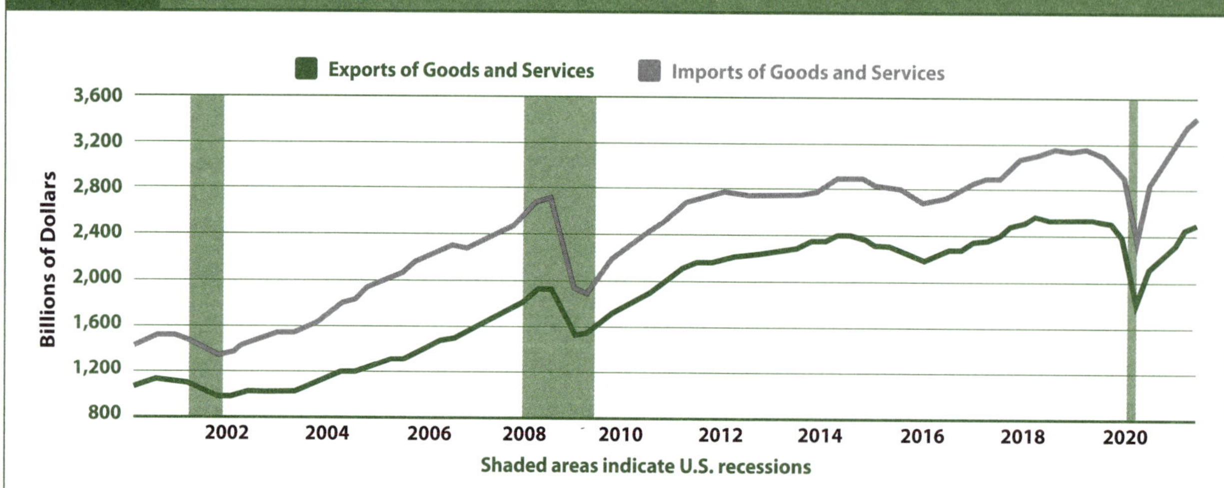


*Source:* U.S Bureau of Economic Analysis

*The Export-Import Bank of the United States assists in financing and facilitating U.S. exports of goods and services.*

benefits and costs may be unevenly distributed or concentrated. A nation is more prosperous on net with **free trade**—the ability to buy and sell goods and services from foreign countries without tariffs, quotas, or other restrictions. Still, it is also true that not everyone in the country is better off. In the face of generally favorable international trade, some people will find their jobs or businesses displaced by foreign competition.

Countries increase production and export goods and services in areas in which they have a relative comparative advantage through skills or resources. At the same time, they import goods and services unavailable domestically or less efficiently produced. **Comparative advantage** refers to the ability of a business in one nation to produce a good or service at a lower opportunity cost than a business in another nation. Benefits of trade include more efficient resource allocation, greater productivity, and greater choice for consumers and firms who purchase imports. The benefits come about through competition, specialization, and the advantages of large-scale production ("economies of scale") enabled by trade. Costs can include losses of jobs, wages, and entire firms as imports create competition and motivate the relocation of production.

The benefits of comparative advantage can be thrown off track by politics. This helps explain the case for the "fast track" authority mentioned above. Why would Congress need to restrict itself to a straight "up or down" vote on a negotiated trade agreement? Why not allow amendments to be proposed and voted on as with other measures?

The answer lies in the interest group effect outlined in Chapter 8. A good trade agreement will create large overall gains in an economy, but they will be diffused over the entire economy. Specific sectors, on the other hand, will find concentrated benefits or costs. The U.S. steel industry will get a large benefit from restricted trade in steel, even as the economy would be better off with the ability to buy steel from all over the world. Members of Congress from steel-producing areas have every reason to try to amend a broad free trade agreement to protect steel. But others in Congress want to protect their favorite industries, too.

With the interest group effect in full operation, a trade agreement may get amended beyond recognition. Further, the agreement may then not be acceptable to the negotiators for other countries who hammered it out over months or years of talks. A simple "up or down" vote can thwart the interest group effect while still letting Congress exercise its constitutional authority. In the end, the overall benefits of a trade agreement can win the day, and yet it's much harder if multiple special interest amendments have to be fought off first.

## Civics Questions & Economic Answers

### Do free trade agreements assure free trade between countries?

No. Free trade agreements generally lower or eliminate tariffs on most of the goods and services traded between nations. Free trade agreement may be bilateral (between two nations) or multilateral (among more than two countries). Whatever the number of countries, even the most comprehensive trade agreements have "carve outs" that exclude some areas from free trade. Under the wide-ranging United States-Mexico-Canada trade deal (USMCA), described later in this chapter, Canada still has a "carve out" for its dairy industry. This exception to free trade includes steep tariffs, quotas, and price supports for its dairy industry. Canada charges among the world's highest tariffs on imported ice cream at more than 95 percent.

### If free trade can make both countries better off, why would a nation impose trade restrictions?

National security is one common reason for blocking free trade in some goods. As an example, in March 2018, the Trump administration imposed a 25 percent duty on steel and 10 percent duty on aluminum imports into the United States. The argument was that the United States must maintain adequate steel manufacturing capacity should it be needed in a time of war.

Another argument for import restrictions is to protect an infant industry. A nation may seek to establish a new industry, but the new small industry may not be able to compete with larger international rivals. The idea is that these "infant industries" must be protected until they can attain needed efficiencies. Such **protectionist** policies would be imposed in the short term but later removed when the new industry was ready to compete internationally. American's first Secretary of the Treasury, Alexander Hamilton, made such an argument in his 1790 Report on Manufactures as Hamilton argued for the need to protect infant industries to establish an industrial base.

A final reason a country may establish protectionist policies is to shield domestic jobs from competition. In an effort to protect domestic agricultural jobs, many developed nations maintain extensive programs of tariffs and quotas on their farm goods. In Europe, such policies have led to surplus production of agricultural goods that some have referred to as mountains of butter and lakes of wine.

### What kinds of protectionist tools can be used to restrict free trade?

There are a number of tools used by nations to restrict international competition and trade. Import tariffs are one of the top tools a government uses when seeking to enact protectionist policies. In general, all forms of import tariffs are charged to the importing country and documented at government customs. Import tariffs act as a tax and raise the price of imports for a country.

Import **quotas** are non-tariff barriers that limit the quantity of products that can be imported over a set period of time. The purpose of quotas is to limit the supply of specified products coming in. Quotas may also be put in place to prevent **dumping**, which occurs when foreign producers export products at prices lower than production costs. An **embargo**, which completely prohibits the importation of designated products, is the most severe type of quota.

Product standards can also be a barrier that limits imports. Some countries may have lower regulatory standards in the areas of food preparation, intellectual property enforcement, or materials production. This can lead to a product standard requirement or a blockage of certain imports due to regulatory enforcement. Overall, restricting imports through the implementation of product standards can often lead to a higher volume of product production domestically.

Government subsidies can also be used to promote domestic businesses. Generally,

*A WTO public forum in Geneva, Switzerland, in 2014.*

subsidies provide businesses with cash payments or special savings such as interest-free loans and tax breaks. Export subsidies provide an incentive for domestic businesses to expand globally by increasing their exports internationally.

### Can economic sanctions be used as a foreign policy tool?

The United States maintains sanctions programs against many countries around the world.[2] The Office of Foreign Assets Control (OFAC) of the Department of Treasury administers and enforces economic sanctions based on U.S. foreign policy and national security goals. In many cases, sanctions involve trade restrictions or even an embargo. The United States maintains near-total economic embargoes on Iran, Cuba, North Korea, and Syria.

### What is the World Trade Organization (WTO)?

The current rules-based multilateral trading system is rooted in the WTO, established in 1995 to succeed the General Agreement on Tariffs and Trade (GATT). Formed in 1947, the GATT was part of the post–World War II effort led by the United States and Europe to build a stable, open, and prosperous global economy. The WTO is based in Geneva, Switzerland, and has 164 members that represent 98 percent of world trade.

The WTO operates the global system of trade rules and helps developing countries build their trade capacity. It also provides a forum for its members to negotiate trade agreements and to resolve the trade problems they face with each other.

## QUESTIONS for DISCUSSION

1. Explain the concept of comparative advantage.
2. What are some arguments countries make for trade restrictions (such as tariffs or quotas)?
3. Describe some areas of the federal government that are involved with international trade.

# USA Free Trade Agreements

PRIMARY SOURCE

The United States has free trade agreements in force with 20 countries, via 14 free trade agreements, as described in Table 1.

**TABLE 1 Nations with Free Trade Agreements with the United States**

| Year Initiated | Agreement |
|---|---|
| 2004 | Australia Free Trade Agreement |
| 2006 | Bahrain Free Trade Agreement |
| 2015 | Dominican Republic – Central America Free Trade Agreement |
| 2004 | Chile Free Trade Agreement |
| 2012 | United States – Colombia Trade Promotion Agreement |
| 1985 | Israel Free Trade Agreement |
| 2001 | Jordan Free Trade Agreement |
| 2012 | United States – Korea Free Trade Agreement |
| 2004 | Morocco Free Trade Agreement |
| 2009 | Oman Free Trade Agreement |
| 2012 | U.S.-Panama Trade Promotion Agreement |
| 2009 | Peru Trade Promotion Agreement |
| 2003 | Singapore Free Trade Agreement |
| 2020 | United States – Mexico – Canada Agreement |

**MAP 1 Nations with Free Trade Agreements with the United States**

*Source: World Trade Organization*

*President Barack Obama greets South Korean President Lee Myung-bak at a State Dinner at the White House following the passage of a free trade agreement with South Korea in 2011.*

## QUESTIONS for DISCUSSION

1. Pick two of the free trade agreements the United States maintains and research their details. How do they work? What goods or services are covered under the agreements? Are any excluded?
2. What geographic pattern do you see in the nations that have free trade agreements with the United States?
3. The first free trade agreement the United States signed was with Israel. What is the history of that agreement?

Contemporary Connection

## NAFTA to the USMCA

The United States-Mexico-Canada Agreement (USMCA) went into effect July 1, 2020. The USMCA replaced the North America Free Trade Agreement (NAFTA), a trade pact eliminating most trade barriers among the three North American countries that went into effect in January of 1993. Most economic analyses of NAFTA concluded that it was beneficial to all three North American economies and to the average citizen of these nations. However, studies also show that there were short-term harms borne by a small minority of workers in industries particularly exposed to trade.

The USMCA agreement is an updated version of the 25-year-old NAFTA trade deal. During President Donald Trump's 2016 presidential campaign, he promised to renegotiate NAFTA, frequently referring to it as a flawed trade deal. The USMCA agreement includes major changes on auto production rules, labor and environmental standards, intellectual property protections, and some digital trade provisions. Some examples of the changes between the two agreements include:

- Under the USMCA, automobiles must have 75 percent of their components manufactured in Mexico, the United States, or Canada to qualify for zero tariffs. This is up from 62.5 percent under NAFTA.

*Leaders of the United States, Mexico, and Canada sign the USMCA in 2018.*

- USMCA requires that about 45 percent of automobile parts must be made by workers who earn at least $16 an hour by 2023. This wage is substantially higher than most manufacturing workers earn in Mexico. Further, Mexico agreed to pass new labor laws that protect workers and migrants and make it easier for Mexican workers to unionize.
- Canada agreed to open a small part (about 3.5 percent) of its dairy market to U.S. farmers. Under NAFTA, Canada imposed very high tariffs on all dairy imports, making the market effectively closed to American farmers.
- USMCA extends the terms of copyright to 70 years beyond the life of authors (up from 50 under NAFTA). It also includes provisions to deal with the digital economy such as prohibiting tariffs on things such as music, e-books, and movies.
- Unlike NAFTA, which was designed to last indefinitely, the USMCA has a 16-year sunset clause. The agreement will expire in 16 years and also is subject to review every six years, at which point any of the three nation partners can decide to extend the agreement.

## QUESTIONS for DISCUSSION

1. What are the costs and benefits to the United States from the changes contained in the USMCA from the prior NAFTA agreement?
2. Why did the United States fight hard to have the USMCA require Mexico to pass new labor laws?

## Web Quests

**Enter any of the links below and use the questions to get you started on your own web quest.**

### World Trade Organization

*Visit the webpage of the World Trade Organization.*

**https://www.wto.org**

1. Briefly describe the history of the WTO.
2. How does a country become part of the WTO?
3. What countries currently have trade disputes in front of the WTO?

### Office of the United States Trade Representative

*Visit the webpage of the Office of the United States Trade Representative.*

**https://ustr.gov**

1. Who is the leader of this office? What is this person's background and training for the appointment?
2. Pick one free trade agreement the United States maintains with another country and write a brief summary of the agreement.

### Meet FRED

*Visit the St. Louis Federal Reserve's FRED database.*

**https://fred.stlouisfed.org**

1. Make a graph of U.S. next exports of goods. What do you observe?
2. Make a graph of U.S. next exports of services. What do you observe?
3. Make a graph of U.S. next exports of goods and services. What do you observe?
4. Pick one other country that FRED has trade data for and graph U.S. net exports of goods and services with this nation. What do you observe?

# CHAPTER 17

# What Is Civil Society? What Role Might You Play?

*The American Red Cross, a nonprofit humanitarian organization, provides support after a fire and explosion in Manhattan's East Village, 2015.*

# Robert L. Woodson Sr.: Civil Rights and Neighborhood Empowerment Leader

Robert L. Woodson Sr. is an important participant in what is called civil society. But he did not start out that way. Woodson was born in 1937 in South Philadelphia. His father, a World War I veteran, died when he was young. His mother raised five children but struggled financially.

Woodson had a troubled childhood and didn't do well in school. He dropped out of high school and joined the U.S. Air Force at age 17. While in the military, he completed a high school equivalency program. After leaving the Air Force, he was admitted to Cheyney State College in Cheyney, Pennsylvania, the oldest historically black college in the country.

As a graduate student at the University of Pennsylvania, he became involved in the civil rights movement. He managed several community development projects and directed the National Urban League Department of Criminal Justice. Always something of a maverick, he disagreed with civil rights leaders at the time who believed that schoolchildren should be bused to schools outside of their neighborhoods to achieve racial balance in schools.

*Robert L. Woodson Sr.*

### KEY ECONOMIC CONCEPTS

**civil society**
**human capital**
**non-government organizations (NGO)**
**nonprofit organizations (NPO)**
**self-interested behavior**
**social entrepreneur**
**voluntary exchange/trade**

Woodson changed course again. He founded the Woodson Center in 1981. He became a pioneer of what became known as the neighborhood empowerment movement. His focus was on youth. His approach was to help low-income neighborhoods address their problems through their own actions rather than depending on government assistance. Woodson focused on troubled youth living in tough neighborhoods. For example, he established Violence-Free Zones in many communities. There you might find him or his local colleagues counseling gang members and eventually hiring them to patrol basketball courts so their younger brothers and sisters could play in peace.

Woodson's programs have helped thousands of community groups across many states. His work has done much to reduce gang violence, school absences, and police arrests. His programs also helped provide ownership opportunities in former public housing units.

Woodson's work is a small part of what happens in America's vast civil society. Civil society might be thought of as a third sector, different from business and government, which includes a highly diverse set of voluntary organizations supported by voluntary donations of time and money. Read on to learn more.

*Volunteering at a soup kitchen is an example of being engaged in civil society.*

## The Civics Context

### Civil Society

Are you a member of an after-school club? Ever play in a community soccer, football, or baseball league? Have you run or walked in a 5K fundraiser to raise money for a homeless shelter? Have you volunteered at a soup kitchen or a thrift shop? If you have been involved in these projects or something similar, then you, like Robert Woodson Sr., are engaged in civil society.

**Civil society** includes the thousands of voluntary organizations that are largely untouched by government or business. Civil society includes private schools and universities, advocacy groups, charitable organizations, professional associations, religious organizations, cultural institutions, and more.

Civil society provides a wide range of services. Many organizations provide education. Others provide services to the poor and underserved. Still others provide important information for citizens, defend citizen rights, engage in advocacy, and offer alternative policies for government, the private sector, and other institutions. Examples include the American Bar Association, American Civil Liberties Union, Rotary International, Ford Foundation, American Enterprise Institute, Human Rights Watch, Red Cross, Salvation Army, Sierra Club, Freedom House, National Organization for Women, the Heritage Foundation, and more than a million others.

Most economists and political scientists agree that a democratic system is not sustainable without a well-functioning civil society. It fills gaps left by the public and private sectors. It gives individuals the opportunity to directly engage in community life. Civil society helps the public and private sector function better largely through voluntary activity.

## The Economics of Civil Society

Civil society has institutions that come in many shapes and sizes. Most often it includes nonprofit organizations. A **nonprofit organization (NPO)** is an enterprise that is granted tax-exempt status by the Internal

Revenue Service. Its income is used to address the cause it has identified rather than being used to earn profits. The tax-exempt status of NPOs provides an important incentive for motivated individuals to start up such organizations. There are about 1.3 million NPOs in the United States.

**Non-government organizations** or **NGOs** are another form of NPO. NGOs are often involved in international humanitarian or economic development projects. There are about 1.5 million NGOs in the United States. NGOs typically focus on international humanitarian projects such as relieving hunger. Others concentrate on economic development projects such as launching innovative ways of providing clean water to local villages.

Social enterprises are relative newcomers to civil society. These are projects run by **social entrepreneurs**. Social enterprises might be NPOs, but they might also be businesses. The idea is to be innovative in approaching a social problem. So, a social entrepreneur might run a coffee shop that hires people just out of jail or prison to help them develop work skills and earn a steady income. Another might be a financial institution that makes microloans to help women start small businesses.

Finally, grassroots associations are another form of civil society. They are different from NPOs and NGOs. While NPOs and NGOs often hire paid staff, grassroots organizations are characterized by depending on volunteers to get things done. It could be a storefront church, a chess club, or a neighborhood soup kitchen.

Four economic concepts will help us to better understand the contributions of civil society to our nation and the world:

- Voluntary exchange
- Incentives to care for others
- Investments in human capital
- Contributions to gross domestic product (GDP)

*Volunteers plant a tree.*

Civil society exists because of **voluntary exchange and trade** (see Chapter 1). NPOs receive voluntary donations from individuals, foundations, and corporations. Donations go toward supporting religious organizations, arts and culture, education, health, human services, disaster relief, the environment, and so forth. More than 60 million people donate their time as volunteers to NPOs. If you could put a price tag on all of the donated time, it would approach $200 billion. Remember, no one can force an individual to donate time and treasure to these causes.

All of this voluntary exchange might strike you as odd. Back in Chapter 1, we discussed that self-interested behavior is a feature of being human. **Self-interested behavior** means that we are pursuing outcomes that we value. It is easy to see self-interested behavior in our decisions as consumers. When people buy new running shoes on Amazon, many will carefully check the quality and the prices of various alternatives. Consumers of running shoes are trying to purchase shoes that best align with their self-interest.

It is harder to see self-interested behavior in the context of civil society. And yet many decisions we make are about caring for others. This is a big part of our lives. We vote, do volunteer work, visit people in need, and make donations to charities. Remember, economic thinking suggests that people respond to incentives in predictable ways. If this is true, then there must an incentive that encourages us to be generous in caring for others. Adam Smith, the founding economist, is well known for telling us about self-interest within a market economy. However, in his early work *The Theory of Moral Sentiments*, he explains why we are generous:

> How selfish soever man may be supposed, there are evidently some principles in his nature which interest him in the fortune of others and render their happiness necessary to him though he derives nothing from it except the pleasure of seeing it.[1] (page 9)

Smith says that part of human nature is to care for others—that is our incentive to be generous. He must be right. According to the National Philanthropic Trust, Americans gave $471.44 billion in 2020. Individuals make up nearly 70 percent of all giving. The remainder comes from foundations, corporations, and the estates of individuals who have passed away.[2]

Now, let's turn to investments in human capital. A significant number of NPOs are involved in education. In economics, formal schooling at private schools and universities is an investment in human capital. **Human capital** refers to the knowledge, skill, and work habits that enable workers to be productive. There are about 35,000 private K–12 schools in the United States, serving about 10 percent of all students. There are about 1,660 private colleges in the United States. About 20 percent of all college students attend a private college or university. There is a strong relationship between formal education attainment and income. Because of these civil society organizations, people give money to improve the lives of students, most of whom they will never meet.

But human capital involves more that formal schooling. The mission of many NPOs is to improve the lives of others, and that often means supporting programs to serve the disadvantaged. NPOs across the nation help people to become healthy, eat healthy food, have temporary shelter, get over addictions, develop communication skills, and learn basic career skills such as being on time and having a good work ethic. These programs all represent examples of investments in human capital.

The Brookings Institution is an NPO based in Washington D.C. that has made many contributions to human capital. Its overall mission is to conduct in-depth research that leads to new ideas for solving problems that are facing society. Brookings brings together more than 300 experts from all over the world to provide high-quality research and policy recommendations. One focus of its research offers serious advice for young people for improving their human capital.

Brookings scholars Isabelle Sawhill and Ron Haskins have found that achieving economic success—joining the middle class—is highly probable if individuals follow what they call the "success sequence."[3] Using data from the U.S.

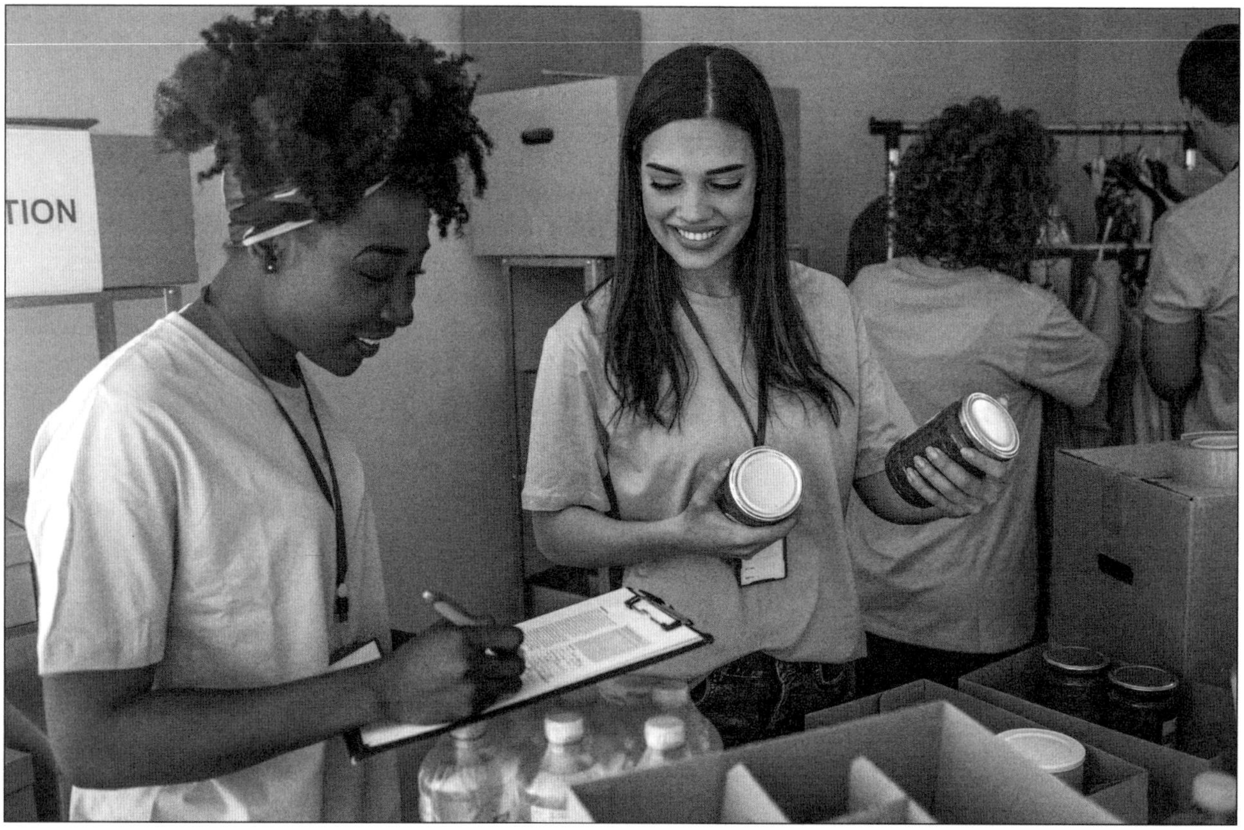

*Volunteers sort donations for a food drive.*

Census Bureau, they found that about three-quarters of Americans reach the middle class when they

- graduate from high school;
- get a full-time job; and
- wait until after age 21 to become parents.

Sawhill, Haskins, and other scholars believe that young people can benefit from knowing and following the success sequence. It provides youth from all backgrounds with a sense of agency, taking responsibility for what is happening in their lives. Some critics say that this emphasis on agency deflects policy leaders away from other social problems. They may have a point. But the research is clear that following these commonsense norms can make a big difference in the lives of young people. It is a data-supported, nonpartisan approach to lift people out of poverty.

Finally, it is easy to see that civil society enhances the lives of individuals. It not as easy to see its direct economic contributions. In Chapter 6 we explained that gross domestic product (GDP) is the total value of all goods and services produced within the United States during a certain period of time. Civil society provides a large contribution to GDP. The National Council for Nonprofits report that NPOs spend nearly $1 trillion annually for goods and services. NPOs spend money on computers, software, rent, food, and so forth. Even with these large numbers, NPOs' contribution to GDP may understate the real contribution to economic well-being. When a park is cleaned up or children are tutored by NPOs, good things happen that are not captured in official statistics because they are not directly paid for. Moreover, NPOs employ over 10 percent of America's private workforce.[4]

## Civics Questions & Economic Answers

### Does the federal government provide funding to NPOs?

Yes. Federal and state governments cooperate to provide funding to NPOs, which, in turn, provide community services. Meals on Wheels programs are a good example. Meals on Wheels programs deliver meals to the homes of low-income senior citizens. Federal funds come to the states and are then allocated to local NPOs. An average local Meals on Wheels program receives 35 percent of its budget from the federal government. So, while federal spending is an important part of their budgets, these programs still depend on additional funding sources—voluntary giving—to carry out their mission.

### Why might local NPOs be more effective in addressing issues such as poverty and violence than federal programs?

Programs directly administered by the federal government face challenges. Economist F. A. Hayek argues that information is widely dispersed. It is difficult for a government bureau in Washington D.C. to know what is necessary to serve people in a local community. Such needs are better understood by people operating at the local level.[5] NPOs in local communities have their "boots on the ground." For example, they are likely to know who needs help with nutrition or violence. Robert Woodson Sr.'s Violence-Free Zones are an example of programs run at the grassroots level.

The federal government is relatively good at promoting uniformity through regulations and at moving large sums of money. But when a social problem calls for custom-tailored local solutions with smaller amounts of money, civil society organizations have the edge.

### Has the increase in federal spending to reduce poverty affected voluntary giving?

This question interests many economists. It is called the *crowding out hypothesis*. Crowding out occurs when individuals reduce giving to a NPO as a resulting of government funding for that NPO. As an example, private donors might give less to a food bank that gets new federal anti-hunger funding. The logic is straightforward.

*People pick up trash at a local park.*

Why should individuals donate to a charity when taxpayers are doing it for them?

But wait. It might be a little more complicated. People give for many reasons including feeling good about themselves and, as Smith points out, caring for others. So, it would be extreme to see private donations completely crowded out (reduced dollar-for-dollar as government funding went up). Some studies even find "crowding in," or an actual increase in private donations when a NPO gets government grants. After a natural disaster, people may give more to the American Red Cross even as the news reports that there is increased government disaster assistance.[6] "Crowding out" is a long-standing concern, but it also appears that "crowding in" is possible.

## QUESTIONS for DISCUSSION

1. What is civil society?
2. How is civil society different from the public sector and the private sector?
3. What is an NPO?
4. How does Adam Smith explain why people are generous to others?
5. What role do NPOs play in investing in human capital?
6. What is the success sequence?
7. What role do NPOs play in increasing GDP?
8. What advantage do NPOs have over programs administered directly from Washington D.C.?
9. What is the crowding out effect?

# Charitable Giving in the United States and Around the World

PRIMARY SOURCE

The Charities Aid Foundation in the United Kingdom, among other things, periodically tracks the donations made to charities by individuals. One study presents the amount of charitable giving by individuals as a percentage of total GDP. Figure 1 shows the percentage of GDP donated to nonprofit organizations by individuals in 24 nations.

**FIGURE 1** Charitable Giving by Individuals as a Percentage of GDP

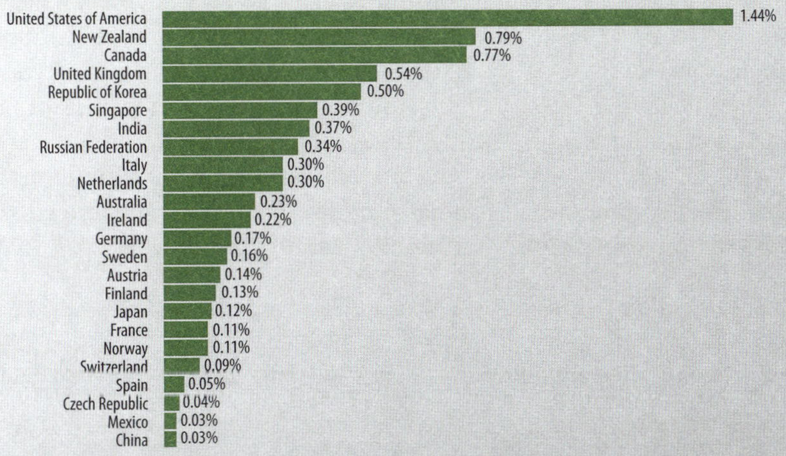


As you can see, the highest-ranking country in charitable giving as a percentage of GDP is the United States. The United States is followed by New Zealand, Canada, and the United Kingdom.

Nations in other parts of the world also in the top 10 include Singapore, India, and Russia. The study found that the amount of charitable giving was not related to levels of taxation and levels of government spending. Finally, the study found that there was a relationship between charitable giving and other aspects of civil society such as volunteering time and helping a stranger.[7]

## QUESTIONS for DISCUSSION

1. What do you think explains the high level of charitable giving in the United States as well as other nations including New Zealand, Canada, and the United Kingdom?
2. Why do you think there would be a relationship between volunteering time and giving? Explain.

Contemporary Connection

## Your Role in Today's Civil Society

Feeling inspired? Want to get involved helping others? It's easy to join civil society:

- Volunteer for an existing NPO.
- Start a grassroots association.
- Start your own NPO.

### Volunteer

Maybe you wish to do something to improve the environment, help the homeless, tutor young students after school, fight cancer, or help provide shelter for animals. There are many NPOs in your community that would welcome your help as a volunteer (or perhaps as an employee). Ask around and do some web searches, and you are almost certain to turn up organizations in which you have an interest.

### Start a grassroots association

Do you see a need in your school or community that you think you can help address? You don't have to work through an existing NPO. Think about starting your own grassroots association with friends or family. Identify a need that interests you. Maybe you can put your finger on something that others are not already doing. Here are three examples just to get you thinking:

- Perhaps a nearby elementary school has an after-school program. Maybe you and your friends wish to set up an association to work as volunteer tutors.
- Love chess? Think others would benefit from learning how to play? Start a club at school. Meet after school, at lunchtime, or maybe during a study hall.
- Worried about the hungry in your community? Organize a fundraiser with your friends and donate the proceeds to a local food bank.

### Start your own NPO

Do you have an innovative idea about how to help others? You might consider starting your own NPO. You would be in good company. In fact, many high school and college students have done just that.

There are several steps involved. There may be an organization in your community that can help you with the resources to get started. A few of the steps involve the following:

- Do research on the problem you wish to address.
- Develop a business plan, which means setting out your goals, your specific strategy to address the problem, how you will raise funds, and so forth.
- Appoint a board of directors.
- File an application with the state agency that allows you to incorporate your NPO.

The Food Recovery Network (FRN) is an example of a how a small, student-led NPO became a national operation. FRN today is a large movement working to fight hunger, but it had humble beginnings. Four students from the University of Maryland noticed that a lot of food was going to waste in their dining hall. They began to explore how food could be recovered and delivered to people who needed it. Now there are 181 student chapters on campuses in 45 states. FRN has recovered millions of pounds of food. FRN includes a network of 4,000 students, alumni, dining providers, national partners, and local businesses that are all involved in recovering food that would otherwise have gone to waste and using it to help feed the hungry.

## QUESTIONS for DISCUSSION

1. What might be a project in your school or community that could interest you in getting involved?
2. What are three ways that you could get involved in civil society?
3. What are some of the steps in starting an NPO?

## Web Quests

**Enter any of the links below and use the questions to get you started on your own web quest.**

### JA Worldwide

*If you have some interest in an NGO that prepares young people for employment and entrepreneurship, you might check out JA Worldwide at the following link:*

**https://www.jaworldwide.org**

1. What is the mission of JA Worldwide?
2. What are one or two of the programs run by JA Worldwide?
3. In what ways does JA Worldwide have a global reach?

### Alexis de Tocqueville on American civil society

*Americans have been engaged in civil society for a long time. Alexis de Tocqueville was a French aristocrat, diplomat, political philosopher, and historian who traveled America in 1831. His book,* Democracy in America, *is one of the most influential books of the 19th century. You may wish to read about his observations regarding civil society in the early days of the republic. Click on the link below and read Volume 2, Section 2, Bullet 5.*

**https://xroads.virginia.edu/~Hyper/DETOC/toc_indx.html**

1. How does de Tocqueville explain why Americans tend to form so many associations?
2. How is today's civil society similar to what de Tocqueville observed in 1831?
3. How is today's civil society different from what de Tocqueville observed in 1831?

### Food Recovery Network

*If you would like to take a deeper dive regarding the story of the Food Recovery Network, click on this site:*

**https://www.foodrecoverynetwork.org/chapters**

1. How did the Food Recovery Network get started?
2. Describe its operations today.
3. What is the impact of the Food Recovery Network?

### National Council of Nonprofits

*Interested in learning more about what it takes to start an NPO? Visit the National Council of Nonprofits:*

**https://www.councilofnonprofits.org/tools-resources/how-start-nonprofit**

1. What are the main steps in starting an NPO?
2. What do you think would be your biggest hurdle in starting your own NPO?

CHAPTER 18

# A Citizen's Guide to Financial Independence

# A Former Waitress Teaches Others How to Prosper

Today, Suze Orman is well known for her work as a financial advisor. She has written 10 *New York Times* best-selling books about personal finance, she was the TV host of *The Suze Orman Show* between 2002 and 2015, and she is now the host of the *Suze Orman Women and Money Podcast.*

Today, she is financially successful and teaches others how to succeed. But back in 1980, she had a different story. Back then she was working as a waitress and had been given around $50,000 in loans from friends and family to help her start her own restaurant. A broker ended up investing and losing the entirety of what had been loaned to Suze. What went wrong? Isn't investing for the future a good thing? Well, it turns out that the broker had invested Suze's money in a rather risky investment strategy: trading options.

Is there a way to invest for your future without taking on such a huge risk? As will be shown, your relationship to your government depends partly on how financially independent you are. This chapter will show you some methods for moving toward financial independence without taking a great deal of risk.

*Suze Orman*

### KEY ECONOMIC CONCEPTS

**exchange traded fund (ETF)**
**indexed funds**
**managed funds**
**S&P 500 (Standard & Poor's 500 Index)**

## The Civics Context

As a citizen you may cast votes and engage with elected officials to seek change. If you are able to move toward financial independence, then you can have a direct effect on your own life without having to win anybody's political support. Consider the roles you may play in the economy and how these roles interact with government:

If you are an *employee*, you are working for someone else. You know you have a paycheck coming in, unlike those who open their own small businesses. You may have less flexibility in your work schedule, and you have a boss to answer to. Your role as an employee is regulated and mediated by government at all levels through its policies on labor and employment.

If you are an *entrepreneur* and you've chosen to open your own business, then you are "working for yourself." The rewards are potentially much greater than for employees of a larger organization, but so are the risks. Again the government sets the tone for your business, sometimes promoting, sometimes regulating, and almost always taxing it.

At any point in your economic life you may be a *saver* by spending less than you receive and putting that amount into a bank or other financial institution. That relationship will be affected by institutions such as the Federal Reserve and your state bank regulators.

At various points you may be a *borrower*, and at other times a *lender*. People generally tend to borrow money during the early stages in life when they're pursuing a higher education, buying a

*Spending less than you receive is the single most important rule for financial success.*

house, or starting a business. People tend to enter into the lending stage later in life once they're more financially secure. Most of this happens in regulated financial markets.

Another role you can play in the economy is that of an *investor*. In this role, you commit money to a financial asset such as a stock or bond, hoping to receive a return in the future. As with the aforementioned roles, you operate in the context of "rules of the game" set by government.

Our economic system, with its mix of governmental and market institutions, works best if people are able to build financial independence. We have social safety net programs like unemployment compensation to help people through temporary hard times. We also have more permanent safety net programs for the elderly and for disabled individuals. But what can you do to build your own financial success? Let's have a look.

## The Economics of Building Financial Success

Building financial success starts with investing in human capital—that is, increasing your knowledge and skills to become a productive employee or entrepreneur. This means you want to stay in school and obtain your high school diploma. From there, you can decide what form of additional human capital best suits your needs. It could be anything from learning a skilled trade to a four-year college degree or graduate study. The important thing is to acquire knowledge and skills that make your labor valuable to others. In terms we saw earlier, you want to develop your own personal "comparative advantage."

The single most important rule for financial success is: *Spend less than you receive*. This is not easy for people on low incomes, but it points the way to future success by moving into a position to earn more or by budgeting to spend less. When you spend less than you receive and save the difference, it becomes possible to have an emergency fund—savings equal to three to six months of essential expenses.

With an emergency fund of savings in place, you will be prepared when various unexpected (yet inevitable) things break and need repair. For example, when you have unexpected car repairs you'll be able to pull savings out of your emergency fund rather than, say, having to pull money out of long-term investments to cover the expense. Or, if you have an unexpected emergency surgery for your beloved pet, you'll be able to pay the veterinarian bill from your emergency fund rather than putting it on a credit card.

If you work somewhere that offers an employer-sponsored savings plan, this will typically be your best first step in investing for your retirement. You'll see those plans labeled as "401(k)" or "403(b)," for the section of the tax law that authorized them. Many firms offer an "employer match" that adds to the money you put into your account. Standard and smart advice says you should take full advantage of an employer match.

*Long-term investments make the most of compound interest.*

As you save and invest, you get an important boost from the power of compound interest. Compound interest is the interest earned on both the original amount invested (principal) and the accumulated interest. In other words, you're earning interest on interest. This is why the standard advice is to *start investing early* to be able to make the most out of the compound interest on your investments.

To finance their operations, corporations issue shares of stock. Those who buy the stock become fractional owners of the company and receive financial returns. Stock ownership has long been seen as accessible only by upper-income individuals. However, in recent years, changes in technology and markets have made stock ownership widely available, even to those without much money to invest. This has brought both opportunity and risks, but for those willing to educate themselves, simple strategies can promote financial fitness with relatively little risk.

One such strategy for long-term investing has three key parts:

1. **Start investing early**. This provides the advantages of compound interest. Even for those who come to investing later in life, starting is better than waiting.
2. **Buy and hold**. This strategy says most investors should "buy and hold," rather than "buy and sell" (jumping in and out of markets). The long-term benefits of holding stock are well established in the U.S. economy. In the short term, any stock investment can be risky.
3. **Diversify**. This advice says not to "put all your eggs in one basket." A small investor concentrating on one stock faces a large risk from the company's potential bad performance or even its bankruptcy. Today there are investments available that spread an investor's "eggs" across many financial baskets. These include everything from high-flying technology stocks to low-risk assets issued by established utility companies.

## Civics Questions & Economic Answers

### Is it realistic to assume people of limited means can become financially fit?

A common reaction is to say that personal financial advice does not apply to people of limited means—they simply can't save or invest. The implication would then be that our society should expand our social safety net because people cannot become financially fit on their own. To be sure, people with low incomes face challenges securing adequate housing, medical care, and many other things. However, volunteers who counsel low-income adults report success from financial education programs that help people carefully budget and spend income, develop emergency funds, and avoid financial mistakes. These volunteers also report that low-income adults frequently have not taken full advantage of available social safety net programs.

There are two different visions of individuals and government behind this question. Some people prefer a larger governmental safety net and consider a slower growing and less dynamic economy as a worthwhile tradeoff if it means lower income individuals have a better quality of life as a result. Others believe a more dynamic and growing economy generates more opportunity for all members in society, leading to a more prosperous nation.

### How can people without special expertise build wealth using financial markets?

Because of some 20th-century innovations, the advice above to "buy and hold" and to diversify your investments does not require special expertise. Specifically, mutual funds were established to take small amounts of money from many investors, pool those funds, and invest in many stocks on their behalf. On their own, investors would find it difficult to own shares of stock in many different companies. But when their money is pooled together in mutual funds, owning these diversified shares is made easy through a single stock market purchase. Those investing at work in 401(k) or 403(b) plans will often have financial counseling available.

Investors often find *indexed* mutual funds to be particularly useful. Such a fund does not try to pick winning stocks, but instead buys and holds many stocks that track a particular stock market index or other key stock market indicator. The first indexed mutual funds, for example, were set up to buy stock in the 500 large corporations represented in the **Standard & Poor's 500 Index (S&P 500)**. These mutual funds have an astonishing record of success when bought and held over the long term. Another form of investment that can track a stock market index such as the S&P 500 is called an **exchange traded fund (ETF).** An ETF is traded throughout the day (and its pricing fluctuates throughout the day) while the stock market is open, whereas a mutual fund is priced just once per day when the stock market closes. But the idea is the same: pooling investors' funds to give access to many different stocks.

### What is the government's expected role in preventing fraud in financial markets?

The U.S. Securities and Exchange Commission (SEC) has a key role. The SEC is a large independent agency of the U.S. federal government, tasked with regulating the securities markets and protecting investors by enforcing the law against market manipulation. The SEC's stated mission is to (a) protect investors, (b) maintain fair, orderly, and efficient markets, and (c) facilitate capital formation. The SEC requires publicly traded companies to submit quarterly and annual reports, and the agency maintains an online database called EDGAR (the Electronic Data Gathering, Analysis, and Retrieval system), where investors can access information filed with the SEC.

## Does buying and holding indexed funds actually work?

As we saw, an indexed mutual fund does not try to pick winners but is instead designed to hold everything in a particular stock market index or other indicator, such as the S&P 500. But not all mutual funds are indexed. Some of the funds are managed mutual funds that deliberately try to pick "winning" stocks. The portfolio manager generally has a research team, and these individuals work together to try to figure out which combination of stocks will maximize the investor's rate of return. The portfolio manager decides which stocks to purchase and when they will be bought or sold.

Intuition tells many people that an expert picking winning stocks will beat a strategy that does not try to pick winners. That intuition, however, is incorrect. **Indexed funds** designed to mirror the S&P 500 have historically *beaten* the returns of **managed funds**! You heard that right: Indexed mutual funds and ETFs set to index themselves to the S&P 500 more often than not *get better returns* than the funds that are managed by an "expert." Further, indexed mutual funds tend to have lower fees involved. Managed funds have higher fees associated with their purchases to pay the salaries of the research team.

There are countless reports and articles confirming that the S&P 500 historically outperforms managed funds. It's not impossible to beat the returns of the S&P 500 in any given year, but a managed fund consistently beating the S&P 500 year after year for an extended time is extremely unlikely.[1]

## How can a regular citizen who is a novice investor stay informed about the current performance of managed versus indexed funds?

To keep up with how the S&P 500 index is doing compared to actively managed funds, look at the data and reports published by SPIVA (this stands for S&P Indices Versus Active, published by a division of S&P Global).

Comparing managed funds against their benchmark (in this case, matching some comparable funds against the S&P 500) is one way to evaluate performance. The following are the percentage of large-cap funds in the United States that underperformed the S&P 500 (data as of June 30, 2021):[2]

FIGURE 1 Percentage of Large-Cap Funds that Underperformed the S&P 500 — Over 10 Years

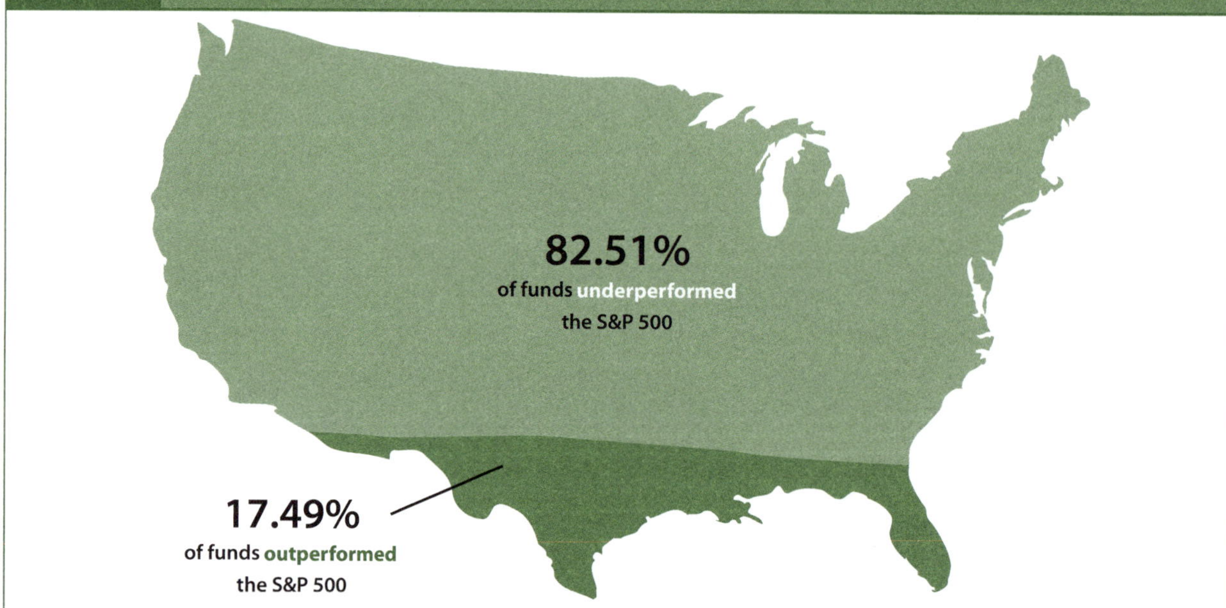


*Source:* S&P Global

- In the past year, 58.2 percent of funds underperformed the S&P 500.
- In the past three years, 67.64 percent of funds underperformed the S&P 500.
- In the past five years, 72.67 percent of funds underperformed the S&P 500.
- In the past 10 years, 82.51 percent of funds underperformed the S&P 500.

Even the top performing funds that were able to outperform the S&P 500 find it hard to surpass the benchmark in consecutive years. What if we took the top-performing managed funds that succeeded in outperforming the S&P 500, and we tracked how many were able to outperform the index in subsequent years? Out of the 819 large-cap funds in June 2019, 244 (i.e., 29.8 percent) of large-cap funds managed to beat the S&P 500 in the first 12-month period ending in June 2019. Only 128 out of the 244 "winners" (i.e., 52.5 percent of the 2019 "winning" funds, or 15.6 percent of the original 819 large-cap funds) managed to again beat the S&P 500 in the next 12 months ending in June 2020. Even more astounding, only 30 (i.e., 12.3 percent of the initial 244 "winners," or 3.7 percent of the total 819 large cap funds) were able to beat the S&P 500 for a third year in a row (by the end of June 2021).[3]

Another way to evaluate the performance of managed funds is to measure their persistence to do exceedingly well. One can create different thresholds for what it means to be successful. Let's have one definition of success be the funds that perform within the top quartile (the top 25 percent) of funds. Looking at all the domestic funds during the time period of June 2019 through June 2021, only 4.8 percent of the superstar funds that were in the top quartile in June 2019 were able to remain as winners in the top quartile at the end of this two-year period. And if you widen the time horizon to five years (beginning in June 2017), only 2.37 percent of all domestic funds managed to remain in the top quartile in June 2021 at the end of the five-year period. Meanwhile, only 3.08 percent of all large-cap funds managed to remain in the top quartile during this five-year period, and 0 percent of the mid-cap funds were able to accomplish this (that's right, *none*!).[4]

If in the future actively managed funds start outperforming the S&P 500, consulting SPIVA will be the way to find that out. But for now, choosing an actively managed fund gives the average investor a low probability of beating the average returns of the market as measured by the S&P 500.

## How can an average citizen who is a novice investor reduce risk when investing?

Two important forces to reduce investment risk are diversification and time. First, instead of buying an individual stock with the hope that it'll do well, make sure your investment is well-diversified. One way of doing this is to buy a mutual fund that tracks a market index, as previously discussed.

Second, try not to pull your money out of your investments prematurely. Jumping in and out of the market is risky. The risk of holding stocks is lower when you hold them for a lengthy period of time.

From 1950 to 2019, the S&P 500 saw positive returns for 55 years during the 70-year period. What's more, there were double-digit positive returns during 43 of the years. There were negative returns for only 15 years throughout the 70-year period.[5]

## How can a citizen ensure a comfortable retirement?

The foundation of retirement income is Social Security. Individuals pay in during their working lifetimes. As they pay in, their taxes pay current retirees. Then when workers retire, they have qualified for benefits paid by the taxes of the current workers at that point in time.

However, Social Security benefits by themselves are not high enough to provide for a comfortable retirement. Thus, individuals who want more must save for retirement. Retirement systems are subject to controversy, with some favoring much more generous Social Security benefits and others insisting that it's up to individuals to make their own provisions for retirement.

You may save in ordinary accounts for retirement, but there are also individual retirement accounts (IRAs) that receive favorable tax treatment of two different kinds:

With a traditional Individual Retirement Account, you receive the tax benefits up front. Your contributions to your traditional IRA are tax deductible. This means that your contributions go into the IRA pre-tax (without that income being taxed), which makes your tax liability lower that year. Because you received your tax benefit at the time you made the contribution, this means that later down the road when you go to withdraw the funds from your traditional IRA, these funds will be taxed as regular income. Similar rules apply to traditional 401(k) and 403(b) plans: tax savings now but not later. A Traditional IRA does not have an income limit, meaning you are eligible to invest in a Traditional IRA even when you have a high annual income.

With a Roth IRA, you do *not* receive any tax benefit up front. This means if you invest a portion of your salary into your Roth IRA, the contributions go in as after-tax income. You will not lower your tax liability for that year. That said, because you don't receive any tax benefit at the time of contribution, you will receive your tax benefit later on: You will not owe any taxes when you go to withdraw your funds upon retirement! People might prefer a Roth IRA if they expect their investment to grow thanks to compound interest and they don't want to owe taxes on the millions of dollars they expect their investment to grow into, if they expect to be in a higher tax bracket later in life when they want to withdraw the funds, or as a safeguard to the political uncertainty of a future tax rate. (If tax rates increase in the future before you are able to withdraw your retirement funds, the higher tax rate won't impact the retirement funds that

are placed in a Roth IRA because you have already paid your tax burden upfront at the time of contribution.) However, there are income limits eligibility to contribute to a Roth IRA, meaning those with high incomes beyond a given threshold aren't eligible to make a contribution to a Roth.

Both Roth and Traditional IRAs have contribution limits (the amount you are allowed to contribute in a given year). The contribution limits and the income eligibility thresholds change slightly from year to year (and also differ depending on your tax filing status), so you'll want to look up the figures for the current year.

Your decisions about retirement saving are yours to make. The public policy decisions about whether and how to subsidize retirement saving belong to the overall political system.

*A decision to start early with retirement planning helps lay the foundation for future financial security.*

## QUESTIONS for DISCUSSION

1. How does an actively managed mutual fund differ from an indexed mutual fund?
2. Historically, which type of investments tend to have greater returns over the long term: managed mutual funds or indexed mutual funds? Provide some relevant statistics to support your answer.
3. What does it mean to "not put all your eggs in one basket"? What are a few ways one can mitigate risk when investing?
4. What are a few benefits of choosing a Roth IRA over a Traditional IRA? Why might someone opt to instead invest in a Traditional IRA?

# An Online Compound Interest Calculator by the SEC

PRIMARY SOURCE

There are several compound interest calculators online. One is the Compound Interest Calculator within the website Investor.gov, which is run by the U.S. Securities and Exchange Commission (SEC). (The direct link is https://www.investor.gov/financial-tools-calculators/calculators/compound-interest-calculator.)

You can specify various aspects to make the estimate of the future value of your investment more accurate for yourself. These inputs include your initial investment, the amount you plan to contribute every month, the number of years of contributions, the estimated interest rate, and the compounding frequency. (Will your interest be compounded annually, semiannually, monthly, or daily?)

**FIGURE 2 Investment Growth Over Time**

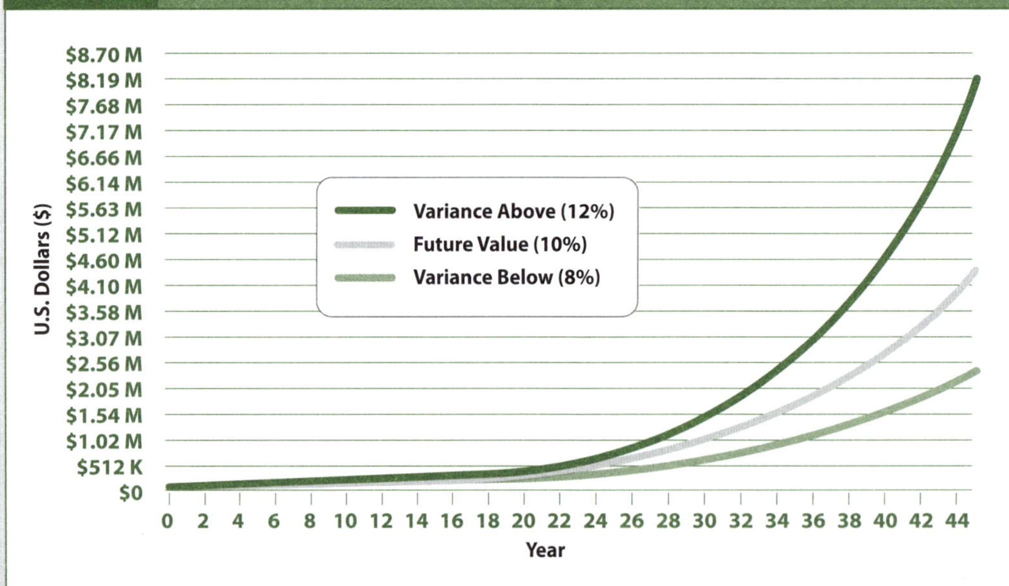


*Source:* Investor.gov

The results shown in Figure 2 are produced when you enter the following specifications:

- Initial Investment: $0
- Monthly Contribution: $500
- Length of Time in Years: 45
- Estimated Interest Rate: 10
- Interest Rate Variance Range: 2
- Compound Frequency: Annually

In 45 years, your total investment would be about $4.3 million if your average annual interest rate ends up being 10 percent. If your average annual interest rate ends up doing a little better than that—say, 12 percent—then you're looking at somewhere around $8.1 million. If your average annual interest rate ended up being around 8 percent, then you're still looking to have around $2.3 million by the time you retire.

Keep in mind, you can tweak all the above listed specifications to better fit your own budget and financial goals. Perhaps you plan to invest longer than 45 years, or you plan to contribute a greater amount toward your investments. Play around and see the difference that each change makes for the estimated future value of your investment.

## QUESTIONS for DISCUSSION

1. Which will result in a greater total amount of money in your investment account: annual compounding or semiannual? What about monthly versus daily?
2. What are a few different things you can change to allow your investment to grow more? (For example, you can invest for a longer period of time. What else can you do?)

Contemporary Connection

## Choosing Your Career Path

Before selecting a career, it is important to make sure that the services you plan to supply are actually in demand. Do others want to hire people with the types of skillsets and knowledge that you'll be acquiring? Jobs in the STEM fields tend to be in high demand. STEM stands for Science, Technology, Engineering, and Mathematics. You may want to consider majoring in something related to these fields, whether you pursue college, technical school, or some other route.

When making a career decision, you'll want to consider: your comparative advantage (What are you good at? What do you tend to excel at more than others?), your interests (What do you enjoy doing?), and the market demand for each line of work along with the expected salary range for each career path.

Also keep in mind that if you enjoy a particular activity but you decide not to pursue it as your career, you can still incorporate such an activity into your life. Perhaps you love music. You don't have to be the lead singer of a band or even work in the music industry to enjoy music as a hobby. You could volunteer to join the band at your local church and perform during the service on Sundays, or perhaps you'll make it a point to go to a certain number of concerts every year.

Maybe you get great enjoyment out of various types of art and you're considering specializing as a landscape painter, or a sculptor, or a wildlife photographer. If you decide to become a teacher, or an optometrist, or an accountant, you can still be an artist and enjoy it as a hobby, and maybe you can still sell your artwork to produce supplementary income.

You can have many hobbies, so even if you don't choose something as your career, you can still enjoy your favorite parts of life! When choosing what career path is best suited for you, it's important to balance many considerations, including your comparative advantage, your interests, the market demand, expected salary range, and flexibility in your work schedule.

### QUESTIONS for DISCUSSION

1. Which jobs and careers do you find interesting? Name three different career paths you're considering. What are some pros and cons of each?
2. Should salary expectations be the sole consideration when you're choosing your career? What other things should you also weigh when making a career decision?
3. If you really enjoy something but decide not to pursue it as your career, what are other ways you can still incorporate that activity into your life? Give an example that is specific to an activity that you enjoy.

## Web Quests

**Enter any of the links below and use the questions to get you started on your own web quest.**

### Calculating Compound Interest

*The Power of Compound Interest Calculator by Signè Thomas.*

https://www.signethomas.com/materials/investmentcalculator

1. Select the **Basic Version** of The Power of Compound Interest Calculator. What happens if you start investing at age 22 versus if you wait until age 30 to start investing? For Person A, enter 22 as the "start age" (the age you plan to start investing) and enter 67 as the "end age" (the age when you plan to retire and pull out your investment). Enter 10 percent as the annual interest rate (your expected annual rate of return), and enter $6,000 as the amount invested annually. For Person B, keep everything the same but enter 30 as the start age. What happened to your total investment by delaying investing for those 8 years when you're in the early stages of your adult life? (Be sure to scroll down to view the full results.)
2. What happens if you delay retirement and work a few extra years? Let Person A's specifications stay the same as before (start investing at age 22 and stop investing to retire at age 67), but let's change Person B's specifications. Enter 22 as the age Person B plans to start investing, and enter 75 as the age Person B plans to stop investing to retire. Leave the annual interest rate as 10 percent and the amount invested annually as $6,000. How much additional money does The Power of Compound Interest Calculator estimate someone's investment to be worth if they continue working, saving, and investing up until age 75 rather than retiring at 67?
3. Select the **Advanced Version** of The Power of Compound Interest Calculator. With the Advanced Version you are able to play around with different scenarios where you may want to invest different amounts during different stages of your life. Perhaps you have a goal to always invest at least $6,000 each year, but you set a goal to invest $10,000 instead of $6,000 every 5 years. Or, perhaps you have a goal to always invest at least $6,000 each year while you're in your 20s, $7,000 each year while you're in your 30s, $8,000 each year in your 40s, and so on. Play around with various scenarios that you think may be pertinent for your own life.
4. Now use the **Advanced Version** of The Power of Compound Interest Calculator to see what happens when Person A invests only for a few years in the early stages of their adult life (but leaves the investment in their brokerage account or their IRA to keep compounding until they decide to retire), compared to when Person B invests the same amount of money each year for a longer period of time but got a later start when it comes to their initial investment. (Before beginning, you may want to reset the Advanced Calculator to clear out the specifications you entered during Part 3 of this web quest.) Enter 10 percent as the annual interest rate and $6,000 as the annual amount invested for each person. For Person A, enter age 22 for the "start age," and enter age 67 as the "end age" (when they plan to retire). For Person B, enter age 32 as the "start age" and enter age 67 as the "end age." Then, for Person A, clear out the fields for ages 33 through 67 so that it shows $0 being invested for those years instead of $6,000. (To view the full results, be sure to scroll down to the bottom of the page.) Who ended up having more in their retirement account upon retirement at age 67? Was Person B ever able to "catch up" to Person A, given that Person B contributed a lot more money into their brokerage account (or their IRA) over the years?

**Occupational Outlook Handbook (OOH)**

*This website is created by the U.S. Bureau of Labor Statistics and uses real-world data of people across the United States to provide statistics and other information about various occupations.*

**https://www.bls.gov/ooh**

1. Select three different jobs you might potentially be interested in pursuing. Compare the median pay, the number of new jobs (projected), and the growth rate (projected) for each.
2. Within the list of "Occupation Groups," select "Computer and Information Technology." All of these fall within STEM, but they require different skillsets and even different levels of education for entry-level positions. What do computer and information research scientists do as part of their job? What level of education is required for an entry-level position for this occupation? What is their median pay? Compare this to the job description, entry-level education, and median pay for a computer programmer. Which of these occupations has the better job outlook? (Click the link for each occupation to view additional information, including the projected job outlook.)
3. Compare and contrast two occupations within the "Architecture and Engineering Occupations."
4. Click the category for "Entertainment and Sports Occupations" within the "Occupational Groups" list. What do you notice about the median pay for the occupations in this list?
5. What does "median pay" mean? Is it reasonable to expect to make the figure listed as the median salary when you're first starting out? Why or why not?

## CHAPTER 1

1. Adam Smith, *An Inquiry into the Nature and Causes of the Wealth of Nations* (Indianapolis: Liberty Fund, 1776/1981).

## CHAPTER 2

1. George Washington to Benjamin Harrison, 18 January 1784, Founders Online, National Archives, last modified June 13, 2018, http://founders.archives.gov/documents/Washington/04-01-02-0039

2. Alexander Hamilton, James Madison, John Jay. *The Federalist Papers: Number 10* Mineola, New York. 2020.

3. Adam Smith (1776, 1981) *An Inquiry into the Nature and Causes of the Wealth of Nations.* Indianapolis: Liberty Fund.

4. Adam Smith (1759, 1982) *The Theory of Moral Sentiments.* Indianapolis: Liberty Fund.

5. Adam Smith (1776, 1981) *An Inquiry into the Nature and Causes of the Wealth of Nations.* Indianapolis: Liberty Fund.

6. Alexander Hamilton, James Madison, John Jay. *The Federalist Papers: Number 62* Mineola, New York. 2020.

## CHAPTER 3

1. See "Enlightenment Man" in *The Economist*; London Vol. 389, Iss. 8609 (Dec 6, 2008): s31-s32, and "The Birth of Google" by John Battelle (August 1, 2005): https://www.wired.com/2005/08/battelle/?tw=wn_tophead_4

2. See the Fraser Institute's website: https://www.fraserinstitute.org/economic-freedom/

3. See the *Economic Freedom of the World: 2021 Annual Report* by Gwartney, James, Robert Lawson, Joshua Hall, and Ryan Murphy. 2021. *Economic Freedom of the World: 2021 Annual Report.* Fraser Institute. Vancouver, Canada.

4. See Wick, Katharina and Erwin H. Bulte. (2006). "Contesting Resources: Rent Seeking, Conflict and the Natural Resource Curse." *Public Choice*, 128 (3/4). 457-476. https://www.jstor.org/stable/25487568

5. See "Free Gao Zhisheng - China has brutalized the human-rights lawyer for a decade." Sept. 11, 2014. https://www.wsj.com/articles/free-gao-zhisheng-1410195980

"China: Further information: Disappeared activist at risk of torture: Gao Zhisheng." April 14, 2019. https://www.amnesty.org/en/documents/asa17/0199/2019/en/

6. "Hong Kong security law: What is it and is it worrying?" by BBC News. June 30, 2020. https://www.bbc.com/news/world-asia-china-52765838

7. See "Hong Kong's national security law: 10 things you need to know." July 17, 2020. https://www.amnesty.org/en/latest/news/2020/07/hong-kong national-security-law-10-things-you-need-to-know/

"Hong Kong: How life has changed under China's national security law," June 30, 2021. https://www.bbc.com/news/world-asia-china-57649112

8. See "'Hong Kong people made history again': Over 600,000 vote in democrats' primaries as co-organiser hails 'miracle' turnout" by Rachel Wong; July 12, 2020. https://hongkongfp.com/2020/07/12/hong-kong-people-made-history-again-over-600000-vote-in-democrats-primaries-as-co-organiser-hails-miracle-turnout/

"Hong Kong's traditional opposition parties lose out to localist challengers in fierce weekend primary for coming Legislative Council election," by Tony Cheung, Natalie Wong, and Lilian Cheng; July 13, 2020. https://www.scmp.com/news/hong-kong/politics/article/3093015/hong-kongs-traditional-opposition-parties-lose-out-localist

"Hong Kong police say 53 were arrested for trying to use strategic voting to win election, veto budget & shut down govt," by Kelly Ho; Jan. 6, 2021. https://hongkongfp.com/2021/01/06/hong-kong-police-say-53-were-arrested-for-trying-to-use-strategic-voting-to-win-election-veto-budget-shut-down-govt/

"Security chief says mass arrest of democrats 'necessary' due to 'malicious' plot to paralyse Hong Kong," by Candice Chau; Jan. 6, 2021. https://hongkongfp.com/2021/01/06/security-chief-says-mass-arrest-of-democrats-necessary-due-to-malicious-plot-to-paralyse-hong-kong/

"Hong Kong Charges 47 Democracy Activists With Subversion Under Security Law," by Robert Olsen; Feb. 28, 2021. https://www.forbes.com/sites/robertolsen/2021/02/28/hong-kong-charges-47-democracy-activists-with-subversion-under-security-law/?sh=1c7037e14327

## CHAPTER 4

1. See Robert A. Lawson and J.R. Clark, "Examining the Hayek–Friedman hypothesis on economic and political freedom," *Journal of Economic Behavior & Organization*, Volume 74, Issue 3, 2010: 230-239.

2. See the video "WSJ Opinion: Was Milton Friedman Wrong On China?" and the accompanying article "Was Milton Friedman Wrong About China" by William McGurn, published by the *Wall Street Journal* on June 28, 2021. https://www.wsj.com/articles/was-milton-friedman-wrong-about-china-11624918231

3. See p. 10 of Milton Friedman's *Capitalism and Freedom* (originally published in 1962; third edition published in 2002).

4. See the 2021 Economic Freedom of the World Annual Report, which uses 2019 data.

5. For further information summarizing empirical studies and analysis involving economic freedom, see: Niclas Berggren (2003). "Economic Freedom: A Survey." *The Independent Review*. 8(2). 193-211; Joshua Hall and Robert Lawson. (2014). "Economic Freedom of the World: An Accounting of the Literature." *Contemporary Economic Policy*. 32(1). 1-19.

6. See p. 17 of the third edition of *Capitalism and Freedom* by Milton Friedman (originally published in 1962; third edition published in 2002).

7. For information regarding the gender ratio in China, see https://statisticstimes.com/demographics/country/china-sex-ratio.php

## CHAPTER 5

1. Robert A. Margo What Is the Key to Black Progress? *In Second Thoughts: Myths and Morals of U.S. Economic History* Edited by D. N. McCloskey pp 65- 69 Oxford: Oxford University Press, 1993.

2. Ibid

3. Ibid 67

4. Ibid 67

## CHAPTER 6

1. A. R. Slabaugh, W. Brandimore, and George S. Čuhaj, *Confederate States Paper Money: Civil War currency from the South* (Krause Publications, 2012).

2. M. S. Niederjohn, A. S. Harrison, and J. R. Clark, "Will the Economy Pick the Next President?" *Social Education*, 80.2 (2016), 96–100.

3. http://www.miseryindex.us/indexbyyear.aspx

4. Erik Brynjolfsson and Avinash Collis, "How should we measure the digital economy?" *Harvard Business Review*, 2019. https://hbr.org/2019/11/how-should-we-measure-the-digital-economy

# NOTES

## CHAPTER 7

1. See Ayn Rand's "The Nature of Government," which originally appeared in the December 1963 issue of *The Objectivist Newsletter*, and can be read online at https://fee.org/articles/the-nature-of-government-by-ayn-rand

2. The information provided in the description about the time lags and forecasting issues involved with trying to properly time changes in fiscal policy is in large part thanks to the ideas presented in Chapter 11 ("Fiscal Policy: The Keynesian View and The Historical Development of Macroeconomics") from the 17th edition of *Economics: Private and Public Choice* (2021) by Gwartney et al. See p. 225-226 of that textbook for further details.

3. This story involving Milton Friedman and the suggestion to have workers use spoons instead of shovels can be found in many places, including: https://www.aei.org/carpe-diem/milton-friedman-shovels-vs-spoons-story/, https://quoteinvestigator.com/2011/10/10/spoons-shovels/, and https://marginalrevolution.com/marginalrevolution/2019/08/spoons-are-in-aisle-9.html

4 The graph of "Federal Debt: Total Public Debt / Population" was accessed from FRED (Federal Reserve Economic Data) on December 28, 2021. The graph is annualized (by taking the average of the quarterly figures). In 1970, the U.S. federal debt amounted to 1.84059 million dollars per thousand individuals (or in other words, about $1,841 per person in the U.S.). By 2020, the U.S. federal debt had soared to 79.05008 million dollars per thousand individuals (or in other words, $79,050 per person)!

5. The graph of "Federal Debt: Total Public Debt as a Percent of GDP" was accessed from FRED on December 28, 2021. The graph is annualized (by taking the average of the quarterly figures).

6. Our World In Data: https://ourworldindata.org/grapher/life-expectancy-vs-health-expenditure?minPopulationFilter=1000000&country=USA~GBR~CHE~SWE~MEX~CAN

## CHAPTER 8

1. Molly F. Sherlock Focus. In *The Plug-In Electric Vehicle Tax Credit*. Congressional Research Service, May 14, 2019, https://crsreports.congress.gov/product/pdf/IF/IF11017

2. Ishaq Nadiri and Theofanis Mamuneas. *The Review of Economics and Statistics* (1994) vol 76, issue 1, pp 22-37.

3. James D. Gwartney, Richard L. Stroup, Dwight R. Lee, Tawni H. Ferrarini, and Joseph P. Calhoun. *Common Sense Economics*, Third Edition, New York: St. Martins Press, 2016.

4. Congressional Research Service. *The Renewable Electricity* Production Tax Credit: In Brief. April 29, 2020. https://sgp.fas.org/crs/misc/R43453.pdf

## CHAPTER 9

1. Prepared by Larry DeWitt, Social Security Administration Historian's Office, https://www.ssa.gov/history/idapayroll.html.

2. See *Pollock v Farmers' Loan & Trust Co.*, https://www.law.cornell.edu/supremecourt/text/157/429.

3. https://www.cbpp.org/research/federal-tax/where-do-federal-tax-revenues-come-from

4. https://taxfoundation.org/2021-tax-brackets/

5. https://ourworldindata.org/taxation

6. https://www.taxpolicycenter.org/briefing-book/how-do-us-taxes-compare-internationally

## CHAPTER 11

1. See Harold Seymour, *Baseball: The Early Years* (New York: Oxford Press, 1960), p. 212.

2. See Harold Seymour, *Baseball: The Early Years* (New York: Oxford Press, 1960), p. 212.

3. Adam Smith, *An Inquiry into the Nature and Causes of the Wealth of Nations* (Indianapolis: Liberty Fund, 1776/1981).

4. *Matsushita Electric Industries v Zenith Radio Corp.*, 475 U.S. 574, 589 (1986).

5. Clyde Wayne Crews Jr., *Ten Thousand Commandments: An Annual Snapshot of the Federal Regulatory State* (Washington, D.C.: Competitive Enterprise Institute, 2021).

6. See https://www.law.cornell.edu/supct/html/04-108.ZS.html

## CHAPTER 12

1. An important Supreme Court case related to the constitutionality of the Fed, *McCulloch v Maryland* of 1819 will be discussed in chapter 11.

2. This article explains the Fed's current monetary policy tools: https://www.stlouisfed.org/education/teaching-new-tools-of-monetary-policy

3. Miranda, L. (2015). *Hamilton: an American Musical* [MP3]. Atlantic Records.

## CHAPTER 13

1. Adapted from W. R. Sanford and C. R. Green, *Basic Principles of American Government* (Amsco School Publications, Inc., a division of Perfection Learning, 2019).

2. M. D. Mitchell and P. J. Boettke, Applied Mainline Economics: *Bridging the Gap between Theory and Public Policy* (Mercatus Center George Mason University, 2017).

3. https://www.census.gov/data/tables/2021/econ/qtax/historical.html

4. Dissent in 1932 case of *New Sate Ice Co v Liebmann*

5. https://www.census.gov/newsroom/press-releases/2021/2020-census-apportionment-results.html

6. Quoted in Joanna Cagan and Neil deMause, *Field of Schemes* (Monroe, Maine: Common Cause Press, 1998), p. 137.

## CHAPTER 14

1. U.S. Citizenship and Immigration Services: https://www.uscis.gov/citizenship/learn-about-citizenship/should-i-consider-us-citizenship

2. Adam Smith [1759] *The Theory of Moral Sentiments* (Indianapolis: Liberty Fund, 1982) p. 26.

3. U.S. Census Bureau: https://www.census.gov/newsroom/press-releases/2021/2020-presidential-election-voting-and-registration-tables-now-available.html

4. U.S. Census Bureau: https://www.census.gov/newsroom/press-releases/2021/2020-presidential-election-voting-and-registration-tables-now-available.html

## CHAPTER 16

1. https://www.igmchicago.org/surveys/free-trade/

2. https://home.treasury.gov/policy-issues/financial-sanctions/sanctions-programs-and-country-information

## CHAPTER 17

1. Adam Smith [1759] *The Theory of Moral Sentiments* (Indianapolis: Liberty Fund,1982).

2. National Philanthrope Trust https://www.nptrust.org/philanthropic-resources/charitable-giving-statistics/

3. Ron Haskins and Isabell Sawhill *Creating an Opportunity Society*. Washington D.C. The Brookings Institute 2009 https://www.brookings.edu/wp-content/uploads/2016/07/CreatinganOpportunitySociety1.pdf

4. National Council of Nonprofits https://www.councilofnonprofits.org/economic-impact

5. F.A. Hayek *The Fatal Conceit: The Errors of Socialism*. Chicago: The University of Chicago Press. 1988.

6. James Andreoni *Do Government Grants to Charities Crowd Donations Out or In?* National Bureau of Economic Research. https://www.nber.org/reporter/2019number1/do-government-grants-charities-crowd-private-donations-out-or

## CHAPTER 18

1. See the article "Active fund managers trail the S&P 500 for the ninth year in a row in triumph for indexing" by Bob Pisani, published by CNBC on March 15th, 2019: https://www.cnbc.com/2019/03/15/active-fund-managers-trail-the-sp-500-for-the-ninth-year-in-a-row-in-triumph-for-indexing.html. The article states, "Indeed, while a fund manager may outperform [the S&P 500] for a year or two, the outperformance does not persist. After 10 years, 85 percent of large cap funds underperformed the S&P 500, and after 15 years, nearly 92 percent are trailing the index." For the ninth year in a row, the majority (64.49 percent) of large-cap funds lagged behind the S&P 500. The author concludes that "active managers continue to show dismal performance against their passive benchmarks."

Also see "Special Topic 3: The Stock Market: Its Function, Performance, and Potential" in the 17th edition of *Economics: Private and Public Choice* by Gwartney et al. (2021), which states that the top 20 managed mutual funds of the 1990s outperformed the S&P 500 by 3.9 percent per year over that decade. But be careful if you're thinking of selecting a given managed fund based on successful past performance, because the same 20 funds that were at the top in the 1990s underperformed the S&P 500 by 1.3 percent per year in the following decade.

Also see Ch. 7 ("How Good is Fundamental Analysis? The Efficient-Market Hypothesis") in *A Random Walk Down Wall Street: The Time-Tested Strategy for Successful Investing* by Burton G. Malkiel (2016), which states that only 14 managed mutual funds (out of thousands available) were able beat the S&P 500 for nine consecutive years during 1999-2007. Nevertheless, only *one* of the those top fourteen managed funds was able to beat the S&P 500 Index the following year in 2008!

2. These data (and the graphic depicting the data) were collected on Dec. 12th 2021, from the URL https://www.spglobal.com/spdji/en/research-insights/spiva/ (published by SPIVA within the website of the S&P Dow Jones Indices)

3. See the "U.S. Persistence Scorecard Mid-Year 2021" report published by SPIVA. https://www.spglobal.com/spdji/en/documents/spiva/persistence-scorecard-mid-year-2021.pdf

4. Ibid.

5. See Exhibit 1 ("Annual Return for Stocks, 1950-2019") in "Special Topic 3: The Stock Market: Its Function, Performance, and Potential" in the 17th edition of *Economics: Private and Public Choice* by Gwartney et al. (2021). Source for that exhibit: Global Financial Data (www.globalfindata.com), and Standard 7 Poor's (www.standardandpoors.com).

# GLOSSARY

## A

**absolute advantage**: The ability of a business or an individual to produce more units of a good or service than some other producer, using the same quantity of resources. See also **comparative advantage**.

**antitrust**: Laws and regulations that are meant to encourage competition by limiting the market power of an individual firm.

**Articles of Confederation**: The first constitution of the United States, adopted in 1789; supplanted in 1789 by the U. S. Constitution. The Articles established a weak role for the federal government and a strong role for state governments.

## B

**benefits**: Positive consequences resulting from a choice. Benefits may be monetary or non-monetary.

**benefits of voting**: Positive outcomes associated with voting such as satisfaction from fulfilling a citizen's duty and cheering on favored candidates and issues.

**bond**: A certificate issued by a government or a corporation promising to repay borrowed money, plus interest, to the owner of the bond. Bonds acknowledge loans made by investors (individuals or institutions).

**boycott**: The act to refuse to buy a product or do business with a company or other organization as a way of expressing disapproval. The Montgomery bus boycott of 1955 and 1956 against segregated seating of African American is an example.

**business cycles**: Patterns of up-and-down movements that occur in economic activity over time. Business cycles are measured in part by increases or decreases in Gross Domestic Product (GDP).

## C

**capital resources**: Goods used to produce other goods and services. Capital goods include tools, equipment. buildings and machinery.

**cartel**: A group of producers acting together in an effort to restrict production and control the prices of their products.

**central authority**: A high-level concentration of government power, as contrasted with power dispersed among different government branches and localities.

**central planning**: A form of economic control under which a government decides in advance what goods should be produced, how they should be produced, and how they should be allocated among people.

**checks and balances**: A structure built into the U.S. Constitution intended to limit the central government's power by distributing decision-making authority across different branches of government.

**civil liberties**: Personal freedoms such as freedom of speech, freedom of the press, freedom to peaceably assemble, and freedom of religion. Some scholars distinguish between **civil liberties** (personal freedoms protected by the Bill of Rights) and **civil rights** (essential and inherent protections), while others use the terms as synonyms.

**civil rights**: Guarantees of equal protection under the law such as the right to vote, the right to a fair trial, and the right to use public facilities. Some scholars distinguish between civil rights (essential and inherent protections) and civil liberties (personal freedoms protected by the Bill of Rights), while others use the terms as synonyms.

**civil society**: An arena in which people interact with one another voluntarily on the basis of shared interests and purposes. Churches, labor unions, business associations, charitable organizations, book clubs, garden clubs, and bowling leagues are among the many organizations that make up civil society.

**command economy**: An economy in which the government or some other central authority makes the decisions about what goods and services will be produced, how they will be produced, and how they will be distributed. Contemporary examples of command systems are Cuba and North Korea.

**Commerce Clause**: Article I, Section 8, Clause 3 of the U.S. Constitution, which states that Congress shall have power "To regulate Commerce with foreign Nations, and among the several States, and with the Indian Tribes." The Commerce Clause took the power to impose tariffs away from the states and created a "free trade zone" within the United States.

**communism**: An economic and political theory that calls for a society in which property is publicly owned and government power is concentrated in a single political party whose leaders control the economy and society generally. In the 20th century, the Soviet Union controlled a powerful communist empire until its collapse in 1991. Today, North Korea and Cuba are communist nations, and there are communist political parties in various parts of the world.

**comparative advantage**: The ability of a business in one nation to produce a good or service at a lower opportunity cost than a business in another nation. See also **absolute advantage.**

**competition**: In business, rivalry among producers and suppliers, acting independently, in their efforts to win customers by offering the best deal. In a market economy, competition acts as a control on self-interested behavior by guiding the market toward high-quality products and services offered at low (that is, competitive) prices.

**constitutional monarchy**: A form of government in which a ruler acts as head of state within the limits of a written constitution. Most constitutional monarchies have a parliamentary system and a prime minister who serves as the head of government.

**Consumer Price Index (CPI)**: A statistic calculated by the Bureau of Labor Statistics (BLS), the CPI represents changes in the prices of goods and services commonly bought by consumers. It is widely used as a measure of inflation.

**contract**: A legally binding agreement between consenting people; contracts can be enforced by the courts.

**Contract Clause**: Article I, section 10, clause 1 of the U.S. Constitution, which states that "No state shall...pass any...law impairing the Obligation of Contracts," thus ensuring that contracts, including those dealing with debts, can be enforced.

**corporation**: A business owned by shareholders who possess ownership rights to the firm's profits.

**cost**: What people pay to buy something—as in That skateboard will cost you $78. Also, a consequence resulting from a choice or an act—as in That speeding ticket is going to cost you $160. Costs may be non-monetary—as in Learning Spanish cost me a lot of effort. See also opportunity cost.

**costs of voting**: Negative outcomes associated with voting such as waiting in line and interference with work.

**cryptocurrency**: A digital or virtual currency that is secured by cryptography, which makes it nearly impossible to counterfeit or double-spend. Many cryptocurrencies are decentralized networks based on blockchain technology—a distributed ledger enforced by a disparate network of computers.

**currency**: a medium of exchange for goods and services. In short, its money, in the form of paper or coins, usually issued by a government and generally accepted at its face value as a method of payment.

## D

**deadweight loss**: a cost to society created by market inefficiency, which occurs when supply and demand are out of equilibrium.

**deflation**: A sustained decrease in the average price level of all goods and services produced in an economy.

**demand**: The amount of a good or service that consumers are willing and able to purchase at specific prices.

**discount loans:** Short-term loans from a central bank.

**dumping**: The sale of a product in another nation at a price lower than the price charged in the producer's home markets.

## E

**economic expansion**: A period of economic growth; a time when people spend and receive more and more money. Economic expansion is measured in part by increases in Gross Domestic Product (GDP).

**economic freedom**: An environment in which individuals are able to make their own choices, engage in voluntary exchanges with others, enter and compete in markets, and possess and use private property, as long as their actions do not infringe upon the same rights of others.

**economic growth**: An increase in the production of goods and services over time. Economic growth is often measured by changes in Gross Domestic Product (GDP).

**economic indicators**: A piece of economic data, usually of macroeconomic scale, that is used by analysts to interpret current or future investment possibilities. These indicators also help to judge the overall health of an economy.

**economic institutions**: Established arrangements and structures that affect the security of property rights, enforcement of contracts, and the prevalence of voluntary exchange. The formal and informal customs arising from economic institutions are informally known as the "rules of the game."

**economic recovery**: A period of economic expansion following an economic downturn. Economic recovery is measured in part by increases in Gross Domestic Product (GDP).

**economic system**: The framework of rules that form the relationships regarding what goods and services are produced, how they are produced, and how they are distributed. See also rules of the game.

**economic way of thinking**: An approach to analyzing human behavior by reference to individual choices, costs, incentives, rules of the game, gains from trade, and unintended consequences.

**economics**: The study of human behavior that emphasizes choices people make about how to use scarce resources.

**Electoral College**: The electors chosen by the states in a presidential election, taken as a group. Like any political Institution, it has costs and benefits.

**embargo**: A government order that restricts commerce with a specified country or the exchange of specific goods.

**eminent domain:** The right of a government to take private property for public use with proper compensation without the owner's consent.

**employed**: Adults who are working in either full-time or part-time jobs.

**entrepreneur**: A person who introduces new products, or improved technologies or production methods, and decides which projects to undertake, often within a newly created enterprise.

**estate taxes**: A levy on estates whose value exceeds an exclusion limit set by law. Only the amount that exceeds that minimum threshold is subject to tax.

**exchange traded fund (ETF):** A type of financial asset that operates much like a mutual fund in pooling investors' resources to purchase a collection of assets. Unlike mutual funds, ETFs experience changes in value as they trade throughout the day.

**excise taxes**: A legislated tax on specific goods or services at purchase such as fuel, tobacco, and alcohol.

**exports**: Goods and services produced by people in one country and sold to people in another country.

**external benefit**: An advantage or positive result that goes to people other than those who benefit directly from an action. For example, homeowners who paint their homes or make other outside improvements provide an external benefit to neighbors. See also **externality**.

**externality**: A positive or negative effect of a transaction on somebody who is not directly involved in the transaction. Informally: a spillover effect.

## F

***Federal Baseball Club of Baltimore, Inc. v National League of Professional Baseball Clubs***: A 1922 U.S. Supreme Court case in which the Court ruled that major league baseball was not engaged in interstate commerce and was not a monopoly as defined by the Sherman Antitrust Act.

**Federal Deposit Insurance Corporation (FDIC)**: A corporation sponsored by the U.S. government that insures bank deposits in order to maintain public confidence in the banking system.

**Federal Funds Rate**: The interest rate banks charge one another for loans. This is a key interest rate controlled by the Federal Reserve.

**Federal Open Market Committee**: The branch of the Federal Reserve System (FRS) that determines the direction of monetary policy specifically by directing open market operations (OMOs). The committee is made up of 12 members: the seven members of the Board of Governors; the president of the Federal Reserve Bank of New York; and four of the remaining 11 Reserve Bank presidents on a rotating basis.

**Federal Reserve Act of 1913**: A federal law that set up a central bank, the Federal Reserve System, to regulate banking and the supply of money.

**Federal Reserve System**: The U.S. central bank, designed as an independent agency to coordinate the activities of all financial institutions in the country. It is commonly called the Fed.

***Federalist Papers***: A series essays written by Alexander Hamilton, James Madison, and John Jay, between 1787 and1788. These essays advocated for ratification of the U.S. Constitution.

**financial institution**: An organization, such as a bank or a brokerage firm, that collects funds and provides services for the management, investment, and safekeeping of funds.

**fiscal policy**: The use of taxation and government spending to increase or decrease total demand in an economy for goods and services. Loose fiscal policy is intended to increase total demand, while tight fiscal policy is intended to reduce total demand.

**free trade**: The policy that allows goods and services to be bought and sold among countries and states without tariffs, quotas, or other restrictions.

**free trade zone**: A region in which trade between nations or states takes place without tariffs, quotas, or other restrictions. The Commerce Clause in the U.S. Constitution allowed for the creation of a free trade zone among the states.

## G

***Gibbons v Ogden***: An 1824 decision by the U.S. Supreme Court that confirmed the power of the federal government to regulate interstate commerce.

**gift taxes**: A federal tax paid by an individual who transfers something of value to another individual without receiving something of similar value in return.

**globalization**: The expansion of international trade, communications, and transportation across regions, nations, and cultures.

**gross domestic product (GDP)**: The market value of all final goods and services produced within the borders of a nation during a specific period of time, such as a quarter or a year. GDP is often used to measure economic growth and to mark periods of economic expansion and contraction.

## H

**holding company**: A company that holds the stock of other companies. It is sometimes called a parent company.

**human capital**: The knowledge, skills, and work habits that enable workers to be productive.

**human resources:** The knowledge and skills of people in the workforce used to produce goods and services.

## I

**imports**: Goods and services bought from people in another country.

**incentives**: A benefit offered to encourage people to act in certain ways. Incentives can be monetary, such as a paycheck, or non-monetary, such as praise.

**Incentives to vote**: These are rewards derived from voting. Often older adults have stronger Incentives to vote than do younger voters.

**income inequality**: A measure of unequal earnings among residents of a society. Income inequality is always present, but it may increase or decrease over time and may vary sharply across societies.

**income taxes**: a type of tax that governments impose on income generated by businesses and individuals within their jurisdiction.

**indexed funds**: ETFs or mutual funds constructed to track the components of a stock market average such as the S&P 500. By design, they are not intended to outperform the market, but instead to match the market characterized by the index.

**inflation**: A sustained increase in the average price level of all the goods and services produced in an economy.

**inflation rate:** The percentage change in the level of inflation measured from a prior period.

**information costs:** Costs incurred from the time and effort it takes to cast an informed vote.

**infrastructure**: Basic facilities such as roads, ports, bridges, airports, and railways that support economic activity.

**interest group**: A voluntary organization of like-minded citizens who act as advocates for members of their group. Interest groups include business owners, farmers, consumers, the elderly, environmentalists, and so forth. See also **interest group effect**.

**interest group effect**: The condition when elected officials face incentives to support legislation that provides concentrated benefits to the members of interest groups at the expense of others such as voters and consumers. Interest group effects are likely to happen when the benefits of a piece of legislation are concentrated on the members of an interest group and the costs are spread out over many. See also **interest group**.

**interest rates**: the amount a lender charges a borrower and is a percentage of the principal—the amount loaned.

**investment**: The use of income today in a way that may yield gains in the future. For example: a business invests when it spends some of its income to build a factory or buy new equipment. An individual invests when she deposits some of her income in a retirement account, or improves her knowledge and skills through continuing education or training.

**investors**: Individuals and firms who use income in a way that may yield gains in the future—for example, by purchasing stocks and bonds or by spending money to improve productivity.

**invisible hand**: A metaphor created by Adam Smith in *The Wealth of Nations*. As used by Smith and subsequently by other economists, the term suggests that the operation of free markets promotes positive social outcomes even when those outcomes are not intended by individuals involved. The positive outcomes occur, Smith claimed, as if the market transactions had been guided toward those ends by an invisible hand.

## J-K-L

**Jim Crow laws**: Local and state laws in force in the South from about 1876 to 1965, requiring that African Americans be segregated from white Americans in most public settings.

**labor force**: The category of all adults who are working (the employed) plus those who are seeking work but unable to find it (the unemployed). The size of the labor force can change over time as the economy expands and contracts and as people make choices about work and other priorities.

**labor force participation**: The percentage of adults employed or seeking employment.

**labor market**: Any place or situation in which employers are trying to hire workers at various wages and workers are trying to find jobs at various wages. See also **market**.

**labor union**: An organization of employees, established for the purpose of improving wages, fringe benefits, and working conditions. Unions negotiate with employers on behalf of all unionized employees in a given company rather than having each employee negotiate an employment contract on their own behalf.

**laissez-faire**: A policy of minimal governmental government regulation of voluntary transactions in an economy.

**lobbying**: The effort by members of interest groups to inform legislators about how policies may affect their group. Lobbying also includes efforts to persuade legislators to support or oppose various government policies.

## M

**managed fund**: A mutual fund that strategically selects, buys, and sells stocks in an effort to outperform the market under the guidance of a portfolio manager.

**market**: Any place or situation in which people buy and sell goods and services. Markets can arise when people meet face-to-face or through technological arrangements such as telephone conversations.

**market economy**: An economy based on individuals' choices and voluntary exchange; consumers are free to spend their money as they wish, to enter into businesses or to sell their labor as they think best. In market economies, prices are determined by supply and demand; information suggested by rising or falling prices guides decisions about how to allocate goods, services, and productive resources.

**market price**: The price at which the quantity demanded by buyers equals the quantity supplied by sellers.

**Marx, Karl**: A German political philosopher and economist (1818-1883); the founder of modern communism.

**mass media:** Communication platforms that seek large audiences, such as television, newspapers, and associated websites.

**media bias**: Favoritism toward particular individuals or ideas by communication outlets.

**Medicare**: An entitlement program that provides health care insurance for people aged 65 and over.

**mercantilism**: A loosely defined set of ideas that identified the wealth of a nation with its possession of gold and silver. Mercantilism suggested that colonies have an obligation to assist the mother country in gaining wealth and that the government of the mother country should managing the overall economy by offering monopolies and subsidies and by intervening in trade.

**misery index**: A measure of economic pain, calculated by adding the unemployment rate to the rate of inflation. Higher sums mean more economic pain.

**mixed economy**: An economy that has some characteristics of a command economy and some characteristics of a market system. Many modern economies are mixed economies.

**monetary policy**: Government actions that influence the money supply and the banking system, exercised to influence the economy. In the United States, monetary policy is conducted by the Federal Reserve System. Loose monetary policy is intended to increase total demand, while tight monetary policy is intended to reduce total demand.

**money**: Anything commonly accepted as payment for goods and services.
**money supply**: The total quantity of money in the economy. Money resulting from loans is part of the money supply, along with coins, currency, and deposits in savings accounts and checking accounts. Bank lending affects how much money there is in the economy overall.
**monopoly**: A market that is difficult to enter, typically with only one supplier producing a unique product.

## N

**narrative**: An overall story or viewpoint that underlies media coverage or political discourse.
**national debt**: The amount of money the U.S. government owes, that is, the total sum of the deficits it has accumulated.
**national deficit**: The amount that U.S. federal spending exceeds total federal tax revenue for the current year. When a government runs a budget deficit year after year, the national debt grows.
**natural resources**: Productive elements available from the environment; they include land, water, wildlife, timber, and climate. As an economy's access to natural resources improves, it becomes capable of producing more output.
**non-governmental organizations**: Types of nonprofit organizations that are independent of government and often are involved in international humanitarian or economic development projects.
**nonprofit organizations**: Organizations that make up civil society. They are granted tax-exempt status by the Internal Revenue Service. Donations to nonprofit organizations are typically tax deductible, which provides an incentive for individuals to make donations. Examples of nonprofit organizations include hospitals, universities, charities, churches and much more. See also **civil society**.
**North American Free Trade Agreement (NAFTA)**: A regional trade agreement (RTA) established in 1994 under President Bill Clinton. Under the terms of NAFTA, the United States, Canada, and Mexico agreed to reduce trade barriers.

## O–P–Q

**objectivity**: An approach to media coverage and politics that seeks to balance coverage of competing viewpoints, avoiding favoritism. (See also **media bias**.)
**opportunity cost**: The value of the next-best alternative, or what someone gives up choosing one alternative over another.
**payroll taxes**: A percentage withheld from an employee's pay by an employer who pays it to the government on the employee's behalf.
**PCE price index**: A measure of price changes in consumer goods and services exchanged in the U.S. economy.
**personal consumption expenditure**: A measure of imputed household expenditures defined for a period of time.
**political freedom**: The presence of institutions that foster and promote free and fair elections while constraining the behavior of government leaders. A democratic country has high levels of political freedom, while an autocratic country has low levels of political freedom.
**political institutions**: Structures and arrangements that influence the outcome of government action, such as the method of how political leaders are selected and the constraints on their behavior.
**pork-barrel legislation**: A package of spending projects bundled into a single bill to obtain funding for projects intensely desired by interest groups. The term reflects disapproval, in that the bundled projects are thought to be unlikely to pass if voted on separately.
**predatory pricing**: A company's strategy of charging prices below its costs to gain control of a market.
**primary effects**: The immediate and visible effects of an action. See also **secondary effects**.
**private property**: Things owned by individuals and businesses; in the United States and other countries that protect property rights, owners of property can control, use, and transfer their possessions, subject to rules intended to prevent harm to others.
**productivity**: A measure of efficiency, based on the amount of goods or services that a person can produce with a given quantity of resources in a given period of time.
**profit**: The money left over after costs have been subtracted from revenues. Profits serve as an important incentive in a market economy.
**profit motive**: The desire to earn profits—often prompting businesses to produce or supply the goods and services consumers want. Businesses that satisfy consumers and produce efficiently are rewarded with profits.
**progressive taxes**: A tax system that imposes a lower tax rate on low-income earners than on those with a higher income.
**property rights**: The exclusive authority of property owners to determine how their property will be used. Property rights may be held by individuals, groups, or governments.
**property taxes**: a tax paid on property owned by an individual or other legal entity, such as a corporation.
**protectionism**: government policies that restrict international trade to help domestic industries.
**public choice theory**: This theory applies economic analysis to the study of government decisions. It assumes that government actions are the result of individuals making self-interested choices in their roles as elected officials, appointed officials, or bureaucrats.
**public goods**: Goods and services that are both *non-excludable* (meaning it is extremely difficult and costly if not impossible to exclude non-paying consumers) and *non-rival in consumption* (meaning that one individual's consumption of the good

or service does not prevent another individual from consuming the good or service at the same time).

**quota**: A restriction on the amount of a product that may be imported during a period of time.

## R

**rational ignorance**: Since the chances of one vote changing the outcome of an election are low, voters have an incentive to not seek out all of the information they need to cast an informed vote.

**real GDP per capita**: A financial metric that breaks down a country's economic output per person and is calculated by dividing the GDP of a nation by its population.

**real Gross Domestic Product**: The total monetary or market value of all the finished goods and services produced within a country's borders in a specific time period. As a broad measure of overall domestic production, it functions as a comprehensive scorecard of a given country's economic health.

**recession**: A period of economic contraction; a time when people spend and receive less money. A recession is measured in part by decreases in Gross Domestic Product (GDP).

**Regional Trade Agreements (RTAs)**: Trade agreements among a limited number of nations, designed to reduce trade barriers. The North American Free Trade Agreement (NAFTA) is an example.

**regressive taxes**: A tax applied uniformly, taking a larger percentage of income from low-income earners than from high-income earners.

**regulation**: Government rules imposed on firms and individuals to achieve a government purpose. Regulations often involve efforts to keep markets competitive and to improve the environment.

**rent-seeking**: Actions by special interests to restructure public policy to redistribute income or wealth to themselves.

**republic**: A form of government in which power is held by the people, acting through elected representatives.

**reserves**: Funds that banks set aside for use in managing the day-to-day operations of the bank or for an emergency. These funds are not lent to customers. Today, banks keep some of their reserves in their own bank vaults, but they keep most reserves in the form of deposits with the Federal Reserve.

**rules of the game**: The formal and informal regulations that govern the economic system. These rules are often set by government; they often act as incentives, influencing people's behavior. Tax laws and government regulations are examples.

## S

**S&P 500 (Standard & Poor's 500 Index)**: An index that tracks the value of 500 prominent publicly traded companies in the United States.

**sales taxes**: A consumption tax imposed by the government on the sale of goods and services.

**scarcity**: The lack of enough resources to satisfy economic wants. Scarcity exists because human wants are always greater than the resources available to satisfy them.

**secondary effects**: The unexpected or indirect effects of an action that become known with the passage of time. See also **unintended consequences**.

**self-interested behavior**: Purposeful action people engage in to make themselves better off, in material or non-material ways. Self-interested behavior might include working overtime to earn more money; it might include volunteer work at a community hospital. The key is whether the acts in question do serve the interests of the person performing them.

**Sherman Antitrust Act of 1890**: A federal law designed to break up monopolies or companies attempting to form monopolies. The Sherman Act authorized the U.S. attorney general to initiate lawsuits against firms regarded as trying to restrain trade by reducing competition.

**slavery**: A condition in which a person is nonvoluntarily owned as property by another person.

**Smoot-Hawley Tariff**: Federal legislation passed in 1930, increasing tariffs on many goods imported into the United States.

**social contract**: An unwritten agreement or consensus among people in a given society, indicating basic values and mutual obligations. Because there is no written form of the social contract, references to its contents are often subject to dispute.

**social entrepreneur**: A person who establishes an enterprise, often a nonprofit organization, to address social problems such as improving health care, the environment, or helping underserved communities.

**social media**: Communication platforms that rely on having users create and share content, such as Twitter, Instagram and Facebook.

**Social Security**: An entitlement program to pay retired workers a continuing income. The Social Security program also provides other benefits including payments to people who are disabled and to spouses or children of a worker who has died.

**socialism**: A political and economic theory that calls for government ownership of industry, and for social policies aimed at promoting equality. Socialist political parties have been influential in Europe and other parts of the world throughout much of the 20th century.

**special-interest group**: A group of people or an organization that seeks special favors or advantages, typically through lobbying government officials.

**specialization**: Confining oneself (or one's business) to providing a narrower range of goods and services than one consumes, and then trading for (purchasing) other goods and services. People who specialize do not try to be self-sufficient.

**stagflation**: Stagnant economic growth (including high unemployment rates) combined with high levels of inflation. The term was first used to describe the U.S. economy of the 1970s.

**stimulus spending**: A package of economic measures a government invokes to stimulate a floundering economy. The objective of a stimulus package is to reinvigorate the economy and prevent or reverse a recession by boosting employment and spending.

**stock**: Shares of ownership in a corporation. A corporation sells stock in order to obtain money to run or expand the business. Stock buyers purchase stocks in hopes of earning a financial gain.

**subsidy**: A form of financial assistance—a special economic favor—provided by government to a business, to individuals, or to some group. Subsidies are often used by government to encourage the production of a good or a service.

**supply**: The amount of a good or service that producers are willing and able to sell at specific prices.

## T

**Takings Clause**: The last clause of the Fifth Amendment to the U.S. Constitution, which concludes with the statement: "nor shall private property be taken for public use, without just compensation." This clause provides protection for private property owners against arbitrary government seizure.

**tariff**: A tax charged on imports.

**Taxation Clause**: Article I, Section 8, of the U.S. Constitution, which gives Congress the power "to lay and collect taxes."

**taxes:** Mandatory payments levied on individuals or corporations by a government entity—whether local, regional, or national

**trade**: The action of buying and selling goods and services, within a nation or internationally.

**transfer payments**: Payments by government to recipients who do not provide any goods or services in return. Examples include Social Security payments, unemployment compensation, and payments to people with disabilities.

**trust**: A form of business organization in which individuals (trustees) are given legal authority to administer the organization for the advantage of its shareholders.

**trust busting**: An informal term for legal actions taken by government to break up large corporations or trusts by enforcing anti-trust laws; trust buster: a political figure who engages in trust busting.

## U–V–W

**unalienable rights**: Rights that cannot be taken away, surrendered, or sold to others. The term "unalienable rights" is used in the Declaration of Independence, which states that unalienable rights to life, liberty, and the pursuit of happiness are given to "all men" by their creator—that is, they are not a gift from government.

**unemployed**: Adults who are seeking work but unable to find it.

**unemployment rate**: The percentage of the labor force that is unemployed.

**unintended consequences**: Results that are not expected or predicted. The term is often used in reference to government policies that produce unwelcome results.

**voluntary trade (or voluntary exchange)**: Transactions entered into freely, in which both sides anticipate that the benefits of the exchange will outweigh the costs. Buying a cup of coffee is an example of a voluntary exchange.

**wealth tax**: A tax based on the market value of assets owned by a taxpayer.

**World Trade Organization (WTO)**: An international organization which succeeded the **General Agreement on Tariffs and Trade** in 1995. With 153 members, the WTO is now a forum in which member countries negotiate reductions in trade barriers.

Note: Page numbers in **bold** indicate tables; page numbers in *italics* indicate figures.

# INDEX

# INDEX

# INDEX



## V



## W



## Y–Z

# IMAGE CREDITS

The following abbreviations are used for sources from which several images were obtained:

AP . . . . . . . . Associated Press
GI . . . . . . . . Getty Images
LOC . . . . . . . . Library of Congress Prints and Photographs Division
NARA . . . . . . . . National Archives & Records Administration
SS . . . . . . . . Shutterstock.com

**Cover Images:** SS. **Preface:** iv Drozd Irina / SS.

**Table of Contents:** viii Kjell Leknes / SS; xi J. Helgason / SS.

**Chapter 1:** 1 Stefan Schäfer; 5 Dan Race / SS; 6 Michael Armentrout / SS; 8-9 Alex Alsemgeest; 10 Kathy Tran Campaign.

**Chapter 2:** 13 Howard Chandler Christy ; 15 Smithosonian National Postal Museum; 16 Barry Faulkner / NARA; 21 GI.

**Chapter 3:** 23 Kim Kulish / GI; 26 Hulton Deutsch/GI; 30 University of Salford; 31 Acton Institute; 32 AP.

**Chapter 4:** 35 Dunya Degismeden / SS; 36 Tore Sætre; 37 David Guttenfelder/AP; 38 David Steele / SS; 40 2p2play / SS; 43 Chrispictures / SS; 44 The Friedman Foundation for Educational Choice; 45 Ivan Marc / SS.

**Chapter 5:** 49 NARA; 52 LOC; 54 LOC; 57 LOC; 58 AP

**Chapter 6:** 61 Denys Kurbatov / SS; 63 Wangkun Jia / SS; 66 Maxx-Studio / SS; 68 Gerald R. Ford Presidential Museum; 69 Wachiwit / SS.

**Chapter 7:** 71 Chris Cobert / SS; 72 James Andrews / SS, Gage Skidmore; 75 GI; 81 Jose Gil / SS.

**Chapter 8:** 83 Roschetzky Photography / SS; 84 Iryna Ishyna / SS; 85 Eisenhower Presidential Library; 86 Missouri Department of Transportation; 92 Joseph Sohm / SS.

**Chapter 9:** 95 Rob Crandall / SS; 97 AP; 99 RomanR / SS; 102 NARA.

**Chapter 10:** 105 Leah Mills / Reuters / Alamy Stock Photo; 106 Al Teich / SS; 109 Pictorial Press Ltd / Alamy Stock Photo; 112–113 LOC.

**Chapter 11:** 117 EQRoy / SS; 119 John Silver / SS; 122 LOC; 124 Government Publishing Office; 128 Gil C / SS.

**Chapter 12:** 131 LOC; 132 LOC; 139 EQRoy / SS; 140 Sol Invictus / SS; 141 Petr Hoffmann / SS.

**Chapter 13:** 143 SpaceX; 144 U.S. Air Force; 146 Flamingo Images / SS; 150 Wangkun Jia / SS; 152 Ringo Chiu / SS.

**Chapter 14:** 155 vesperstock / SS; 159 Rob Crandall / SS.

**Chapter 15:** 165 Grindstone Media Group / SS; 168 DenPhotos / SS; 172 Byron Rollins / AP; 174 A Katz / SS.

**Chapter 16:** 177 olrat / SS; 178 LOC, 181 JIIVEPhoto / SS; 183 Pamela Au / SS; 185 catastrophe_OL/SS; 187 Alamy Stock Photo.

**Chapter 17:** 191 A Katz / SS; 193 Monkey Business Images / SS; 194 Rawpixel.com / SS; 196 Dragana Gordic / SS; 197 Rawpixel.com / SS; 200 Krakenimages.com / SS.

**Chapter 18:** 203 Pressmaster / SS; 204 Al Teich / SS; 205 Rawpixel.com / SS; 206 Krakenimages / SS; 210 Lightfield Studios / SS; 211 Fizkes / SS; 214 Rohatynchuk Mykola / SS.

*Maps, tables, and figures by Jeremy C. Munns*

*All other images are in the public domain or not under copyright.*